WHO SPEAKS FOR JUSTICE

RAISING **OUR** VOICES IN THE **NOISE** OF HEGEMONY

JOAN WYNNE   CARLOS GONZALEZ

Kendall Hunt
publishing company

Cover image © Shutterstock, Inc.

Kendall Hunt
p u b l i s h i n g   c o m p a n y

www.kendallhunt.com
Send all inquiries to:
4050 Westmark Drive
Dubuque, IA 52004-1840

Printed in the United States of America

Joannie

To Catharine and Sharon, who celebrate life with courage, gusto, wit, and kindness, making the world a better place.

Carlos

For all in the crawl space who resist and create.

TABLE OF CONTENTS

PART 1:   A human being is part of the whole 1

A human being is a part of a whole, called by us a universe, a part limited in time and space. He experiences himself, his thoughts and feelings as something separated from the rest . . . a kind of optical delusion of his consciousness. This delusion is a kind of prison for us, restricting us to our personal desires and to affection for a few persons nearest to us. Our task must be to free ourselves from this prison by widening our circle of compassion to embrace all living creatures and the whole of nature in its beauty.

—Albert Einstein

A teacher seeks to develop the genius within the young so that each can arrive at his or her destination—the sharing of one's gifts within the community.

—The Healing Wisdom of Africa

The spirit of agency is believing at the molecular, spiritual level that you can make a difference in the world, not by changing others, people and things, but by opening your spirit enough so that the light of others can shine through you.

—Real World Dialogue

The world is richer than it is possible to express in any single language.

—*Ilya Prigogine*

I still believe the problem is cultural, but it is larger than the children or their teachers . . . the cultural framework of our country has, almost since its inception, dictated that "black" is bad and less than and in all arenas "white" is good and superior. This perspective is so ingrained and so normalized that we all stumble through our days with eyes closed to avoid seeing it. We miss the pain in our children's eyes when they have internalized the societal belief that they are dumb, unmotivated, and dispensable.

—*Lisa Delpit, Multiplication is for white people:
Raising the expectations for other people's children*

To love. To be loved . . . To never get used to the unspeakable violence and the vulgar disparity of life around you. To see joy in the saddest places. To pursue beauty to its lair. To never simplify what is complicated or complicate what is simple. To respect strength, never power. Above all, to watch. To try and understand.

—*Arundhati Roy*

PREFACE

by Joan T. Wynne

My country. My country.
Tis of thee I sing.
Country still unborn
Sweet land yet to be

In our country, cited in the above spiritual (Harding 1981), we often find inspiration from different sources. Some find it in poetry, music, science, in cultural beliefs or religions; some are inspired by parents, friends, children, or mentors; still others by listening to the earth. I've been inspired by each at different times, especially by my mother and my daughter. Yet I've also found that the source which seems to rock my soul is the rhyme, rhythm, spirituals, poetry, epistemology, philosophy, complexity, indeed, the spellbinding story of the African-American struggle to be free in a "sweet land yet to be."

Born white in the south and, thus, drenched in the dirty history of southern Jim Crow laws and slavery, I seem to have drunk this struggle into my blood. I've spent a life time studying that Black liberation chronicle; trying to understand it; making friends with it; but mostly standing in awe of it. Immersed in its tale, though, I have often asked the same question the character, Stamp Paid, asked in Toni Morrison's novel, *Beloved*. After consistently witnessing the savagery of whites during slavery, he asks: "What are these people?" (1987 p. 172). So, part of my story is also investigating just what "these people" are, my white people and me, because I do not want to be "trapped in a history I do not understand" (Baldwin 1963, p. 8). Like James Baldwin, I believe that until I unravel it, I cannot "be released from it." Therefore, I'm always listening for a variety of voices that sing about justice, hegemony, and grace in this "country, my country."

My friend and co-editor of this book, Carlos Gonzalez, in our syllabus for a course that we team-taught for Miami Dade College professors, wrote the following:

> This is an invitation to sit and explore the tension of working, teaching, and profiting from a system that inherently creates distinction and privilege, one that thrives on disparity. If Asa G. Hilliard III[1] is correct, reformation of this system is not really possible. Critical transformation is our best hope.
>
> So, what are we to do as those in the middle? How do we possibly teach and work with the understanding that, at the core of our efforts, there is a seed waiting to sprout, that will eventually put down roots and possibly bring down the bricks and mortar of injustice, privilege, and oppression? This prospect is downright frightening! What would we do next?

Carlos' words helped shape my vision for this book. It, too, is an invitation, a call for being "out-rageous" in declaring ourselves against the hegemonic machine that pulverizes our imaginations, like a cow's flesh in a meat grinder. Hoping to escape that grinder, however, Carlos and I, through this text, propose a challenge—that we gather as often as we can and tell our stories, as encouragement to think more deeply and act more diligently in resistance to the "injustices, the privilege, and the oppression" in schools and the academy, injustices that chop up our spirits, and for many others, their bodies. We picture these pieces, represented in the book by multiple writers' stories, as a catalyst for creative encounters confronting the repression that our students face every day in school buildings, where children of the poor are treated as fodder for prisons and wars; where children of the elite are bamboozled by philosophies of self-aggrandizement and greed; and where the earth has become invisible in concrete camouflage.

Yet rather than a heavily theoretical discussion, we share stories about what philosopher, Martha Nussbaum calls "the frontiers of justice" (2006). For us, that frontier includes all species on the earth as well as all humans. And such conversations in this country, we believe, should begin with a recognition of a crime, one which Civil Rights icon, Bob Moses, brings to light in his essay in this book. To frame his essay, Moses cites James Baldwin who declared, "The crime of which I accuse my country and my countrymen is that they have destroyed and are destroying hundreds of thousands of lives and do not know it and do not want to know it." Baldwin further insists that "It is not

---

[1] Asa G. Hilliard III's passage to which Carlos refers is: "Revolution, not reform, is required to release the power of teaching . . . Virtually, all teachers possess tremendous power which can be released, given the proper exposure. We can't get to that point by tinkering with a broken system. We must change our intellectual structures, definitions and assumptions; then we can release teacher power."

permissible that the authors of devastation should also be innocent. It is the innocence which constitutes the crime" (1963, p. 6).

So, following Moses' lead, we and our students continue to help each other deconstruct that crime of innocence. We assume that our civic duty requires exploring the nation's feigned innocence in the hundreds of years of death and destruction of many cultures in 'this country, our country.' In the classroom as well as in the national dialogue, we argue that learners and citizens alike should heed Bryan Stevenson's suggestion, in his Equal Justice Initiative report on lynching, that "Suffering must be engaged, heard, recognized, and remembered before a society can recover from mass violence" (Lynching 2015 p. 23). The severity and the currency of the repercussions of the crimes referenced by Baldwin and Stevenson as well as the violence against other cultures seem to demand that we address this suffering in *Who speaks for justice?*. Within that context, we like to think of this book as an instigator of what David Lawrence, Jr.[2] calls "creative outrage" (2012).

As we wrote and edited, we strove to carefully parse our words, wanting them to stay as true to our commitment to justice as Diane Nash's actions demonstrated on March 7th during the 50th anniversary of "Bloody Sunday." Returning there, to Selma Alabama, to push forward the country's dream of democracy, one soaked in blood that day 50 years ago, Nash[3] spoke to the media, sat in priority seats to listen to President Obama speak, and, then, stood alongside the President and his family to walk across the infamous Edmund Pettus Bridge. Yet, when Former President George W. Bush walked into the line to cross that bridge with them, Diane Nash walked out of that privileged line.

Explaining later to Amy Goodman on *Democracy Now* (2015), Nash said: "They placed me in the front line. And then George Bush . . . got in the march. And I left. . . . I wasn't marching anywhere with George Bush. The Selma movement stands for nonviolence, peace, democracy, fairness, voting rights." To her, Nash clarified, Bush represented the exact opposite, even torture. She didn't want to be a part of any photographs, she explained to Goodman, which might travel around the globe depicting Bush as one of the leaders of nonviolence. For Nash, his picture would suggest the nonviolent movement had "sold out;" and, more importantly, she insisted, it would be an insult to all of the people who had been murdered in Selma.

---

[2] President of the Children's Movement of Florida and former publisher of the *Miami Herald*.

[3] Nash a leader in the Student Nonviolent Coordination Committee (SNCC); co-led the Freedom Riders; helped plan the Selma march; and is nationally known as a constant "Freedom Struggle" activist.

Well, regardless of what position someone might take on former President Bush's right to be on that bridge, Nash's spontaneous action of walking away from that stately spot shook our conscience, crystalizing what vigilance to one's truth might look like. Forced us to ask the question, "How often have we remained in the lines of privilege, and, thus, compromised our vision for justice, for listening to those who have been silenced?" Nash's daring action that day seemed to model a different way of being in the world. Her releasing attachment to the traps and seduction of privilege that oppress us as citizens, as teachers, as students was not only a gutsy move. It, indeed, also required, as Lisa Delpit once said about Vincent Harding,[4] "principles of steel."

Nash and Bob Moses, another one of our heroes, have dedicated their lives to pushing for full rights of citizenship for all Americans. A citizen-poet-writer who also pushes America toward realizing its dream of freedom for all is Nikki Giovanni. In 1994, she suggested that the ideals of democracy in America still create a powerful imaginative force that she continues to hold onto in spite of the horrors of the nation's history and the terrors of its current global initiatives. But, she declares later in her book, *Racism 101*, that the African-American "spirituals teach us that the problem of the twentieth century is not the problem of the color line. The problem of the twentieth century is the problem of civilizing white people" (p. 56–57).

We seem to have failed to solve that problem. For, in the twenty-first century, Western-Eurocentric people on the planet perpetually ratchet up the bellows and machinations of wars upon wars. In the twenty-first century, public education is becoming more a mouthpiece for corporate interests than interests of a democracy or of the earth and all its species. In the twenty-first century, unarmed black boys, men, and women have been shot down like vermin in a nation that professes "justice for all." Yet as the rapper, Common, sings in *Glory*, "Justice for all ain't specific enough."

So, we wanted the stories in this text to be "specific enough." We wanted to tell of the tragedy and glory of cultures, of humans, of trees, of earth. We wanted to raise all of those stifled intonations. The youth, the ancestors, the elders, the rock, the land, the river, the sea, the cosmic energy. We believe those vibrations and stories will stir us in our perpetual work toward resistance and inspired action. For, as Giovanni insists about story-tellers, "There must always be griots . . . else how will we know who we are?" (p. 19).

And when thinking of us as griots, we were reminded of Archbishop Desmond Tutu when he condensed the history of Africa into this one short quip: He said, "When the white missionaries came to Africa, they had the

---

[4] Historian; writer; social activist; speech writer for MLK, Jr.; Professor of Religion and Social Transformation

Bible, and we had the land. They said, 'Let us pray.' We closed our eyes. When we opened them, we had the Bible, and they had the land" (Tutu 2015). Therefore, the lens we look through, as we describe our individual truths, can become as vital as the truth itself. Recognizing the imperative of seeing our separate histories through multiple lenses can create an intellectual smorgasbord that might entice all citizens to see and reckon with the complexities of living in an inscrutable world, one full of contradictions and ambiguity.

Any ambiguities that unfold in this text, we hope, might also encourage students to recognize not only the inevitable convolutions of life's stories, but also the power and the place of those stories in the scope of research. For, Carlos and I think of research as just a story. Some tell it in statistics; some in ethnographies; some in case studies. But all research is formed within a specific context of socio-political realities. As Deepak Chopra suggests, "We have all walked through different gardens and knelt at different graves" (p. 16). Because of those separate realities of lived experiences, the fact that research studies and discoveries often conflict with one another holds no surprise for us, especially since humans from all walks of life design those studies. Yet it is important to reckon with at least two realities when searching for research validity. These realities are as significant as assessing the validity of the measurements used. The first is that historically the typical researcher came from the colonial elite. The second is that most often now researchers come from the academic elite. So, we hope that students will wrestle with the biases that naturally emanate from the context of researchers' lives. Taking the time to examine our lived experiences can clarify how those events complicate our perspectives in diverse disciplines, whether literature, science, art, music, or education. Furthermore, unpacking the ever-present colonial subtexts of our own lives might liberate our minds from the daily grind of the oppressive institutional demands that often trap us into accommodating injustice.

Recently, raising the issue of the historical Western economic accommodation of injustice, scholar and activist, Noam Chomsky, insisted that: "Racism is a serious problem . . . white supremacy in the United States was even more extreme and savage than in South Africa. . . . Our economy, wealth, privilege relies . . . on a century of horrifying slave labor camps." Drawing from the work of Edward Baptist (2014), Chomsky equated those camps to the horrors of the ones created in Nazi Germany. Baptist, in his book, insists that American slavery, the buying and selling of bodies as investment and capital, created an economic engine in the 18th and 19th century in the south, in the north, and in Europe that drove the explosion of U.S. financial and commercial prosperity and superiority, which is still sustained in this nation. But, for us, Baptist's and Chomsky's condemnation of our history seems to beckon another line from the song, *Glory*, the challenge of John Legend and Common when they proclaim, "Now we right the wrongs of history" (Glory, 2014).

So how do we do that? How do we right the wrongs, not only of our human history, but the history of our abuse of the ecosystem? How do we nurture ourselves and others as we take on such daunting work? How do we, in any corporate or bureaucratic jungle, create what Bob Moses calls, the "crawl spaces," (2001) where we can build healthy relationships? How do we resist injustices and continue to laugh big and loud? How do we stop oppression while learning to sing new songs? How do we dismantle public policies that sustain the plethora of societal injustices, while learning to dance wildly? How do we stop planetary destruction, while eating apple pie? How do we walk in and out of privilege, while strumming a guitar? How do we redeem America's soul, while frolicking with every Mother's child? And how, oh how, do we block out the cacophony of hegemony and begin to live Fannie Lou Hamer's chorus, "Freedom is a constant struggle; make a joyful noise"?

Conscious of the joy amidst the angst in the struggle, Carlos and I offer this text as an enticement to explore each other's stories about our battles to be free, as researchers, teachers, learners, citizens. When editing, he and I tried to write ourselves out of the lines of privilege that we occupy, while seeking to extricate ourselves from the scholastic shackles that we wear. As a counter to our professorial privilege, we listened not just to persons with national reputations in circles of justice, but also to students, friends, and younger colleagues. We invited their writing into our circles—investigating their lessons, challenges, joys, questions. We believe those narratives can lead us to confront together the hegemonic noise of systems that exploit humans and this small planet earth. As Ram Dass suggests, "We're all just walking each other home" (1971).

So, as we're walking each other home, let's consider once again the words of that master of story-telling, James Baldwin, who said, "...while the tale of how we suffer and how we are delighted and how we triumph is never new, it must be heard. There isn't any other tale to tell, it's the only light we've got in all this darkness" (1995 p. 87). Carlos and I believe that it is in our shared stories, true or not, that we can discover what sustains us "from the inside when all else falls away" (Oriah 1999). But, beyond that, perhaps, our joint stories will help us and our students determine ". . . if we can get up, after a night of grief and despair, weary and bruised to the bone, and do what needs to be done to feed [and teach] the children" (Oriah) in our communities, in our schools, and in this "country still unborn."

References

Baldwin, J. (1963). My dungeon shook: Letter to my nephew on the one hundredth anniversary of the Emancipation. *The fire next time*. New York: Vintage Books (p. 6).

Baldwin, James. (1995). *Sonny's Blues*. New York: Penguin Books Ltd.

Baptist, E. (2014). *The half has never been told: Slavery and the making of American capitalism*. New York, NY: Basic Books.

Chopra, D. (1991). *Unconditional life: Discovering the power to fulfill your dreams*. New York, NY: Bantam Books.

Dass, Ram (1971). *Be here now*. New York, NY: The Crown Publishing Co.

Giovanni, N. (1994). *Racism 101*. New York: William Morrow and Company.

Harding, V. (1981). *There is a river: The Black struggle for freedom in America*. Orlando, FL: Harcourt Brace and Co.

Hilliard, A. G. III (1997). "The Structure of valid staff development." *Journal of staff development*. Spring, Vol.18, No.2.

John Legend & Common, video on YouTube.com. https://www.youtube.com/watch?v=HUZOKvYcx_o

Lawrence, D. Jr. (2012). The Principles of Power and Leadership: How to get things done in Miami and America. The Chapman Leadership Lecture. Florida International University, September 12.

Lynching in America: Confronting the legacy of racial terror (2015). *EJI Report*. Birmingham, AL: Equal Justice Initiative. http://www.eji.org/files/EJI%20Lynching%20in%20America%20SUMMARY.pdf

Morrison, Toni (1987). *Beloved*. New York: Alfred Knopf.

Moses, R. P. & Cobb, C. (2001) *Radical Equations: Civil Rights from Mississippi to the Algebra Project*. Boston: Beacon Press.

Nash, D. (2015). Interview. *Democracy Now* http://www.democracynow.org/2015/3/9/civil_rights_pioneer_diane_nash_i

Noam Chomsky on Black Lives Matter: Why Won't U.S. Own Up to History of Slavery & Racism? Mar. 3, 2015. *Democracy Now*. http://www.democracynow.org/2015/3/3/noam_chomsky_on_black_lives_matter

Nussbaum, Martha (2006) *Frontiers of Justice: Disability, nationality, species membership*. Cambridge MA: First Harvard University Press.

Oriah Mountain Dreamer (1999) http://www.oriahmountaindreamer.com/person.html

Roberts, Wally. (2004). E-mail sharing his experience living one summer in Fannie Lou Hamer's home.

Tutu, Desmond. *Seeds in conflict in a haven of peace: From religious Studies to Interreligious Studies in Africa.* Student Non-violent Coordinating Committee (SNCC) e-mail list-serve, April 7, 2015.

PART 1

A human being is part of the whole

A human being is a part of a whole, called by us a universe, a part limited in time and space. He experiences himself, his thoughts and feelings as something separated from the rest . . . a kind of optical delusion of his consciousness. This delusion is a kind of prison for us, restricting us to our personal desires and to affection for a few persons nearest to us. Our task must be to free ourselves from this prison by widening our circle of compassion to embrace all living creatures and the whole of nature in its beauty.

—Albert Einstein

Math, struggles, and slash pines

by Carlos Gonzalez

She told me that she did not think she was going to pass her math class, that the teacher was confusing, that she worked full time, went to school full time, and she did not have the energy or time to go to tutoring. She saw herself taking the class once again, she said. It was five minutes before I was taking students on a tour of the Environmental Center. I was drawn into my student's struggle and for a moment wondered what I had to offer her, if anything. In my work I see so many who juggle too much, who struggle and often don't see a way through their challenges because they are so many.

We walked toward the start of our tour, and I felt the heaviness of this conversation. To me it wasn't just one more student merely giving up on a class, but hers was the voice of so many others. Math was not the real issue. It was life itself, life that seemed unfair, harsh, and impossible. Clearly I was hearing her story filtered through my own heaviness, my own sense of struggle, loss, and pain, the past nine years or so of seeing my mother lost to dementia, the breakdown of family bonds, the loss of loved ones, and at times, the loss of hope.

The week before hearing my student's story, I had read over 140 essays. Some of them detailed suicide attempts, painful separations, failed dreams, loss on a scale that surprised me and reminded me how we are more alike than we are different. And as I walked to the entrance of the Center, the air plant growing on the tree caught my attention. It did not do so in a subtle way. It spoke to me and asked me to tell a particular story. This beautiful being, although voiceless, was asking to speak to my student and to me.

The clarity of the communication surprised me. It was now evident to me that I needed to have overheard my student mention her math class. It was also evident that what I was going to do for the next seven hours of teaching was to repeat the message, not so much because of my math challenged student but because I, too, needed to hear a good word. I needed a reminder. We needed a story, this story, as Barry Lopez reminds us, "more than food to stay alive" (1990, p. 8).

The Environmental Center is a nine-acre preserve. One enters it through a colorful mosaic gate and is immediately presented with a radically different space. The Center is on the edge of campus, the edge of time, and a text that often is misread or not read at all. It is a reminder of what parts of South Florida used to be, of how the landscape looked before development. It offers a glimpse of a bygone era where slash pines covered the area and the human footprint was less obvious. It is also a clear reminder of the feeble efforts to preserve the often tenuous relationships between humans and other life forms. It is a place where one can experience great peace and also be in touch with a sense of deep loss. It is filled with life and reminders that death is also part of life and the cycle of beginning and endings is infinite.

So what did the epiphyte say to me? This was no joke. Adaptation = Learning. The rest follows.

As I stood before my students, I told them how at some point, millions of years ago, I was guessing, the ancestors of this plant learned that living on the soil was not to its advantage, and somehow learned to live on the tree canopy, gathering food and water from the falling leaves of the host tree and in the process providing a home for small animals such as frogs and lizards.

This particular air plant was about to bloom, and we could see the emerging structure of the flower, an elegant manifestation of perfectly adapted design. We looked at the plant, I caressed its leaves. Students looked at me as if I were on some kind of drug. I assured them I was not. I told them the message from my plant friend: To adapt is to learn and to take on life's challenges and use them to create what is necessary for survival and the possibility to thrive. We took a moment. I answered some questions. We were quiet. Some were looking at their phones. I hesitated to take steps away from the air plant, but I knew then that I would be able to hear its message the rest of the day. And we walked to the little sliver of slash pine forest.

It was only a hundred feet or so away. At the head of the trail, a beautiful specimen of a tree stands tall. It's probably 60 or more years old. As I came upon it, I told them that this tree was a Ph.D. in South Florida; that it had learned this area so well that it had specialized in living here and nowhere else. This particular species of slash pine, *Pinus elliottii* var densa, is endemic to South Florida (Pine Rocklands—Miami-Dade County). Students looked at me funny. I stared back. I kissed the tree. I thanked it. By now, everyone had been pushed over the edge of weirdness, and they just looked at me and smiled.

I continued with my message and repeated the mantra the epiphyte gave me: Adaptation is learning. It is the means that all of life has to continue to exist. Change is a constant. Adaptation is a dance with change. It is the engagement of the core challenge associated with change. It is the "yes" in all creatures to life, possibility, and existence.

I told them the little I know about slash pines, that there are other relatives of this tree, but that this species is only found here. I pointed out how this particular pine learned to use the wet and dry seasons, the poor soil conditions, frequent fires to manifest a beauty that is a gift to witness and appreciate. I celebrated the tree in front of me. Everyone did so as well. A little attention, at least, from the more hard to reach. We took a moment to breathe deeply and notice the scent the tree gives off. I was filled with wonder. Some were too. Others looked at their phones. They were receiving messages at the time, but not from the epiphyte, the slash pine, or me.

So many unique elements of this tree's knowledge and manifestation of life exude in this place, the fringes of this campus where concrete replaced its kin. Its bark is fire resistant, a useful trait given lighting strikes that in the past burned the under story. These fires took place in the wet season and were not destructive. They were energy deposits into the area that these trees knew how to use. The slash pine drops its seeds after a fire into the ash-enriched limestone and the seeds take root.

The specialization worked well for thousands of years. It stopped working once large numbers of people moved into the area. The Dade County slash pine did not specialize in humans, however. It did not take us into account and our aversion to fire. Not surprisingly, the slash pine has lost out to our home building and fire suppression. In a matter of less than 100 years or so, about one to two percent of the endemic slash pine forest is left (Pine Rocklands—Miami-Dade County). This tree adapted to the area but has not been able to adapt to our presence.

The lesson in this is difficult. It presents us with many questions. Primarily, "What's our responsibility and role in preserving those life forms that don't have the capacity to adapt to the rapid change we are creating?" and "How do we address those who are not able to learn at the pace of change all around us?" These were big questions, but not the thrust of what I was hoping I was conveying to my students. The message of the air plant, though a species that supposedly lacks judgment, seemed more direct: To adapt means to learn. To stop learning or not learn fast enough means death.

So about one to two percent of the original Dade County slash pine forest is left. Our campus has a couple of patches where once the entire area was dominated by these trees. We walked away from this small patch and felt ambivalent.

The beauty of the trees is obvious; their fate also seems sealed. But. There is always a "but" that carries the possibility of surprise. On the way out of the slash pines, I spotted one solitary atala butterfly heading for its morning breakfast. This small dark blue butterfly with a red belly and metallic blue dots on its wings echoed the epiphytes message and gave it a slightly different intonation.

We paused before leaving the forest and observed the atala dancing amongst the flowers. I mentioned how this exquisite creature was believed to have been extinct as of 1965 and that in 1979 a small population had been discovered in Key Biscayne (Pine Rocklands). The atala had almost disappeared because it, too, specialized and had adapted exclusively to the South Florida environment. Like the slash pines, it found itself challenged to live because we interfered with its environment and eliminated the coontie plant, a once prevalent plant of the hammocks and rock pinelands. The coontie, an ancient cycad, is the sole host plant for the atala. This specialization meant that when the coontie was virtually eliminated from the area, the atalas disappeared as well (Pine Rocklands).

I told students to pay attention to this story. That it offered a detail that was not fully developed in the earlier message of the air plant. What was interesting about this story was that the atala did not die off. Against significant odds, it came back. It was not supposed to survive. But an effort to encourage gardeners to plant the coontie allowed the butterfly to return. This was not an all-out plan by a monied government agency or environmental group. Butterflies are not big money makers! And so I reminded them and me that not all is loss. Not all is a sealed fate. Sometimes we get surprised by the beauty of small miracle stories that don't allow us to give up. More significantly, the atala reminded us that there's always a possibility for the creature with the greatest ability to adapt, us, to do so and allow others who may not have the same capacity to survive and thrive.

Our journey through the Environmental Center came to an end as we approached the chickee next to the lake. We sat there and felt the cool breeze. The pitched roof thatched with native palm fronds, the cypress columns, and the setting offered a perfect conclusion. We were sitting under a structure built by members of the Miccosukee Tribe of Indians. The structure was one last reminder of adaptation, where lessons from math, life's struggles, and slash pine can collide.

References

Lopez, B. (1990) *Crow and Weasel*. Canada: North Point Press. p. 60.

Pine Rocklands. Miami-Dade County Government (n.d.). Retrieved April 21, 2015 from http://www.miamidade.gov/environment/pine-rocklands.asp

Generations Connect: Variation on "Om Namah Shivaya"

by Carlos Gonzalez

> Patience
> For now there is destruction
> Later
> much later
> gate gate paragate parasamgate
> under the rubble
> a strong vulnerable sprout breaks ground
> and embraces
> the sky.

I began to write this piece above as I was listening to the wind rustling the leaves of the trees in the valley below. I'm sitting on a grassy knoll, under the overhang of what serves as the front porch of the Straw Bale Lodge donated to Narrow Ridge, a retreat in Tennessee, by Mac Smith, a former professor in Miami who taught for 30 years at the college where I've worked for 22 years now. He also launched a series of programs that have blossomed into a several communities that focus on Earth literacy.

I'm not sure why I need to write the paragraph above, but it seems important to name him, name the place where I'm working, and in doing so remind myself that the work I do is somehow tied to others who have come before me. This "before me" part has been important in the past. Connecting to the ancestors has been a lifeline that in some of the more challenging times of teaching has allowed me to find my way when the path was unclear or encumbered by my own confusion. What I'm noticing more and more is that those who follow are becoming more relevant. What is dawning on me is that I am now becoming more of an elder or lifeline to those who come after me.

I'm also realizing that I'm coming to the end of the summer of my teaching life. I sense the beginning of the fall season and note a number of things.

One that stands out vividly is the notion that the kind of education that I'm interested in is not one that easily translates into objectives and goals. I realize that I'm interested in the ancient notion of education, which the word itself suggests, is to draw out, to invite into awareness. This is what I consider to be my role as a teacher in relationship to my students. It's also the type of role, that when I'm at my best, students invite me to play and they play as well. Together we draw out for one another what is already there but may be overlooked. And the drawing out is not exclusive of learning a skill. It involves and requires so much more than merely writing an essay, resume, or figuring out a complicated calculus.

These reflections and my writing came after spending an afternoon touring Narrow Ridge, an Earth Literacy Center and community in East Tennessee in the foothills of the Smokies, where my school sends students every spring. I came up this time as a chaperone. As I live among 13 young people for this short time, I'm challenged to hold the tension of living from one's ideals while often finding that the choices made don't come close to reflecting those. Like the young people I have accompanied, I live with the disorder of my own mind and life, wanting to live consistently within my ideals and coming up short time and again. This understanding does not jive well with my notion of being an elder.

The disconnect and discomfort in my own mind regarding elderhood is part of the generational gap and chasm that has existed for far too long. The young and old don't relate to one another enough by living and working close together. The segregation that started with industrialization and children being put in schools that were away from their grandparents and parents most of the day, and that were modeled after the factories the parents worked in, planted the seeds of a wisdom deficit that we keep bumping into and find no real way to address. We have become an uninitiated culture unaware of how to be. This is true of young people and of those who are not quite old but getting there.

These particular 13 students remind me in their youthful exuberance of wanting to be, and of being aware of life itself, of exploring the possibilities of living in a way that affirms rather than denies life. They are able to do this so freely and quickly as they step away from the constraints of the classroom and find themselves in a quiet space meant to invite awareness rather than distraction. When joining them at meals, it is clear as I hear them share that they also search for ways to live with the brokenness and disjointedness of life. Our lives are lived in the up-rootedness of urban spaces, where neighborliness is often absent, where green spaces are islands engulfed not only by roads and buildings, but surrounded and steeped in the "always on" culture of social media and smartphones. What's different, it seems, for them is that their desire for wholeness has not yet spiraled down through the challenges of living long enough to experience many of the obstacles inherent in existence itself. They haven't yet experienced the tendency that happens as we grow older to give up or grow disillusioned and disheartened by the alienated culture.

Narrow Ridge is named after a line in Martin Buber's book *Between Man and Man* (2002). It's a pertinent thought that can serve as a signpost for all of us: "I do not rest on the broad upland of a system that includes a series of sure statements about the absolutes, but on a narrow, rocky ridge between the gulfs where there is no sureness of expressible knowledge but [only] the certainty of meeting what remains, undisclosed" (Buber, 2002, p. 218).

The narrow ridge of which Buber and this place remind us is that tenuous spot where we meet all of life not as objects but as subjects. It's a tenuous spot because we do not stay on the ridge easily. We walk it with great care and humility, honoring and becoming aware of the ultimate mystery of existence and life itself. Too much effort or too much trying, and we fall off the ridge. Too little effort and too little awareness and the same thing happens. I'm not even sure that we can use the word tenuous. The narrow ridge is a point that seems out of reach for most. For me, I don't know if I'm on it for more than mere moments, and then off again.

On this particular day, without the use of a textbook or PowerPoint, my students and I got a small glimpse of living in that balance and awareness, of living as Daniel Berrigan says in his introduction to Dorothy Day's autobiography *The Long Loneliness*, of living ". . . as though the truth were true" (Day, 1981, p. xxiii). This happened as we walked up and down hills and saw and heard the story of Narrow Ridge. We spent a couple of hours not only walking, but seeing first hand a physical manifestation of a vision where humans attempt to live in conscious awareness of their own place in the Universe. Through its relationship to the land, built structures, and governance, the Narrow Ridge community shows visitors how a small community tries to walk the ridge together, to navigate between a culture of mass consumption and one of great care.

As we walked, we visited with a number of the human residents of Narrow Ridge. Each offered us a part of their story. Each left us with a bit of the stirring that happens within when we meet another person who has tried her best to live life in service, in love, in truth.

In the process with these 13, I was reconnected with the question of what happens when young and old gather to intentionally learn from one another. And all along the ridge, I'm thinking again and again about the lifeline of ancestors and my own role as an emerging lifeline to others. As often happens from these gatherings when we invite the ancestors, ourselves, and the young together on a journey, we learned the unexpected.

Near the end of our week at Narrow Ridge, we took a day trip to Eagan, just south of the Kentucky border. Eagan is a border town, on the margins so to speak, and as such has been a mining town since the early part of the twentieth century. As we approached the town, it was clear to see that we were entering another America, one that was rich in beauty, culture, and so-called resources, but one that had been used as the source of cheap energy for more than 100 years. All around us we could see the effects of coal extraction, sides of mountains cut in perfect angles, exposing veins of coal that were the remains of our prehistoric ancestors. Our bodies also knew we were in a different America. Many of us had difficulty breathing the air. It was as if the air had become heavy. In reality, the air was heavy with the coal dust of the mountain that was being removed right in front of our eyes.

The point of this trip was to visit the site of a mountain top removal. This is a euphemistic term for something much more gruesome. We were there to witness the decapitation of a mountain, a slow execution fueled by my own, our own, desire and need to cheaply power our modern way of life. I say cheaply because none of us have paid the full cost of the coal that has been extracted from the mountains there. But the mountain and the whole communion of beings who call it home have and are paying the full price.

Eagan felt like a developing country where large landholders control most of the land and do with it what they will, even when this means that area residents suffer dearly with the poisons that are the detritus of extracting energy—either in the form of food (always in the form of some kind of monoculture) or of fossil fuel to keep the economy running.

It was raining on this day and what we could see was the torrents of brown runoff coming down from the side of the mountain. Every barren or almost barren hillside was a flowing river of milk-chocolate-colored water, all flowing to the bottom where mountain streams brim with a cocktail of chemicals and dirt that kills most if not all of the fish and wildlife who call these streams home. The effects on humans of this runoff is equally disastrous as flash floods because the erosion is now commonplace. No trees on the mountain means no roots to hold the soil in place. We are an uprooted culture in so many different ways.

We tried getting to the top of where the coal company had removed the mountain, but we could not. The rain was too much and the road was becoming impassable. Instead, our guide, Gary Garret, a resident of Eagan, an elder in training, and a volunteer at the Clearfolk Community Center, showed us a cemetery on the side of the road. It was the part of the mountain top that had not been carved out for coal. The cemetery stripped of the mountain all around was left as an island of the dead, a monument to short-sightedness on all levels. That it had not been carved out like everything else was a miracle. We suppose that it was left there to respect the remains of the residents who once called the mountain home. But what we witnessed was obscene. The dead in that cemetery like the living have no real resting place as the mountains continue to be chopped up and killed. Chief Seattle's words rung in our ears:

> And when the last Red Man shall have perished, and the memory of my tribe shall have become a myth among the White Men, these shores will swarm with the invisible dead of my tribe, and when your children's children think themselves alone in the field, the store, the shop, upon the highway, or in the silence of the pathless woods, they will not be alone. In all the earth there is no place dedicated to solitude. At night when the streets of your cities and villages are silent and you think them deserted, they will throng with the returning hosts that once filled them and still love this beautiful land. The White Man will never be alone (Smith, 1887)

As we left Eagan, we more fully recognized the value of the solar panels we had noticed in Narrow Ridge during our first tour of the retreat. They are a small response to the mountain top removal/decapitation/execution. As we traveled back to our little oasis, many of us thought and talked about memory and the loss of memory that our culture is based upon. The key to the complete loss of this memory is tied to the disrupted way we learn or don't learn from one another. Without the generations coming together and sharing what's of value, what's of interest, all we have left is a flattened ecosystem both outside and inside of us.

For the youth in the group, the anxiety and questions of what to do with the gift of life in light of the enormity of the challenges before us, how to live in a world that feels out of sorts in its speed, focus, and ultimate goals were offered as the base of much of the conversations during the week. The elders and elders in training, who clearly did not have any specific answers to these heartfelt questions, but, who, because of the grace of sometimes living with some awareness, could point out sign posts that have kept them close to the narrow ridge. The opportunity to be in communion with these young people served as a balm for the achiness of spirit that too often plagues those who have awakened from the dominant culture's hypnotic spell to merely consume and forget. For me, and I suspect for the others above 40 in the group, coming together to enter into dialogue with young people offered the blessing of renewal, a reminder to remain vulnerable, open, and strong all at once.

Walking the narrow ridge in this regard has something to do with that blessed space that is described by many spiritual traditions as sensing the divine presence not in some far off place but in the midst of the current time with its mixture of beauty along with the oppression, hurt, and ugliness of a human constructed system bent on domination of the many for the benefit of the few. Walking the narrow ridge is a movement from disconnection to communion and awareness.

When together we face the youthful not knowing, the pain of the current moment, and the elder's understanding of the inherent incompleteness of all of our efforts, we can sense, if there is honesty and grace in the container of sharing, that we offer one another what is needed. We bring ourselves with all of our limitations into a space of healthy interrogation of life's ambiguity.

Any uncertainty about the future becomes an entry point to the mystery that all we need is right before us, that we are the ones we have been looking for all along. In this meeting place, or narrow ridge, the now of this moment allows all of us, young and old, to be fully ourselves and stop the continuous effort to cover over our inherent qualities as *Homo sapiens*, a species among many, a species with a deep desire to reflect upon its own place in the family of life.

As I look back at my own teaching life, I realize that my development and growth as a teacher often takes off as I enter or create the kinds of diverse communities where the old and young come together in a spirit of listening and sacred sharing. These communities have never been committees. They have always involved effort in either joining or creating them. Sometimes they emerge suddenly and with great force. Their intensity brightens up the path for all who participate. They exist in the margins, in moments—lasting long enough to serve as reminders to all who are there to witness to wake up to possibility, empathy, and action.

Over the years, this practice of not just stepping outside of the classroom but outside of the philosophical underpinnings of a schooling system based on transaction and objectification, has served to bring me back to myself as a learner, a seeker, and one who wants to live with integrity. Interestingly, I have been able to experience this not only outside of the physical structure of schools such as a place like Narrow Ridge, but also even within the walls of my own institution, that I sometimes in frustration and playfulness call Rockland, the psychiatric hospital in Ginsberg's "Howl" (1956).

I point this out, because the magic of this time in Narrow Ridge had more to do with this community container than the actual place. The container can be created anywhere, even in the midst of systemic craziness. I believe that the narrow ridge Buber describes is any space where such gatherings of the young and the elder as well as peers can emerge with integrity; we need these to help us find our way and balance. I know I need these to find my heart and soul when both become opaque or clouded over.

I started this essay with a short poem inspired by an ancient chant to Shiva, the Hindu deity associated with creation and destruction. I did so honoring the pattern within me of creation and destruction. The poem is a reminder that all is not lost. When we find ourselves in the rubble and off the ridge, we have work to do. In this precious and precarious time, the need to connect old and young and form diverse communities of wisdom is not optional because these communities are the medium and the narrow ridges by which and in which all that is vulnerable and truthful can take root, emerge, reach for the sky, and create anew.

References

Buber, M. (2002). *Between Man and Man*. London: Routledge Classics. p. 218.

Day, D. (1981). *The Long Loneliness* (Reprint Edition, ed.). New York, NY: Harper and Row. p. Xxiii.

Smith, H. A. Early Reminiscences. Number Ten. Scraps from a Diary. Chief Seattle: A Gentleman by Instinct – His Native Eloquence. Etc., Etc. *Seattle Sunday Star*, October 29, 1987, p. 3. Retrieved April 21, 2015 from http://courses.washington.edu/spcmu/speeches/chiefseattle.htm

Constitutional Eras for "We the People"[1]

by Robert P. Moses

Almost 55 years ago, in August of 1960, nine months before the Freedom Riders[2] made the route infamous, Ella Baker and Jane Stembridge of SNCC[3] put me on a Greyhound bus in Atlanta, headed to Mississippi. Representing the sit-in movement, but more deeply aware of my ride, I slid to the back of the bus as it approached Anniston Alabama, where the state trooper climbed onboard to take a look. A newly minted SNCC scout, little did I know that I was riding into history and an insurgency grounded in the Mississippi Amzie Moore NAACP World.

Amzie, home from WWII, turned himself into a tree for Delta blacks to transform themselves, in spite of whomever and whatever, from second to first class citizenship. A first-class insurgency, that's what Amzie had in his mind and managed to layer, in all due time, into mine.

In all due time, two and one-half years later, in the early darkness of a winter evening in February 1963, Jimmy Travis slips behind the wheel and Randolph Blackwell crowds me into the front seat of a SNCC Chevy as we leave the Greenwood Voter Registration Office. We were to drive from Greenwood to Greenville on U.S. 82 straight across the Mississippi Delta. Jimmy zigzagged out of town to escape an unmarked car that had been circling the office, but as we headed west on 82, the car spots us, trails us, and sweeps past near the turn off for Valley State, firing a hailstorm of bullets. Jimmy cries out, slumps over; I reach over, grab the wheel, fumble for the brakes; we glide off the icy highway, snuggle into the ditch—a bullet-tattooed

---

[1] A keynote address written and delivered by Bob Moses at Emory University, Atlanta, GA. January 20, 2015.

[2] A series of bus trips through the American South to protest segregation in interstate bus terminals, begun in 1961 by African-American and white civil rights activists.

[3] Student Non-Violent Coordinating Committee of the Southern Freedom Movement.

Chevy, windows blown away, a hole in Jimmy's neck. 1963, the year that began with a grease gun terrorist highway attack, ended with the assassination of a President. First-class black insurgents were not the only ones paying dues.

This is a talk about an abstract American idea, the American concept of a Constitutional Person—a talk to help make that invisible abstraction visible. America's Constitutional people need outfits, clothes, so they can be seen in the stories we Americans carry in our heads about who we are, where we are, and where we are headed: This, therefore, is a talk about the American Lived Constitution.

The concept of Constitutional People is everywhere in America's ongoing story. Over 156 years ago, on June 16, 1858, in front of 1,000 delegates to the Republican State Convention in Springfield Illinois, a candidate to be Senator of Illinois opened his talk with these words: "Mr. President and Gentlemen of the Convention: If we could first know where we are, and whither we are tending, we could then better judge what to do, and how to do it" (Lincoln 1858)

But flash forward for a moment to the words of another citizen and president. In 1988, when Kingman Brewster died,[4] it fell to Sam Chauncey[5] to say how Kingman should be remembered and to plan a memorable space in the Grove street cemetery where all presidents of Yale rest. Sam designed a low black marble wall to enclose Kingman's grave. On it he etched two sentences that encapsulate the interface between constitutional and common law; two sentences to illuminate how, on planet Earth, the ocean of lore humans inherit ought to instruct and inform the constitutional law humans create: "The presumption of innocence is not just a legal concept. In common sense terms it rests on that generosity of spirit which assumes the best, not the worst, of the stranger"[6] (Carter, 1999, p. 292).

Now lurch backward in time. In 1749, A West African boy, nine years old and captured, sailed the middle passage to Virginia and survived. In August of that year, a Scottish born merchant slave trader peered into the pluck of that nine year old and bought him. Up and coming Charles Stewart bought Somerset of West Africa to be his personal slave (Blumrosen 2005).

Twenty years pass, it's 1769. Stewart is 44; and Somerset, 29, accompanies him to London to help care for Stewart's sister's family when her husband

---

[4] Diplomat, Harvard law professor, and President of Yale University, 1963–1977.
[5] Administrator for Brewster, and son of Henry Chauncey, founder of Educational Testing Service.
[6] Tombstone inscription are words from Brewster's writings.

dies. London is awash with Africans from the British Empire. Slaves and runaways, beggars and workers, sea-goers and artisans, and Somerset, running errands everywhere for his master, meeting blacks on the streets, in the stores, along the docks, makes a plan. He arranges a baptism, acquires English Godparents and flows, on October 1, 1771, into London's stream of Insurgent Runaway Slaves (Blumrosen, p. 10).

Charles Stewart, feeling "betrayed and publicly insulted," posted notices to get Somerset back. And on November 2, slave catchers deliver Somerset to a ship bound for Jamaica. Seven days later, Somerset's Godmother, Elisabeth Cade pays to petition the Court of Kings Bench for a writ of Habeas Corpus to release him (p. 10).

Lord Mansfield, the Chief Justice, issues a writ requiring Captain Knowles to explain the reason for detaining Somerset on the Anne & Mary vessel. Six days later, Somerset appears before the King's Bench with Captain Knowles, who declares: "Charles Stewart, a colonial from America, delivered his slave, Somerset, to be sold in Jamaica" (p. 7). But Lord Mansfield releases Somerset pending a hearing, suggesting he be set free. West Indian planters, however, want a decision upholding slavery in Britain to keep prices stable in the commodities markets.

Lord Mansfield cautions them that if they think the question of great commercial concern is the only method of settling the point in the future, they should prepare an application to Parliament. But Parliament, content to let the matter rest at the Kings Bench refused the merchants a hearing.

On June 22, 1772, while the clerk called the case of "James Somerset, a Negro on Habeas Corpus," Lord Mansfield, bewigged, the chief justice of the oldest and highest court in England, mounted the bench to deliver his judgment:

> The state of slavery is of such a nature, that it is incapable of being introduced on any reasons, moral or political. . . . It's so odious, that nothing can be suffered to support it but constitutional law. Whatever inconveniences, therefore, may follow from the decision, I cannot say this case is allowed or approved by the law of England; and therefore the black must be discharged (p. 24).

So why did Slave Owner Stewart feel "betrayed and publicly humiliated?" Almost 200 years pass, and the matter at the heart of that matter resurfaces in a provocative letter that novelist James Baldwin wrote in 1962 in a letter to his brother's son, James:

> The crime of which I accuse my country and my countrymen . . . that they have destroyed and are destroying hundreds of thousands of lives and do not know it and do not want to know it. One can be . . . tough and philosophical concerning destruction and death . . . But it is not permissible that

the authors of devastation should also be innocent. It is the innocence which constitutes the crime (Baldwin pp. 5–6).

It was then in 1772 as in 1963, a question of innocence. After all, saturated with the lore humans inherit, Stewart's generosity of spirit saw the "best" not the "worst" in a nine year old "personable" African stranger. But Stewart who could not clothe his personal property with English Common Law and imagine Somerset into a Constitutional Person, instead imagined himself, a slave owner, an innocent, a victim, "betrayed and publicly humiliated" by an abstraction.

Flash forward in history again. In 1960, after Jimmy caught that bullet in his neck, Snick[7] regrouped to converge on Greenwood, and black sharecroppers lined up at the Court House to demand their right to vote. When Snick field secretaries were arrested, Burke Marshall, the Assistant Attorney General for Civil Rights under Robert Kennedy, removed our cases to the Federal District Court in Greenville and sent John Doar to be our lawyer. From the witness stand I looked out at a courtroom packed with black sharecroppers from Greenwood, hushed along its walls, packed onto its benches, and attended to the question put by Federal District Judge Clayton: "Why are you taking illiterates down to register to vote?" (Moses, 2010)

Wrong question Judge: These delta blacks are dressed up in their new outfits: constitutional clothes. Can you see them and incorporate them in the story you carry in your head about who they are, where they are, and where they are headed?

This conundrum of constitutional outfits, the ongoing dilemma about who gets to wear what constitutional clothes, surfaced at the 1787 Constitutional Convention, and resurfaces time and again: In Lincoln's House Divided speech; in Judge Clayton's question; in Ferguson; in the nation's theory of "undocumented "people"; in the national education conundrum of constitutional, but naked school children, sent to school, with no constitutional clothes.

In all due time, we have circled back, in our story, to Abraham Lincoln, that 1858 Republican Senate candidate, who went on to invoke a House Divided: "A house divided against itself cannot stand. I believe this government cannot endure, permanently half slave and half free. I do not expect the Union to be dissolved—I do not expect the house to fall—but I do expect it will cease to be divided. It will become all one thing or all the other" (Lincoln, 1858).

---

[7] Student Non-violent Coordinating Committee (SNCC)

Don't be fooled, the conundrum of Lincoln's House Divided speech was not the Nation, the Union, nor the "it" in "It will become all one thing or the other." Not even close: SNCC was on the witness stand a century later precisely because the country had figured a way around that "it." No, Lincoln's conundrum was that other two letter word, "We." At the 1787 Constitutional Convention, James Madison rose to clarify the background that paved a path into Lincoln's conundrum. It seems now to be pretty well understood that the real difference of interests lay, not between the northern and southern states. The institution of slavery and its consequences formed the line of demarcation.

Move forward in time to April 1952. President Harry Truman, in the middle of the Korean war, declared that an impending steel strike "would immediately jeopardize and impair our national defense" and ordered the secretary of commerce "to take possession of all or such of the plants, facilities, and other property of the steel companies" (Truman 1952) as he may deem necessary in the interest of national defense (Corwin 1953; Loftus 1952).

The Steel Seizure case, which followed Truman's declaration, culminated in a Supreme Court injunction prohibiting the secretary from obeying the president's order. Six justices explained their reasons, separately, for deciding the order was unconstitutional. But the opinion of Justice Robert H. Jackson has most clearly withstood subsequent legal scrutiny:

The actual art of governing under our Constitution does not and cannot conform to judicial definitions of the power of any of its branches based on isolated clauses or even single Articles torn from context. While the Constitution diffuses power the better to secure liberty, it also contemplates that practice will integrate the dispersed powers into a workable government (Clayton 2002 p. 69).

In advance of any practice, the founding fathers at the Constitutional Convention of 1787, who contemplated the actual art of governing when the institution of slavery and its consequences formed the line of discrimination, faced a conundrum. While the 1787 Constitution contemplated a class of Constitutional People in its "We The People" Pre Amble, and diffused power, the better to secure their liberty, it also contemplated a class of Constitutional Property, outfits for Somerset's constitutional clothing designed as Article IV, Section 2, Paragraph 3: "No person held to service or labor in one state, under the laws thereof, escaping into another, shall, in consequence of any law or regulation therein, be discharged from such service or labor, but shall be delivered up on claim of the party to whom such service or labor is due" (Constitution). Thus, "We the People" does not include slaves.

The Somerset clause contemplated a Constitution that diffused power—the better to secure slavery—because as James Madison understood only too well, slavery was the indispensable practice required to integrate the dispersed powers into a workable government. Without slavery as its economic engine, the nation and the government were not "workable."

America, the land of democracy and freedom, is also a crime scene, the crime of which I accuse my country and my countrymen. . . . We have the wolf of terrorism by the ear, and we can neither hold on to it, nor can we let it go; but it is not permissible that the authors of destruction should also be innocent. Weapons of mass destruction! *It is the innocence which constitutes the crime.*

For three quarters of a century, the Government of Constitutional People and Constitutional Property tried workability all the while, a Young People's Project, Africans, central actors in the Constitutional Drama, acting out, coming of age insurgencies, invisible, mutating viruses, popping up here and there, infecting the Constitutional Scene. Until, inevitably, in the persona of Dred Scott, the central character in the 1857 decision by Roger B. Taney, Chief Justice of the Supreme Court, their project metastasizes into a catalyst of mass destruction that divides Lincoln's House, sets into motion the War of the Constitutional People over Constitutional Property, and drops the curtain on America's first Constitutional era. The Era lurched to an end, but its conundrum refused to expire: Who were we, if "we" was still the problem?

Constitutional Era 2

The moon was quite young when the bell tolled, the young black men rushed into the chapel to get their guns and Margaret Caldwell, left home, her face hid, stepped over a body lying in the street near a store, before going back home where her husband's brother's wife and three children cowered with her against the sound of the white mob roaming the streets. There Margaret stayed until her minister came to bring the news that both husbands were dead, and he carried two bodies upstairs. Margaret's husband's body had to be tied together and the minister laid both bodies out to prepare for burial. Late that night the train from Vicksburg to Jackson stopped in Clinton and Modocs, traveling confederates imagining themselves into a tribe of wild Indians marched into the Caldwell house, threw open the windows, sang, danced, cursed, and challenged the two dead men to get up and meet them. It was a Thursday evening during the Christmas season in Clinton Mississippi; it was 1875. The second Constitutional Era was getting underway.

Margaret's husband, Charles Caldwell had commanded the Negro militia company that marched in formation from Jackson to Edwards on October 9, 1875, carrying armaments for the militia company there. But Ohio's state elections were scheduled for October 13, and Ohio Republicans sent a delegation to Ulysses Grant, informing the President that if he sent troops to Mississippi, Ohio, "which had voted by a wide margin against ratification of the Fifteenth Amendment,[8] the state would fall to the Democrats. Grant sent no troops, but later told Lynch, the black senator from Mississippi, that "I made a grave mistake."

Republicans blinked: In 1875, President Grant yielding to the request of the Republican delegation, put into motion a practice that integrated America's dispersed powers into a workable government, the better to secure Jim Crow, slavery by another name (Blackmon 2008).

Democrats winked: In 1875, Redeemed, Democrats overthrew the Mississippi Government by terror, violence, and murder, and contemplated a written Constitution that diffused power the better to secure white supremacy, a practice which integrated dispersed powers into a workable government, the better for white people to secure freedom.

On a Thursday evening during the Christmas season of 1875, when the moon was quite young and the bells tolled, Margaret Caldwell, her face hid, stepped over the body of her husband Charles (Lemann 2006)

For the Presidential race of 1876, Rutherford Hayes, saved by Grant and reelected governor of Ohio, ran against Samuel Tilden, Democratic governor of New York. Terror and murder rampaged against black men across Louisiana, Mississippi, South Carolina and Florida, and when the election ended in a stalemate at the electoral college, a deal was cut: The Compromise of 1877: The nation got a workable government: Hayes and the Republicans got the Presidency, federal troops were withdrawn from the South, and white southerners established a political confederacy. The Nation finally knew who we were and whither we were tending and, therefore, better judged what to do and how to do it.

And the clarity of the "what and how" of those judgements sharply resonate when listening to Billy Holiday sing "Strange Fruit." Her ironic juxtaposition of words such as "southern breezes, gallant South, and sweetness of magnolias" alongside the words that spoke to the lynching horrors resulting in "bulging eyes, twisted mouths, and burning flesh" (Margolick 2000 p. 25) dramatically captured the contradictions of the perverted betrayals of Black people, sanctioned by corrupted government policies, both southern and national.

---

[8] The 15th Amendment: "the right of citizens of the United States to vote shall not be denied or abridged by the United States or by any state on account of race, color, or previous condition of servitude."

On Wednesday May 14, 1919, an article appeared on the front page of the *Vicksburg Evening Post*. It read in bold letters, "NEGRO ATTEMPTS RAPE OF YOUNG WORKING GIRL." The name of the 22 year old alleged, attempted rapist was Lloyd Clay, a young black man who worked as a day laborer. The young working girl, it later turned out, had a secret older white man as her lover, who ran from the room she rented when discovered by the landlord. He fled to his black chauffeur whom he hired to take his lover on midnight drives. Confronted later, the chauffeur, and two other black men hauled into the Jackson jail, told the entire story to the authorities. All three men were released and told to leave the state (Clay 1919).

The crime of which I accuse my country and my countrymen.

Sheriff Frank Scott, W. M. Hudson and Deputy Charley Gantt used bloodhounds to track down the would-be rapist. The dogs initially led them to a white man, but a second attempt brought them to the A and V Railroad Station where they arrested Lloyd Clay.

That they have destroyed and are destroying hundreds of thousands of lives

After the white townsfolk heard that an arrest had been made, white men and boys began to gather at the Warren County jailhouse. Immediately after Clay was arrested, Mattie Hudson's father took her into town to pick out her assailant from a lineup of several black men. As Hudson stood before the lineup, she stated assuredly that none of the men there had attacked her and none had entered her room (1919).

And do not know it and do not want to know it.

Around 8:00 p.m. a mob used blow torches and a 16 foot piece of railroad iron to break down the jailhouse doors and bend open the iron jail cell bars. About 40 men made their way past Sheriff Scott and twelve of his deputies as they took Clay from his cell. The mob tied Clay up, placed him in a truck, drove him a short distance from where Mattie Hudson boarded, and demanded that Hudson identify Clay as her assailant. On the third day she did (1919).

It is not permissible that the authors of destruction should also be innocent.

Clay's burnt to crisp remains were placed in a plain wooden box. Early the next morning the coroner contacted Hattie Clay, Lloyd's mother who consented to have his remains interred in a cemetery for paupers, misfits and "bad" Negroes. Neither family nor friends escorted Clay's body to his final resting place. The city paid the total cost of his funeral, 15 dollars (1919).

Between 1882 and 1930 Mississippi lynched over 700 young black men: Rounding the numbers, for a half a century, 50 years or 600 months, on average, every six months, seven black men were Mississippi lynched, or, for

50 years, on average, every year 14 black men were Mississippi lynched (Waldrep 2005). On June 13, 2005, the U.S. Senate issued a formal apology for innocence, that it never criminalized lynching, but Trent Lott and Thad Cochran, Mississippi's Republican and Democrat Senators retained their innocence and did not sign (Lemann 2006).

It is the innocence which constitutes the crime.

On March 30, 1908, Green Cottenham was arrested by the sheriff of Shelby County, Alabama, and charged with "vagrancy." After three days behind bars, 22 year-old Cottenham was found guilty . . . and immediately sentenced to a 30-day term of hard labor. Unable to pay the array of fees . . . Cottenham's sentence was extended to nearly a year of hard labor. The next day, under a standing arrangement between the county . . . and U. S. Steel . . . Cottenham was sold and the sheriff turned him over to Tennessee Coal, Iron and Railroad Company, a subsidiary, for the duration of his sentence. The Company gave the county $12 a month to pay off Cottenham's fine and fees, sent him to the Pratt Mines on the edge of Birmingham. Green Cottenham toiled under the lash with 1000 other black men in "Slope #12." Slaves in all but name, almost sixty of the men died of disease, accidents or homicide before the year was over. Green Cottenham was dead from disease after five months (Blackmon 2008 p. 1–2).

In our first Constitutional era, 1787 to 1865, young black men suffered neither prison cell nor the lynch mob. They were Constitutional Property. During our second Constitutional era, 1875 to 1954, young black men were routinely rounded up for vagrancy and imprisoned briefly for debt, before being conscripted to work in a system of involuntary servitude. They were Constitutional People turned back into Constitutional Property.

We can thank Douglas Blackmon, who grew up in Greenville Mississippi and is the former Atlanta Bureau Chief of the *Wall Street Journal*, for the book, *Slavery by Another Name: The re-enslavement of Black Americans from the Civil War to World War II*. His story of tens of thousands of black youth criminalized for walking the railroad tracks, charged with vagrancy, jailed for non-employment, conscripted to die in the coal mines should shake the conscience of the nation. In his book, Blackmon threw a searchlight on Circular 3591 issued by Attorney General Francis Biddle on Dec. 12, 1941, a directive that ruptured the illusion that slavery had ended in America. And it warned the legal community that any person or entity who violated the 13th Amendment "would be prosecuted as a criminal":

> It is the purpose of these instructions to direct the attention of the United State Attorneys to the possibilities of successful prosecutions stemming from alleged peonage complaints which have heretofore been considered inadequate to invoke federal jurisdiction. It is requested that the spelling

out of peonage be deferred in favor of building the cases around the issue of involuntary servitude and slavery disregarding entirely the element of debt (Blackmon, pp 377–78).

All the Civil Rights Movements of the 20th Century took place against the background of WWI and WWII and the insurgencies of colonial peoples across the planet for political voice. African Americans, an internal colonial people during this era, mounted their own insurgencies for political voice. No wonder Japan's attack on Pearl Harbor galvanized President Franklin Roosevelt to seek an end to the conscription of black men into involuntary servitude and slavery; as soldiers he needed them ready to answer Japan's sure to come question: "Why are you, black soldiers, over here fighting us?"

In Clarksdale, as World War II got under way, black day-laborers could "go at six in the morning to the corner of Fourth and Issaquena streets . . . trucks from the plantations would appear at the corner. The drivers would get out and announce their pay scales. The Hopson place always paid at the high end of the going rate" (Lemann 1991 p. 71). In the fall of 1944 an estimated 3,000 people gathered at the Hopson plantation outside of Clarksdale to watch eight bright red machines pick forty-two acres of cotton. Richard Hopson ran the plantation office and the previous spring he had penned a letter urging all the plantation owners in the Delta to "change as rapidly as possible from sharecropping to complete mechanized farming . . . to alleviate the Negro problem" (p. 71).

Three years later, David Cohn, a literary lawyer put the following dilemma to the Nation: "Five million people will be removed from the land within the next few years. They must go somewhere. But where? They must do something. But what? They must be housed. But where is the housing?" (Lemann 1991 p. 51). In December 1946, the Chicago housing authority moved a few black families into a new housing project called Airport Homes, which was in a white neighborhood on the Southwest side. The housing authority proceeded with some care: it obtained the blessing of the mayor; it carefully screened the black families; it moved them in during working hours, when the men in the neighborhood were away. Still more than 1,000 whites gathered to 'greet' the black families. The mayor had to send in four hundred policemen to maintain order; the rioting went on and, finally, after two weeks the black families moved out, back across the housing color line (p. 51).

Ten years later, after the 1954 Supreme Court decision, "Willis wagons" maintained the school color line:

It is obvious in retrospect that the established black neighborhoods were far too small to hold all the black people coming into Chicago [leaving Mississippi's plantations] but [the Mayor's] efforts were directed at finding ways to maintain the color line. His school superintendent [Ben Willis] was immediately faced with the problem of severe overcrowding in the black schools. Instead of integrating the adjacent and usually half-empty white schools, Willis put the black schools on double shifts, eight to noon and noon to four, and installed what blacks called "Willis Wagons"—trailers converted into temporary classrooms—in their playgrounds, thereby creating an urban equivalent of the inferior rural black school systems of the South (Lemann 1991, p. 91).

> I agree with you that there is a natural aristocracy among men. The grounds of this are virtue and talents. . . . May we not even say that that form of government is the best which provides the most effectually for a pure selection of these natural aristoi into the offices of government? (Lemann 1999 p. 43)

So Thomas Jefferson wrote to John Adams in 1813. Adams sent his reply later that year: November 15, 1813:

> Your distinction between natural and artificial aristocracy does not appear to me well founded . . . both artificial aristocracy, and monarchy, and civil, military, political and hierarchical despotism, have all grown out of the natural aristocracy of virtues and talents. We, to be sure, are far remote from this. Many hundred years must roll away before we shall be corrupted.Our pure, virtuous, public-spirited federative republic will last forever, govern the globe and introduce the perfection of man. . . . Your distinction between the aristoi and the pseudo aristoi will not help the matter. I would trust one as soon as the other with unlimited power (Lemann 1999 p. 46).

Flash forward: At the October 29, 1947 meeting of the College Board, the admissions deans who made up the usual attendance at College Board Meetings, were astonished to see James Bryant Conant, President of Harvard, in all his magnificence, as well as the presidents of Princeton, Cornell and Brown (p. 64). Conant had assembled all these "grandees" to persuade the deans that the old dispensation of the College Board was at an end; it was to merge with ACE, the American Council of Education and prepare for the creation of ETS, the Educational Testing Service. George Zook, head of the ACE, also headed President Truman's Commission on Higher Education. Zook submitted his report to the President less than two months later on December 11, 1947, a clarion call to expand American Higher Education:

- The number of students enrolled in institutions of higher education by 1960 should be 4.6 million—triple what it had been in 1940.
- A third of every age cohort should graduate from college.
- Government should substantially finance this expansion by paying for students' tuitions: the first two years of college should be entirely free.
- All discrimination in higher education, especially against Negroes, should be vigorously stamped out (Lemann 1999).

The deans had met two weeks earlier and voted the merger down; they just didn't understand, the deal had already been settled. The question was who would run ETS: Conant via the College Board or Zook, via ACE. Exactly one week after the Zook report was submitted, ETS was chartered with Henry Chauncey a Harvard dean, as president, and Conant as chairman of the Board. The aristocracy was still in charge.

In the aftermath of WWII, in 1948, the nation established universal draft registration to be administered by the Selective Service System, and debated the wisdom of draft-deferment tests for college students. Then on June 25, 1950, North Korea invaded South Korea and Henry Chauncey saw the potential of a Bull Market for his company, ETS, and its products—tests. On March 19, 1951, the Selective Service System signed a contract with ETS to test up to one million college students. Chauncy insisted the test not be called an IQ test: the ability revealed by this test is more properly called "scholastic aptitude," he asserted, the ability to do well in school or college. He devised a scoring system that would bring to mind school grades rather than mental testing: The median score would be 50 and the deferment cut-off, 70. Security at the testing sites matched the life and death matter of the tests. All test-takers were finger printed and the FBI helped to guard the sites. There was the slight issue of one low scoring demographic: Southerners: Only 42 percent made the cutoff score of 70 as against 73 percent of New Englanders. What to do? Establish affirmative action based on regional cut-off scores? Better to keep quiet and, therefore innocent, about the nation's educational line of discrimination and its life and death quota tied to cut-off scores (Lemann 1999 p. 72–76).

Zook's vision lost: the government did not turn universities into extended versions of public school—free to all, the same for all. But so did Conant's vision lose. Conant had wanted to replace a system of higher education based on upper class aristocrats with a system based on Jefferson's "natural aristocrats." But for that to work, "It was essential that people accept this new elite as deserving, selfless, valuable, and dedicated to the public good." To Conant "the spectacle of well-to-do college men being deferred from required military service, to the great resentment of everyone else, under a transparently trumped-up justification, was deeply disturbing." But the testing went smoothly; two-thirds of the takers made the cut-off; the Pentagon found it useful; and soon enough so did universities. The nation set up ETS and the "project of picking just the right aristocrats" (Lemann p. 346).

In the late fifties, Conant took a close look at the nation's public high schools, and in 1961, the same year I returned to Mississippi to work for SNCC on

Amzie's voter registration program, Conant published a book, *Slums and Suburbs*, in which he made the following admission:

> As I read the history of the U. S., this republic was born with a congenital defect—Negro slavery. Or, if one prefers another metaphor, we started life under a curse from which we are not yet free. After the victory of the North . . . the people of the U. S. through their duly elected representatives in Congress acquiesced for generations in the establishment of a tight caste system as a substitute for Negro slavery. As we now recognize so plainly, but so belatedly, a caste system finds its clearest manifestation in an educational system (Conant 1961 p. 8–11).

Conant recognized too little too late.

When the first Constitutional Era had lurched to a close, Stephen Douglas, not Abraham Lincoln, trumpeted "of, by and for the people" in the debate over popular sovereignty versus slavery. So, here is "We The People, one man-one vote," Douglas:

> To throw the force of the Federal Government into the issue, either in favor of the free or the slave states would violate the fundamental principles of the Constitution and run the risk of civil war. The only hope of holding the country together . . . is to agree to disagree, to respect the right of each state and each territory to decide these questions for themselves (Lincoln—Douglas Debates 1858).

And here is "No one has a Right to do Wrong," Lincoln:

> Any man can advocate political neutrality who does not see anything wrong in slavery, but no man can logically say it who does see a wrong in it . . . Douglas contends that whatever community wants slaves has a right to have them. So they have it if it is not a wrong. But if it is a wrong, he cannot say people have a right to do wrong" (Debates, 1858).

In 1964, SNCC had no idea how its work, with MFDP to confront the National Democratic Party and the Nation at the Democratic Convention that year in Atlantic City, was 'dead on' history's mark. In a twentieth-century version of the nineteenth century Lincoln–Douglas debate, Fannie Lou Hamer rose before the Credentials Committee to emphatically interrogate her nation: "I question America! Is this America?" (Brooks 2011 p. 43).

And there, in Atlantic City were President Johnson, Martin Luther King Jr, Walter Reuther and Bayard Rustin, talking like Stephen Douglass, trumpeting popular sovereignty: To throw the force of the National Democratic Party into the issue, either in favor of the MFDP or the Mississippi Regulars, as those four saw it, would violate fundamental principles of the Party and run the risk of destroying it. Thinking like Douglas, they assumed that the only hope of holding the party together . . . was "to agree to disagree, to respect 'the right of the people of each state to decide these questions for themselves."

Yet here are the MFDP and SNCC talking like Lincoln: Any person can advocate political neutrality who does not see anything wrong in Jim Crow Politics, slavery by another name. But no person can logically say it, who does see a wrong in it . . . They contend that whatever state wants Jim Crow Politics has a right to work it out in their state. So they have it, if it is not a wrong. But if it is a wrong, they cannot say a state has a right to do wrong.

The 1941 Attorney General Circular 3591, WWII veterans like Amzie, who came back to a purpose, the 1954 Supreme Court decision, the Montgomery bus boycott, the sit-in movement, the full blown Civil Rights Movement, all signaled an end to America's second Constitutional Era. Certainly the Mississippi Theater of that movement rang the curtain on Mississippi's eighty-nine year reign, 1875 to 1964 as a one party white Democratic state. Moreover, as quiet as it's kept, that effort rang the curtain on the national political party arrangements put into play in the years 1875 to 1877 when Republicans blinked and Democrats winked.

Agriculture dominated the economic arrangements of the first Constitutional Era, 1787 to 1865, Industrial machine technology dominated the second, 1875 to 1954, and Information computer technologies dominate the third, 1965 and into the twenty-first century.

In the first era, Mississippi whites home schooled their offspring or sent them to private schools and on to Princeton and/or the University of Virginia; black slaves learned to read, if at all, on their own dime and at great risk.

In the second era, Conant opened up Harvard and elite Universities to public school students, but nothing interrupted sharecropper education. Sharecropper students, the progeny of slaves, got the education appropriate to their caste and its pre-assigned work.

In all due time, in 1970, ten years after Conant published *Slums and Suburbs*, as the nation transitioned into its third Constitutional Era, the Supreme Court required Mississippi to begin the integration of its public school system. That same year the nation began a forty year documentation of education that included data about four year college graduation. Bad news for Conant and Jefferson. Their vision of a meritocratic national education system producing America's natural aristocrats, had gone South, unless, that is, we agree that the Universe distributes intelligence disproportionately to the wealthy: In 1970, 40 percent of students from the upper quartile of the nation's economic distribution got their Bachelor of Arts (BA) degree; and forty years later, by 2010, the percent had doubled to 80 percent. In 1970 just 7 percent of the bottom quartile of the nation's economic distribution got their BA's and that percent barely nudged for forty years, just 9 percent got them by 2010 (Mortenson 2013). And just this past week we learned that 51 percent of all of America's public school children live in poverty (A new majority SEF 2015).

What we might double down on is the work needed to realize ourselves as a Constitutional People clothed with Human Dignity. And while it is true that we have lurched backwards and forwards over this endeavor in, roughly, three-quarters of a century units of time, we have managed, across two and a quarter centuries, in-spite of ourselves, to extend the reach of "We The People."

The class of Constitutional People that began with white male property owners has expanded to include men and women of all races and income levels with or without property. That expansion has typically required an alliance of the bottom and the top. Certainly that is how I experienced the Mississippi Theater of the Civil Rights Movement—an earned insurgency, a "We The People" force from the bottom found a few allies at the top.

The Pre Amble opens up a constitutional space: "We The People" did not mean "We the President, We the Congress, or We the Supreme Court." It couldn't since none existed at the writing of that document. Neither is it "We the Citizens," for, there was no nation in 1787 for which allegiance could be pledged. If the Pre Amble had begun, "We The Citizens of the several States," we would have a very different America. But it didn't. "We The People" invites everyone living in America, who takes it as their home, into the Constitutional Conversation.

Zook's vision to uplift and universalize into college the reach of Public School Education is the more appropriate vision for this Constitutional Era, the age of knowledge work. The Conant-Jefferson vision of a natural elite based on meritocracy lost out to the Market-based education: Get as much education as money can buy. Even so, "We the People" lies there, biding its time, waiting for its insurgents. Let's lift it up and try to feel its force. Please, say it after me:

"We the People of the United States, in order to form a more perfect union, establish justice, ensure domestic tranquility, provide for the common defense, promote the general welfare, and secure the blessings of liberty to ourselves and our posterity, do ordain and establish this Constitution for the United States of America."

The presumption of innocence is not just a legal concept. In common sense terms it depends on that generosity of spirit, which seeks the best, not the worst, in the stranger.

References

A new majority research bulletin: Low income students now a majority in the nation's public schools (2015). *Southern Education Foundation.* http://www. southerneducation.org/Our-Strategies/Research-and-Publications/ New-Majority-Diverse-Majority-Report-Series/A-New-Majority-2015- Update-Low-Income-Students-Now

Baldwin, J. (1963). My dungeon shook: Letter to my nephew on the one hundredth anniversary of the Emancipation. *The fire next time.* New York: Vintage Books.

Blackmon, D. A. (2008). *Slavery by another name: The re-enslavement of Black Americans from the Civil War to World War II.* New York: Anchor Books, Random House, Inc.

Blumrosen, A. W. and Blumrosen, R. G. (2005). *Slave nation: How slavery united the colonies and sparked the American Revolution.* Naperville, IL: Sourcebooks. Chapter 1.

Brooks, M. P. and Hauck, D. (2011). *The speeches of Fannie Lou Hamer: To tell it like it is.* Jackson, MS: University Press of Mississippi.

Carter, S. (1999). *Civility: Manners, Morals and the Etiquette of Democracy* (New York: Harper Press).

Clay, a Negro charged with attempted rape, hanged and burned. (1919) *Vicksburg Evening Post,* May 17; *Vicksburg Daily Herald,* May 18.

Clayton, C. W. The Supply and Demand Sides of Judicial Policy-Making (Or, Why Be so Positive about the Judicialization of Politics?) *Law and Contemporary Problems* Vol. 65, No. 3, The Law of Politics (Summer 2002), pp. 69–85. Published by: Duke University School of Law. Stable URL: http://www.jstor.org/stable/1192403 Page Count: 17

Conant, J. B. (1961). *Slums and Suburbs.* New York: Signet Books. (p. 8–11)

Constitution. Transcript. http://www.archives.gov/exhibits/charters/ constitution_transcript.html

Corwin, E. S. (1953). The Steel Seizure Case: A Judicial Brick without Straw. *Columbia Law Review* (Columbia Law Review Association, Inc.) **53** (1): 53–66.

Lincoln, A. "House Divided Speech." June, 16, 1858. Abraham Lincoln Historical Society. http://www.abraham-lincoln-history.org/house-divided/ and http://www.pbs.org/wgbh/aia/part4/4h2934t.html

Lemann, N. (2006). *Redemption: The last battle of the Civil War.* New York: Farrar, Straus & Giroux.

Lemann, N. (1991). *The Promised Land: The Great Black Migration and how it changed America.* New York: Vintage Books.

Lemann, N. (1999). *The Big Test: The Secret History of the American Meritocracy.* New York: Farrar, Straus & Giroux.

Loftus, J. Court is Uncertain of Truman's Power to Take over Steel. *New York Times.* April 25, 1952.

Margolick, D. (2000) *Strange Fruit: Billie Holiday, Café Society, and an Early Cry for Civil Rights.* Philadelphia: Running Press pp. 25–27.

Mortenson, Thomas. (2014). Unequal Family Income and Unequal Higher Education Opportunity, 1970 to 2013. *Postsecondary Educational Opportunity.* no. 267, Pell Institute for the Study of Opportunity in Higher Education, Washington DC, September. http://www.postsecondary.org

Moses, R. P. (2010). Constitutional property v. constitutional people. Quality Education as a Constitutional Right: Creating a grassroots movement to transform public schools. Theresa Perry, Bob Moses, Joan Wynne, Lisa Delpit, Ernie Cortez (Eds). Boston: Beacon Press.

The Lincoln Douglas Debates of 1858. Lincoln Home: National Historic Site. http://www.nps.gov/liho/learn/historyculture/debates.htm.

Truman, H. S. Executive Order 10340-Directing the Secretary of Commerce to take possession of and operate the plants and facilities of certain steel companies. *The American Presidency Project.* April 8, 1952 http://www.presidency.ucsb.edu/ws/?pid=78454.

Waldrep, C. (2005). Vicksburg Long Shadow: The Civil War legacy of race and remembrance. Lanham, MD: The Rowman & Littlefield Publishers, Inc. p. 319.

Blockages become gifts

by Carlos Gonzalez

"The impeded stream is the one that sings." (Berry, 2011)

For one week, my students and I read and pondered Wendell Berry's poem, "Real Work" (2011). The last line of the poem is the zinger of an aphorism quoted above that left us all wondering about the many places in our lives where we face obstructions, where the path suddenly narrows or is blocked by something so much larger than ourselves. These moments are never easy and are often spaces that collect fear, shame, and hopelessness. Interestingly, they also can be places where grace emerges if we surrender attachments to moving in the same direction that we have been conditioned to follow, and, instead, allow ourselves to be guided toward the desire of all rivers—the blissful union with the sea.

Time and time again, we are told by prophets and sages that the ocean of bliss for us is not somewhere else, rather within our hearts. The obstacles and impediments are all the delusions and illusions that we create and hold, that take us away from seeking within. These blockages, however, are not curses to fight against, but gifts which call out to us to awaken and surrender to the grace of the present moment, a grace possible to find even when feeling lost in the noise of hegemony.

Reference

Berry, W. (2011). *Standing by words: Essays*. San Francisco: Counterpoint Press (p. 97).

Nature as home ... antidote to war

by Matthew Rubenstein

Being rooted to me isn't as easy as naming a person or talking about the house where I was raised. For me, roots are both physical and blood related. From the giant oak trees penetrating the limestone foundation to the mangroves that soak their roots in the crystal clear waters of Florida Bay, my roots lie within the South Florida wilderness and the people with whom I share it. From the hiking and camping, to sight fishing and lobstering, there isn't a day that goes by that I don't drift back "home." Over my 30 years, breathtaking scenery, adrenaline-filled moments, and hard lessons learned from long tired nights have washed inside me. Along the way, I've shared those soulful saturations with the people whose passions are the same as mine, creating life-long friendships and memories.

From as long as I can remember, I have always been different. I wasn't like most kids. I didn't want to play video games; and as I got older, I didn't want to fill my nights with drinking and the club scene. I was always drawn to adventure and the outdoors, exploring the Everglades and the expanses of untouched wilderness. It's where I first learned a significant lesson in life, Respect! Like all of life, Nature deserves respect. It is delicate and needs to be taken care of—from the animals that call it home to the plants to the weather. If I take care of it, it seems to find ways to take care of me. In a time when technology has taken over, and all emotion is received in an emoji, left to decipher in an email or text, Nature is real. It teaches me to pay attention to all the little details, how to read it, and how to approach its multitude of species. In the everglades if I misjudge something or disrespect it, I will end up paying for it, for nature makes me accountable for my actions. Today, people often don't reprimand or give honest feedback for transgressions. But Nature does, if we stop to listen.

The family I have built around this outdoor haven of mine always seems to last. Many of us have some friends that come and go, but I enjoy the few special ones, who are the staples in my life, who seem to have developed from my experiences in the "great outdoors." From father figures, to brothers and sisters, to my love life, I have found everything I need in the outdoors.

My father left my family when I was nine years old, and my mother gave it her all. She worked hard and provided my sister and me with everything we needed. I never really had a father, but my best friend's father was kind enough to provide me some opportunities and life lessons in the outdoors, experiences that led me to become bonded with animals, trees, plants, water, rocks, other people who share the same values. The bonds of Nature and of those human relationships inextricably bound me to a joy and sometimes to a solitude that keeps me alive.

The roots of the outdoors has such a deep hold on me; I have often turned to it for healing. At the age of 19, I joined the Army and got the opportunity to travel and see the world. Yet I was also deployed to Afghanistan, to an area where I conducted mission after mission to ensure, the Army claims, that our freedoms are kept, and that my family never has to worry about terror stepping foot on our soil. With this responsibility came great sacrifice, and the first place I went each time I came home was straight back where I really am free, the natural world.

While deployed in Afghanistan, I lost my best friend. Every time we had shared some "down time" together, we had shared stories of hunting and fishing. It was our way to escape and dream of the days when we would be back home and wake up to the fall breezes and the crisp air—all the signs that hunting season would be upon us once again. We shared stories and pictures and planned future trips. Neither one of us knew that our last evening together would be his last evening. I longed then for those Everglades, for them to soothe my soul.

Every year there will be a day in a hunt when I just sit back and reflect on the days my friend, my comrade in arms, and I shared together. Each memory brings me a desire to be living my life to his expectations. And I reach back to family and the outdoors. They are the constant in my healing process—a healing demanded by war, its memories, its losses, and its aftermath. And anytime I need to step back and slow things down, and see the world from a different perspective, I go straight back to my roots.

Those roots ground me in what matters most in life. It's often easy to get caught up in day to day struggles, and forget to slow down and live. Working, seeking a degree, taking care of relationships—I can sometimes lose my footing, shake my roots. Growing up in nature helps me see that as fast as we come into this world, we can just as easily be removed from it. I also learned that lesson serving in Afghanistan. We can spend most of our time trying to hide from life, yet in reality life, both vicious and gentle, will find us. Neither does Nature hide reality. If observed closely, listened to attentively, it can offer wisdom, solace, terror, and joy. Hopefully, when it is my time to go, I can retreat back to my roots and watch the sun set for the last time. But if I can't, like most of us, I hope I will have lived my life to the fullest and will take my last breath with no regrets.

PART 2

Develop the genius within the young

A teacher seeks to develop the genius within the young so that each can arrive at his or her destination—the sharing of one's gifts within the community.

—*The Healing Wisdom of Africa*

Despite the rhetoric, teachers and students are succeeding

by Eric Cooper[1]

In his important new book, *Dog Whistle Politics: How Coded Racial Appeals Have Reinvented Racism and Wrecked the Middle Class,* author Ian Haney Lopez defines "dog whistle politics" as veiled references meant to "carefully manipulate hostility toward nonwhites" rather than deal honestly with the racial issues of our time.

American public education is full of these high-pitched battles. Privatizing schools because too many (poor minority) children "fail" to be educated by public systems is one. Another "failure" is that urban (read: "minority") parents are not interested in their children's education. Frankly, having spent significant time working with urban schools and parents, I have never met a parent (whether in Harlem, Chicago, Boston, Seattle, Newark, D.C., San Francisco, or Los Angeles) who is not passionately concerned about the success of a child. Instead, I've met single-parent mothers who hold two or three jobs, working six or sometimes seven days a week just to stay slightly above the poverty level. They are some of my heroes, but in spite of their relentless perseverance, they remain untapped resources in a movement for change.

Teachers are demonized as "failures" in the classroom. Fortunately for all of us, more and more are banding together as agents for justice by believing in the inherent capacity of all students, and seeking strategies and instructional pathways to improve student performance through professional development and collaborative learning.

---

[1] Permission given by Dr. Eric Cooper on e-mail to Joan Wynne on 4/3/2015 for reprint from his blog on Huffington Post: http://www.huffingtonpost.com/eric-cooper/despite-the-rhetoric-teac_b_6993668.html

To add to this narrative, I share an experience from Newark through the words of Dr. Alexis Leitgeb[2], a superintendent in a small Midwest school community and a consulting mentor at the National Urban Alliance (NUA) for Effective Education:

In one of the K-8 schools, I was in charge of teacher professional development. On one particular day, a teacher asked me to come to her classroom because she was struggling with classroom management. In her classroom was an African-American middle-school student named Amos. I observed immediately that the students were not focused on the teacher's presentation and a lot of teaching time was lost. The teacher is very hard working, capable and passionate, but, at the time, did not have the help needed to be effective with this particular class of students. As a consequence, with every visit to that school, I taught the class to demonstrate for the teacher how to engage students through lessons I modeled.

The students started out unengaged in the learning process and chaos was the order of the day, even with the best efforts of the school staff. Throughout the year, more and more teachers began to engage in the professional development we offered, and were always surprised when their students were focused on the subject matter I demonstrated and modeled for their teachers.

Amos, in the back of the classroom, consistently struggled with writing and speaking.

A student mentor program was implemented, and it was here that I became close to Amos. He was a natural for NUA's student-voice initiative, where students become teachers along with their teachers. Amos slowly rose to the top as the leader of the student project. He became so enthusiastic over time that he asked if he could create a website so teachers could read what was taught during my sessions, brainstorm ideas for struggling students, and find a calendar where they could sign up to have a student mentor demonstrate pedagogical strategies in their classroom. We received approval from the school and administration and Amos took off on his own. When he did not feel enough teachers had signed up, Amos took the calendar around to teachers, asking when his group could come in and teach.

Some of the students began to develop ideas on how to use strategies for reading, vocabulary and math.

Toward the end of my final year in the Newark initiative, Amos explained that he and several students were going to attend another school. He indicated that the students who were part of the student-voice project would be speaking to their new principal to bring lessons learned to their new schools.

Right before summer break, when I was leaving and Amos was moving to his new school, I asked to meet his mother. She came after school, and I gave Amos a laptop computer, printer and digital camera so this amazing young student could work at home on schoolwork,

---

[2] Permission granted by Alexis Leitgeb on e-mail to Eric Cooper on 6/11/15 for use of quotation.

creative artwork and design, and videos. I did not want his lack of financial means to prevent him from having the equipment I knew would help him meet his full potential.

Amos went on to the Poetry Out Loud 2015 competition. He made it all the way to the state finals at Princeton and took second place. Amos discovered his strengths—leadership and speaking—while engaged in the student-voice project of the NUA.

There are tens of thousands of stories just like this one, starring teachers who move from being "just a teacher" to justice in teaching, due to their personal commitment to student potential, and, at times, thanks to the professional development and teamwork in which they take part. They don't give up on their students, nor do they give up on each other as they move toward school transformation. In spite of the politics of education, they find a common pathway that leads to improved achievement and social justice.

Let's allow these stories to be told, so that the success Amos has can be taken to scale, and the doomsday cacophony—those dog-whistle politics—about education in America is muted.

Courts to play on

by Omo Moses

When I volunteered to go to Mississippi, I was signing up to get myself together. I followed my younger brother, Taba, cousin, Khari, and father, Bob Moses, to the Sam M. Brinkley Middle School in May 1995, after an unremarkable college basketball career ground to a halt when the George Washington Colonials lost to the Ohio University Bobcats in the Big Apple NIT Classic. I had spent the last decade pursuing the National Basketball Association (NBA) and the accumulation of material things important to most 20 year olds; failing, for the first time, to become the person I imagined. The disappointment arrived at sunrise each morning as I sat, out of habit, on my mother's porch in Cambridge, MA, a ball under my armpit, returning to the street to dribble between passing cars, past phantom opponents. What had been a throne became a coffin. I wouldn't be paraded in the streets like Patrick Ewing after he won his first Olympic gold medal. I wouldn't declare, as Rumeal Robinson had, that I wanted to become as big as the moon to a field house full of high school students. A sign on a pole on a corner wouldn't bear my name as it did his after winning the national championship at the University of Michigan.

Fragments of glory could be gathered from the cracked asphalt of Corporal Burns Park, on the courts at the bank of the Charles River opposite Harvard's Business School, where generation after generation of black and brown-colored boys came to mold themselves into basketball players. I could have competed for status among them (pounding dreams of teenagers; bitter men still looking for a reputation) and the legends (without legs) clinging to the fence, until the debris from bones pestling concrete consigned me to the mob, loitering (seated and standing; their backs to the water) on the curb running the sideline, until it was their turn to claw at the next young player who earned the right to be king of the court.

The burial of my self-portrait—a benevolent, albeit, envied hero, strapped with enough cash, cars, jewels, and eye candy to scatter throughout the neighborhood—was protracted. The possibility continued to arrive at night, soldering desire and fear—that I had one more year of college eligibility, another moment to live before a million eyes. My redemption began with the pain burrowed in ankles already fractured and sprained irreparably. In a rare unmasked moment, I shared with my dad that I would no longer be a basketball player. He offered, *America is filled with courts that you can play ball on.*

Without purpose or clear direction, I asked if I could spend the next year working in his classroom. He was surprised. He had spent the better part of the last 10 recruiting his children to work with the Algebra Project (which he characterized as the family's business). I was the last one he expected to sign up. But, I needed the desolate Mississippi Delta roads which stitched rectangular and square patches of cotton fields, the blues from sharecropper to sharecropper; the obscurity of a classroom punctuated with the infectious curiosity of 7th graders searching for images to attach to themselves; the anonymity of Southern hospitality—to reimagine who I could be. Unlike most of the boys who traveled to Corporal Burns to become Dr. J, my family was stable, my parents made the public schools work, wrapping us in love and the type of experiences that continually expanded what we thought was possible. I left high school with the belief coded in my DNA, that if I put the time in, I would be successful at whatever I put my mind to. Failure, no matter how painful, was just another beginning.

Within a week of my arrival in Mississippi, my dad began declaring, "The young people need to get their act together." There was a sense of urgency in his voice that we didn't share. He talked about jail, saying that if young people didn't do well in math, they were going to end up in jail. The cover of the February 21, 1993 edition of the *New York Times Magazine* had a picture of him with children from the Mississippi Delta beneath the title, "We Shall Overcome This Time with Algebra: Bob Moses and Mississippi Children Focus on a Plastic Learning Screen—A Path out of Modern Bondage." It's difficult to make the connection between success in algebra and serfdom (Silver 2008; NYT, 1993).[1] When I was playing at George Washington, my dad came to town to give a speech to a bunch of mathematicians. A decade before Google and Facebook, he told them that whether they liked it or not they were the leaders of the planet. It was difficult for them to imagine the

---

[1] There is a very high correlation between success in Algebra in high school, graduation from four-year colleges, and work. Students who complete Algebra II in high school more than double their chances of earning a four-year college degree. In Los Angeles, like in most urban districts, 65 percent of the students who didn't pass Algebra by their freshman year dropped out.

role history and the evolution of technology had conceived for them, harder still to enlist them in a struggle for freedom and democracy.

Taba, Khari, and I worked to create a Math Lab out of an unused science classroom: arranging tables laminated with primary colors, building a network with a dozen Macintosh computers, clearing the walls of chipped paint before covering them with affirming words (*math is what you make it*) and images. Taba found a pair of college students (male and female artists) who showed up like Panthers (bobbing afro, black leather jacket, tight jaws) and began sketching with him on the bare primer, first a colored boy standing with a number in his hand before strips of wood patterned into a path extending into a universe of stars and planets and brown, yellow and red children exploring it. A jungle of animals covered a wall. A sketch of my dad was quickly erased as he huffed and puffed at our (affectionate) attempt to memorialize him. Khari—cocky scowl, dreadlocks pointing toward each corner of the room—was immortalized next to the light switch by the door.

Always conscious of how and where he stood in relationship to the people he led and organized, my dad encouraged us to join, from the classroom and school building, the struggle where he and students our age participated on the streets of America during the Civil Rights Movement, confronting the nation on paper and in practice, as they removed Jim Crow from public accommodations and the democratic political apparatus. Jim Crow was the specter drifting through the pages my parents left open in the living room: a crowd of white-colored faces bearing witness to black-colored bodies burning at their feet, Ross Barnett, then Governor of Mississippi, standing in the doorway of a school to prevent black-colored boys and girls from entering, canine teeth extending a white arm's length into black thighs, a pig-colored sheriff struggling to rip the American flag from a five-year-old brown-colored boy as he clutched with two hands his right to be among the "We" that gave birth to the nation.[2]

"It was easier when it was obvious," lamented a veteran of the civil rights movement—to confront the persistent pernicious shove of black-colored people outside the "We" and into a permanent under-caste. Who would deny the contiguous line from slavery, convict leasing, chain gangs, Jim Crow laws, Rockefeller drug laws, stop and frisk and three strikes policies? What is the cumulative impact of this from black generation to generation? How does it show up in the body, mind, and spirit of every black child and the environment that he or she inherits? What is the work that each subsequent generation must recognize and embrace to lift itself up?

---

[2] *We hold these truths to be self-evident, that all men are created equal and We the People of the United States* begin the preambles to The Declaration of Independence and the Constitution; those sacred documents that prophesize America's promise and possibility.

For Taba, Khari, and me—camouflaged in gold herringbone, diamond ear-rings, nugget pinky ring, shorts sagging toward Timberland boots—the work was discovering the obvious parading in and out of the Math Lab and through the halls and classrooms of Brinkley Middle School. There was no epiphany, just a gradual realization of the connections between the conflict and contradictions that rose from the pages left open in my parent's living room, what Brinkley was preparing most of the 99 percent black student body to do, and what we had experienced in the self-proclaimed People's Republic of Cambridge—where, confounding the city's vanguard liberalism the Advanced Placement and honors classes at the high school remained seg-regated. (Khari and I were the only two brown-colored boys in our honors classes for four years.) What became clearer to me was that the Nation's native conundrum transcended generation, region, class, and politics.

The question, *What to do about the slaves and their descendants*, was alive and well in contemporary form: *What to do about black boys*, whether sons of sharecrop-pers or 2nd generation doctors, in both 6,000 and 20,000 dollar per pupil public school systems, above and below the Mason–Dixon line.[3] I've been wrestling with this question for as long as I've been aware of being black. My take on it is that there is either an implicit assumption or explicit accusation that we are complicit in our failure. As a kid, the basketball court and the corner were two places we could go without that burden—we were supposed to be good at hanging on rims and hanging out. In the Math Lab, we con-fronted with other people's children what was buried in our psyches as kids—"Be good at this? Pay attention to that." I learned quickly about the significance of attention—you can't teach someone without it. Because we looked like East Coast rappers, we had a small window of opportunity to earn the trust and respect of the students by demonstrating that we appreci-ated who they were and where they were coming from.

They arrived with a teacher or deputized classmate, in single file or defiantly breaking rank. They sat in groups of five or six on wooden stools pulled from slots underneath the table tops, some erect in anticipation, others wilting. The lessons were structured like a Student Non-violent Coordinating Committee (SNCC) meeting, organized to unleash the energy of the stu-dents by creating space for them to have a stake in what we were learning (Moses & Cobb, 2001; SNCC). My dad usually facilitated while we worked at the tables, helping them reflect on an experience or build consensus about mathematical ideas like equivalence or equality. Eventually I began to facili-tate activities. I would begin with a hand in the air and a request for the stu-dent's attention, relying on the leaders at each table to help their classmates

---

[3] My mom says that in the 60's we struggled in color, but not in kind—referring to the class divide that persists in black and all colored communities.

turn their eyes toward me. The students I relied on weren't necessarily the ones their teachers anointed; they were generally the ones we shot ball with during gym, hung out with during lunch, or in their neighborhood after school. Regardless of the content, the goal was the same—to have a collaborative conversation based on shared experiences. This required that each student exercise leadership as an individual, as a member of a small group and classroom community. More important than paying attention to me was that they pay attention to each other and what was going on around them.

I would watch the students in the marching band parade home after school: plastic Tuba wrapped around a waist, trumpets to lips, snare and base drums, clarinet and sax, boys and girls shedding rigid notes, uniform steps in the parking lot between the school and a row of shotgun shacks as they marched up Ridgeway Street, past St Peters Missionary Baptist Church, an abandoned bar, the parking lot of the adjacent Laundromat and candy store, stopping at each other's stoop until the last instrument arrived in its front yard. Noisy at first, by the time they approached Shady Grove Church on the corner of Ridgeway and California, they were making music. Good days in the Math Lab looked and felt like that.

As my dad pushed us to do more, we began to organize ourselves, partially in response to him, partially in response to a desire to do something that extended beyond the school building and into the crux of our lives. I began to count the students in each class I was able to reach and imagine how many we could reach if we turned our energy and attention toward each other. Dave Dennis, a Freedom Rider out of New Orleans and the Director of the Southern Initiative of the Algebra Project, encouraged us to meet at his office in the Standard Life Building: built in 1929 to attract more business into what was then an industrial city, it had been the largest reinforced concrete building in the world and remained the tallest in Jackson; standing like a decayed minaret beside the King Edwards Hotel (empty since 1967), casting its shadow among the abandoned downtown streets. Dave would bring food, we'd bring students from Brinkley, and talk about how we could take what we were learning in the Math Lab on the road and turn it into a business. The power embedded in the relationships and learning experiences we shared with the students emboldened us to imagine that we—like Curtis, Hollis, Chuck, Charlie, June, Judy, Margaret: the students whose names and faces, bodies, were deserted in the chapters my parents left open—could do something to push America to become America (Banks, 2008).[4]

---

[4] It was only after the Civil War that the United States became America the nation-state. There was a shift there in terminology, too, moving from being the United States of America to "America," from being a fairly loose consortium of separate but united states, pulled apart at times, pulling together at others, into something that was a single word: America.

That's my teacher! Mummy, that's my teacher! I've heard the story a number of times. Stizz the rapper, two years from high school graduation, animated in a polo shirt and skinny jeans, brings it to life as he describes walking through his neighborhood and the pride he felt when an elementary student he taught introduced him to their mom. There's another story the students I work with often share about the rush they feel when they are able to help another student understand a concept or solve a problem. In 1996, Taba, Khari, 8th-grade Algebra Project students from Brinkley, and I, founded The Young People's Project (YPP). YPP is a Math Lab on wheels. Our first enterprise was conducting graphing calculator workshops for teachers and then students in Jackson and the Mississippi Delta to prepare them for the statewide Algebra 1 exam. Over the last 16 years, we have successfully unleashed the energy of thousands of high school students in urban and rural communities across America to work to ensure that mathematics isn't a barrier to high school graduation, college entry, or career. YPP trains and employs teams of high school students, coached and mentored by college students, to conduct math-based workshops for 3rd–8th graders in community and school-based after school programs. We call this math literacy work; enlisting the very students expected to fail (and whose failure is exploited economically) to be resources to their communities (YPP website).[5] Through this experience, they are developing competencies critical to their future success, like teamwork and cooperation, self-confidence, achievement, relationship building, and conceptual and analytical thinking.

When we dribbled from sun up to sun down at Corporal Burns Park, we weren't thinking about our character or the skills we were developing that would enable us to be successful in life. We were all in, NBA or bust. In Mississippi, I began reflecting on the thousands of hours we spent formally and informally training to become basketball players, and how that experience helped shape who I am, how I do things, and what I'm able to do off the court. The pressure to perform, encountered in real time—a man guarding me, the clock winding down before a million eyes—wasn't limited to those moments. My ability and inability to overcome fear in a gymnasium or arena became reference points for how I approach success. As a teenager, I didn't attach these experiences to a future self, other than the image of Michael Jordan spanning the width of my wall finger-tip to finger-tip, or the one of him tilted on a 45 degree angle, ball palmed, tongue out, suspended between the rim and floor. It wasn't until I was much older that I began to intentionally translate and apply what I learned on the basketball court to other areas of my life and other images of myself. It's a lot, but necessary, to tell teenagers,

---

[5] YPP currently operates programs in 10 cities, employing 400 high school and college students who work with 1,600 elementary students annually.

particularly black- and brown-colored youth to "Pay attention to what you're learning while dribbling a basketball or marching home from school."

When my brother and I were eight and ten, my dad moved us from the campus of Harvard University, where he was finishing a Ph.D., to the street across from the Newtown Court housing projects; conscientiously placing us among the children whose failure is predictable and profitable for American business (Whitehead, 2012).[6] It wasn't clear then where the choices our 10-, 11-, and 12-year-old selves made were coming from and where they would lead. Now, at the median of our lives, the various outcomes include: dead; 15 years in jail for murder; school committee member; jail for assault and battery; general contractor; jail for selling drugs; jail for drug use; meter maid; homeless; IT technician; nonprofit executive director; and financial manager. In the shadows of institutions like Harvard and MIT, most of us couldn't see beyond what was in front of us, couldn't imagine making other choices, and had no clue as to how they became available.

For the last 15 years, we have worked to build a healthy organization with the young people who have inherited the corners and courts; a rapper's persona. The "We" now includes my sister Maisha, with whom I share leadership as YPP National Co-directors, and the young people who have grown with the organization (all beginning as elementary, high school, or college students), who now comprise the overwhelming majority of our central and local leadership and participate on the national board of directors (Khari is an advisor to the board). As we strive to grow as human beings and as an organization, we have spent a lot of time thinking about success at an individual level (students and staff), organizational, and community level.

Many of the questions we've been confronted with relate to the work of the Leadership & Sustainability Institute (LSI), which will provide member organizations with access to resources that build their capacity to make tangible progress on issues such as expanding work opportunities, strengthening family structures, and increasing educational equity. In the last three years, we have had the opportunity to work with Root Cause—the nonprofit research and consulting firm based in Cambridge, MA that worked in partnership

---

[6] Between 1900 and 1975, the nation's incarceration rate remained at about 110 prison inmates for every 100,000 people. In 1973 the first drug laws with mandatory sentencing guidelines were enacted and incarceration rates climbed immediately, doubling in the 1980s and 1990s. As of 2010 the rate was 731 per 100,000; among Black and Hispanic adult men 4,347 and 1,755 inmates per 100,000. Private prisons have grown from a billion dollar industry in 1984 to over 30 billion in 2010; its forecasts for expansion influenced by 3rd grade reading and math test scores and the passing of three strikes laws.

with the Campaign for Black Male Achievement at the Open Society Foundations to develop the plan for the LSI—to develop a business plan, and David Hunter to develop an organizational logic model and blueprint (Growth Plans, 2012). This work has clarified how we think about student, staff, and organizational success. As we build central capacity and local leadership, we seek to accelerate our ability to ensure quality programming, achieve targeted outcomes, and meet existing demand. When we began in the Math Lab a decade and a half ago, the Algebra Project provided the space, wisdom, connections, encouragement, and love for us to grow. The work that the LSI is preparing to do is invaluable in that regard. There is a need for black founded and led organizational equivalents to a City Year, Youth Build, Year Up, or Citizen Schools in both scale and ambition that are working to improve the quality of life for black-colored children in America (Black Male, 2012).

In recent discussions with students, success was described as: *happiness, always growing, having a vision and working hard to get there, overcoming obstacles, helping others on the way to success, and the ability to rise after failure.* I asked a childhood friend to join our conversation about institutional obstacles. He sat on the edge of the circle as I hesitated, unsure how to introduce him. He has been Fat Daddy or Fats for as long as I've known him and I felt awkward referring to him by his legal name. A year out of a 15-year prison sentence, he hasn't had a job his entire life. As we began talking about barriers to success, the students struggled to define "institution." Some of the ideas they came up with were *institutions have rules and expectations, they are bigger than you and impact how your life plays out whether negative or positive, sometimes they can be controlled and sometimes not.* Fat Daddy wanted to know why I had invited him to join our conversation. In his mind, these students weren't the young people confronted with the choices he had faced growing up.

He and I sat on the steps of the brick apartments his grandfather had purchased (and where his parents now live) across the street from the Washington Elms projects, a few blocks from where I grew up. *They ain't . . . but they are*, was my response. In my mind we've all inherited an equivalent margin for error. "When your dad was trying to get us to go to do math at the King School on Saturdays I wasn't trying to hear it. I had already made up my mind to go this way." He pointed away from me. "What about the ones who don't wanna join YPP and already made up their minds to go this way?"

A couple weeks ago I had lunch with him, Alex (another childhood friend who made similar choices and also ended up incarcerated) and Barbara Best who lives in Cambridge and works for the national office of the Children's Defense Fund on their Cradle to Prison Pipeline initiative. I thought they should meet. At some point the conversation became me, Alex, and Fats talking about the choices we'd made, where they'd led us, and kids facing similar challenges. We seemed to agree on the need to build relationships with them, particularly the young people who are influential in our neighborhood and in their peer groups, and see if we can get them to experience and think about some other things.

A kid approached on his bike while Fat Daddy and I sat on the steps. He wore a Harvard jersey and shorts. They began talking shit about their game against each other the day before. The kid is wiry, approaching six feet and seemed comfortable confronting adults.

"You play for the high school?" He pointed to the bracelet on his ankle.

"How'd you get that?" He shrugged his shoulders. He'd spent the better part of the last year in jail or on house arrest. Fats tells him to bring five and we'll bring five and play on Sunday. Fat's Uncle Donny pulls up while the kid is riding away. Donny used to take us around the state when we were 10 and 11 to play in tournaments. I asked Fats, "How'd you get a bracelet at 15?"

"I don't know." He was in Billerica. How do you get sent to Billerica, a men's correctional facility, at 15?

Donny said he'd been watching the kid since he was waist high. "He can play; there hasn't been one in 20 years—he was the next you."

I show up early that Sunday to stretch and get some shots in. We are playing at The Terrace, on a court across from the apartments where the Puerto Ricans and Dominicans used to live. The park has been renovated. The neighborhood has gentrified. You get a ticket for smoking weed: the white black brown-colored arms and legs hang in clouds, listlessly from the benches. The court is empty except for a handful of boys whose shots barely touch the rim. There is no evidence of Pat and his heroic deeds. The street sign a block away with Rumeal's name has been torn down (Saslow, 2012). Fats shows up late. He brings Alex and a couple others. The kid comes with his five—three played for the high school. The ball goes up as the afternoon service at the Pentecostal Tabernacle Church on the corner concludes—Dip arrives unannounced in a two-piece suit. He watches from the fence. He had been drafted in the 1980s, led the Big East in scoring and graduated from Providence College. He played in Turkey and got hooked on drugs. When I was a kid he was the king of the court. When I was seventeen he told me I could play in the league. I believed him. Every summer I brought a jersey back for him from college; even then he would school me. 50, his knees are shot. Happy to see him I reach through the fence for his hand.

The kid can play. He can shoot, can handle, has a mid-range game, can stop and pop and get to the rim. He has the talent, skills, and heart to command this generation of black- and brown-colored bodies lured to the chain link, below the nets, attached to the three-point line on Columbia St. We didn't let them win. We played five games, two full-court and refused to let them win. I played well enough for them to ask who I was.

The kid lives across the street from the park. I went to see him a couple days later; he was watching his son who is almost a year old. I told him I was expecting my first any day now; he seemed happy to hear that. We talked about Tommy Amaker's basketball camp at Harvard (I could try to get him in), about Lew Zuchman, a Freedom Rider, member of YPP's board and Executive Director of SCAN, an organization based in New York City that has the best Amateur Athletic Union (AAU) Boys Basketball teams in the country and gets its players into New England prep schools and Ivy League colleges (NY Post, 2012). I told him a little about where I was coming from— he seemed to know about YPP. I asked him about his plans: "What are you gonna do in September when you get the bracelet off?"

References

Banks, R. (2008). *Dreaming Up America*. New York, NY: Seven Stories Press.

Black Male Achievement Fellowship. (2012). *Echoing Green*. Retrieved from http://www.echoinggreen.org/bma-fellowship

Braziller, Z. (2012). Tight-knit Team SCAN enjoys summer of national success. New York Post. August 8. Retrieved from http://nypost.com/2012/08/08/tight-knit-team-scan-enjoys-summer-of-national-success/

Growth Plans. (2012). *The Young People's Project*. Retrieved from http://www.typp.org/growthplans

Moses, R. & Cobb, C. (2001). Radical equations: Civil rights from Mississippi to the Algebra Project. Boston: Beacon Press.

Saslow, E. (2012). Bringing down the house. *ESPN The Magazine*. Retrieved from http://espn.go.com/mens-college-basketball/story/_/id/7649638/ncb-rumeal-robinson-journey-michigan-star-incarceration-espn-magazine

Silver, D., Saunders, M., & Zarate, E. (2008). What Factors Predict High School Graduation in the Los Angeles Unified School District? *California Dropout Research Project*. Report #14 June. UC Santa Barbara: Gevirtz Graduate School of Education.

Student Non Violent Coordinating Committee (www.sncclegacyproject.org).

We shall overcome this time with algebra: Bob Moses and Mississippi children focus on a plastic learning screen – A path out of modern bondage. (February 21, 1993). *New York Times Magazine.*

Whitehead, J. W. (2012). Jailing Americans for Profit: The Rise of the Prison Industrial Complex. *Huffington Post Blog.* Retrieved from http://www. huffingtonpost.com/john-w-whitehead/prison-privatization_b_1414467.html

Can I Write This?

by Laurel Nakanishi

"Ms. Nakanishi, can I write: 'You are like a bird?'"
"Okay," I say, "why is your mom like a bird?"
"No, no, no. You are like my alarm clock . . ."
"Mmm hmm."
"Because my mom is always waking me up in the morning."
"Yes," I say, "that sounds like a great simile."
Jamy A smiles and begins to write.

*

For the last month, I have been teaching poetry to 3rd graders at Orchard Villa Elementary School in Liberty City. These classes are part of the O, Miami Poetry Festival. O, Miami's goal is for everyone in Miami-Dade County to encounter a poem in the month of April. Mrs. Finch's 3rd-grade class has been encountering me.

It is good to be a resident poet in an elementary school. The kids are always excited to see me. I am not constrained by the demands of state testing. I don't have to get caught up in the bureaucracy of the public school system, but I do get to work with public school kids. And thanks to the presence of the classroom teacher, I don't need to spend so much time doing classroom management. And best of all, I get to share my passion for poetry with children. It is, pretty much, the best job ever.

*

From a WLRN radio broadcast:

"This is my first time knowing about poetry, and it is fun. And I get to write my own poetry stories and we could talk about our family," said Kindra Oriental, a 3rd grader.

Oriental is one of the students in the 3rd-grade class learning from poet Laurel Nakanishi.

"Sometimes they'll be like 'Is it ok to write this?' And I'll say 'Yes! Write that,'" said Nakanishi. "Because they aren't sure if they have permission to get that creative or to write about their personal experience in that way."

Nakanishi received her Master of Fine Arts (MFA) in poetry from the University of Montana and is currently studying at Florida International University.

Isaiah Bell is another one of Nakanishi's students.

"When Miss Nakanishi came here I'm like, 'Yes! We need poetry!' Because sometimes in life you have to write yourself a poetry or someone else that needs help cheering up," Bell said.

*

Isaiah sits at the back of the class smiling knowingly. He is one of the students who has taken quickly to poetry writing.

Angel raises her hand. "Can I write: 'In the evening my mom clips my toenails while screaming into the phone'?"

Yes, yes.

*

I have taught poetry to children in Hawaii, Montana, Nicaragua, and now Miami. Each of these geographical locations and the children who live there, pose different dynamics and opportunities for creativity.

Out of all these places, I am least familiar with Miami. When I moved here nine months ago, I was warned to stay out of Liberty City. "You'll get your car stolen!" a friend half-joked. When I watched the local news, Liberty City is often the background for shoots or hit-and-run car accidents. I walked into Orchard Villa Elementary School with these stories in mind. Sitting in the front office waiting area on my 1st day of class, a little girl stared, bemused, at me. She was too young to have learned to look away like her mother did. The adults in the office were extra friendly to me—the only White face in a school where almost everyone else is Black.

Good, I thought, and I tried to be grateful for the discomfort. I am half-Japanese, but few know it from looking at me. My last name is a further mystery: "Nakaskisi?" Not exactly. We practiced pronouncing it on that 1st day of class. "Nakanishi. Nakanishi."

*

Jokira is worried. "Ms. Nakanisi, I don't know how to start."

"Okay, start with what's around you. What do you see?"

"My hand," says Jokira.

"Okay, I want you to describe your hand."

A few minutes later, Jokira is raising that hand.

"Is this okay, Ms. Nakanisi?"

I read:

Poetry

My hand,

brown,

it can write words.

*

At first, they were hesitant. Even after an explanation, examples from professionals and kids, a group brainstorm and a suggested format, the students were still uncertain.

"Can I write this?" They would ask. "Is this okay?"
"Can I write about cat poop?"
"Can I write about a square, squishy monster?"
"Yes," I would say. "That is brilliant!" "Yes, yes, yes, write it."

I think that one of the reasons that my students enjoyed poetry class is because I am so positive. I love them. I love what they write. I love how they see the world. What is most important to me is that they express themselves. I want them to take risks.

They still hold their papers up to me and ask, "Is this okay?"

I am not sure why this class in particular was so hesitant to express themselves. Thinking back to teaching in Montana, I remembered that those kids rarely asked, "Can I write this?" Was that because they were more comfortable with poetry? The Missoula Writing Collaborative has been sending professional writers to public schools for the past 15 years—perhaps they are more used to poetry writing.

Or is it privilege? Do these, mostly White, kids feel entitled to self-expression? Are they more confident because society tells them—these White, mostly middle-class kids—that their ideas matter? I do not know.

My students in Nicaragua began by copying the examples. I would read a poem about birthday cake, and then receive 21 imitations of that same birthday cake. It took about a month to really emphasize that they could have their own ideas. As the students became more and more comfortable, I began receiving poems about solar explosions, giant brains, and wind blowing through the windows. One of my students wrote: "When my mother sweats, it is like the rain in summer."

My students in Hawaii were the most similar to these Liberty City 3rd graders. They were uncertain how to start. They would ask permission before each poem. "Is this okay?" I wonder if this need for reassurance is somehow tied to the way that we test children. In a test there is only ever one correct answer. Students must learn how to block out all of the other ideas and connections in their mind so that they may give the right response. What is the main idea of this text? What is the definition of simile? What is the setting of the story? They must recall and present just that one correct answer.

So how baffling it must be when this White lady with a strange last name walks into your classroom and tells you to write whatever you want. Any answer is correct. Any idea that you have is brilliant. I am affirmative of these students to a fault. I praise them because I want them to gain confidence in their own voice and experience. This sort of confidence is essential to writing. If you do not believe that what you have to say matters, you can never write something that will resonate with readers.

I give my students permission to be weird or silly. I want them to write about the everyday details of their lives. Once they gain this confidence, then we can start working on shaping words into art. But if they are always looking for a "right answer" in their writing, it will never be a poem.

*

Ireanna asks, "Can I write that the stars are tickling?"

*

We are writing about place. I explain that I want them to describe their neighborhood, their house, their room—anywhere they feel at home. I give them examples from my students in Hawaii: "Is your street busy with herds of rusty cars? Is your home quiet as the library?"

Vincent raises his hand. "My neighborhood is loud. They are always shoot-ing guns."

"Okay, write that in your poem," I say. "What do the guns sound like?"

"Pah! Pah!" he says. "Last night there were these boys shooting in front of my house. They were shooting on the street and then some of them ran behind our house. We don't have a gate, that's why. They ran behind and went over the fence."

Suddenly all the words in my head are gone. What can I say to that?

"They're always shooting by my house too. I'm scared of guns," says Katron.

I tell Vincent that his story would make a great poem—"Write it down."

He writes:

I Am From
My city is very loud with the sound of pistols.
I smell the stink of the garbage.
At school, I see Ms. Finch and my paper.
At home, I love to eat crab.
It is so good, I'd eat it 24/7.

It is easy to pigeonhole these kids, to see them only as survivors of their vio-lent neighborhood. But, as Vincent reminds us, there are many other things going on. Yes, there are guns and stinky garbage, but there is also the struc-ture and stability of Mrs. Finch's classroom. There are also delicious crab feasts. There are loving families and wildly fun times riding bikes and playing.

*

Jamy A writes:

Five Things I Love
The hug of my little sister—
she is very special and beautiful.
The strawberry and vanilla ice cream
with a cherry on top that my mom and I share.
The pink diamond sheets on my bed
that sparkle so cute.
The candle burning on the dresser
flickering and casting shadows.
The basketball bouncing up and down
baug, baug, back.

*

I am new to Miami. I moved here nine months ago and I am still trying to figure out this city. Like every other place I have lived and visited, I am finding that it is full of complexity. These young poets are my teachers and I am learning that, unlike a test question, there is no one answer.

Miami is many different things: It is the sound of a basketball and chocolate chip cookies fresh from the oven and gunfire. It is these shining, expectant faces asking "Is this okay? Read this." Maybe, in addition to permission, my students also just want to share their poem. "Ms. Nakanishi, read mine!" They want to share their thoughts and perspective and world with me. How lucky I am to be help in such confidence.

*

Mrs. Finch's 3rd-grade classroom is packed with people—parents, grandparents, sisters, brothers, aunts, and teachers. One by one my students stand up and read their poems:

"I remember when I first started walking.
I was small and everything looked big . . ."

"In the middle of the night
I hear my sister in the kitchen
getting a night snack . . . "

"Ms. Nakanishi's glasses are popping
just like Sienna's hair . . . "

"I remember when I was in a body cast.
My auntie called me Mr. Broke-Down . . ."

"I hear people laughing
at people who are poor
because of their shoes . . ."

"Gazing up at the sky
at night
Stars are tickling . . ."

"My brother snoring with little tears
dropping down like rain . . . "

"Your hugs fill me up with love
like a balloon and spits out all the hate."

A roaring applause!

Breaking silence

by Carlos Gonzalez

Dear Students, I want to break the silence between us and talk to you directly. This will be a rambling piece, but one that I offer as a means to help you navigate through what is probably going to be a couple of years of more institutional education. I do this after 21 years or so of teaching in one place, of loving what I do, and hating with every fiber of my body what happens to many, if not most students, as they weave in and through the many obstacles called college.

Silence and Storytelling

My dad asked me to go with him to the store to pick something up. I sat in the car silently, thinking of the other things I wanted to do. I sat silently because at 18, I had no idea who my dad was or what I would ask him. I felt like a stranger to him. We had not spent much time together. Having fled Cuba with no money and little formal education, he was on a continuous survival mode, and work was priority number one.

That absence early in my childhood and my own quiet personality allowed me to make good friends with silence. Yet it's more complicated than that. It always is. As I look back at that ride now, I would do just about anything to have changed the dynamic of the situation and broken the quiet in that car. There was genuine love between my dad and me, but somehow we could not break through to one another, not at that time.

A couple of months later, toward the end of my freshman semester in college, my dad was killed in a terrible work accident. I can still recall the phone call at about 10:15 am on a clear Monday in early December 1984. I can hear my mom wailing as she came to terms with losing the man she loved. I can feel my heart turning numb, knowing that I would never get to see him walk through our front door covered in the bagasse from the sugar mill. Losing him left a gaping hole in my heart that somewhat healed (but the gaps left by our losses never quite fill in) many years later when I became a father myself. It was then as a grown man that I started to understand my dad and to realize how difficult it is to sometimes let those closest to me into the sounds and rhythms of my heart and mind. We receive from our fathers and mothers what they received from their fathers and mothers. The generational passing down of all that is good in us and the burdens we carry, leave us vulnerable to the very opportunities that call us to be our true selves. By the time my three kids reached their teens, I became aware of how hard it is to be a father and also to be a son. I saw many of the same struggles I faced manifested in my own children as they wrestled with their own voices, with their own souls, and with the challenge of relating to me. (I was not my father, but was psychically one with him.) So I entered into a fellowship of love with my children that included the gifts and flaws that make us so fully ourselves.

Over the years I came to know that the people closest to us often present the strongest challenges to our own constructed worlds. Unfortunately, we often place on these struggling relationships the burden of our own happiness and well-being. We often think the false syllogism: *If I only had a better relationship with. . . . then.* If the struggles are as intense as mine were and are, they often distract us from the very joy and pleasure of the moment in front of us and move us away from the work of consciously walking down our own creative paths. We too often spend our time looking back and licking wounds than on taking a step forward in fulfilling what is our own song. (Have I mentioned already that life is short?)

If we look carefully at these and the many sources of our own wounds, we may find that these strong challenges can become our best teachers, leading us to find life's purpose and mission. Yet, when I look back at my own life and, in particular, my academic journey, I also know that nowhere in my schooling did I ever find an invitation to really explore these experiences, to look at these values and events with the same curiosity and rigor of a text that held important keys to my own well-being.

Schooling for Silence and Conformity

In schools, heart and mind rarely came together for me. Even when studying poetry and literature, the notion of the personal entering the realm of the academic never quite intersected. For me, being in school meant turning away from a part of myself that did not belong. May be this was dictated by my own outsider status as a recent immigrant. When I started college, I had only been living 10 years in this country, and my parents were not fluent in English. My parents, although intelligent and gifted in so many areas, had little formal education. Maybe this and my own introverted personality were factors in my feeling so alienated. But the realities seem more complex and intertwined. Nevertheless, I hold the adults around me, those who attempted to teach me; the schools I attended; the whole educational enterprise responsible for a large part of my inability to break through. After 20 years of teaching, I now realize that I was never invited to share, to look into my own life story as a source of knowledge, wisdom, and guidance for what I was supposed to do with my academic efforts. I know now that this was a loss, a lost connection, but not an anomaly.

For the most part, school was a place where I studied important subjects, the ideas of important people (mostly dead white men), and never quite broke through to realize that within me, I had an important treasure trove of information that might be essential for my own survival and well-being; that reading my life was essential. What I did not have at the time were mentors that could show me how this was done; people with the courage to model the act of looking deep within, not so much for the sake of introspection for introspection's sake, but for the purpose of freedom and liberation. It wasn't until I left college and began teaching that I realized how the significance of allowing the personal into the academy. I remember reading the work of bell hooks and being electrified at the notion that one's inner life needed to be accessed, honored, and shared with others in order to tap into the full experience of transformative learning experiences.

Cracks in the System

Hooks' words were transformative for me. For the first time in my life, I read someone's work that actually expressed what was muddled within my own mind, that ". . .any radical pedagogy must insist that everyone's presence is acknowledged" (1994, p. 8). But how can everyone's presence be acknowledged if her story or his story is not the ground and source of that space? How can we acknowledge presence, when everywhere the academy itself is all about efficiency and productivity? Everyone is a number, an object: students, teachers, administrators.

The challenges of turning away from the process of transforming humans into objects are monumental. No institution where I've been has engaged in this process. On the contrary, from the start of my educational experience,

I was encouraged to cut out the personal and embrace the objective voice of the academy. The process for most starts in kindergarten, and by the time we finish college, most people have thoroughly been indoctrinated to believe that one's personal life belongs deep within, and that if one is to be professional, the personal has to be cut out and left out.

If we look carefully at the process of excluding the personal, for a society like ours to demand efficiency and maximizing profits would make total sense. With those goals, our educational journey must be built on a foundation of de-personalization. We can't possibly honor the quirkiness of the individual; more significantly, we can't possibly let young people believe that their lives, their stories are the source of wisdom and guidance because if we do, how could we control them? Acknowledging their individuality, their power to resist, their self-assertions, their digging for their lived truths clogs the wheels of efficiency.

The funding for schools is not set up for individual meanderings. When we look closely, we see a factory model where everyone who comes through the doors of an institution of higher learning is expected to come out shaped and marked, "ready to consume," and "ready to support production," a model that has served some people really well, while leaving millions without the ability to support even basic needs.[1] I can still recall President Bush's injunction two weeks after the 911 Attacks: "Go down to Disney World!" (CNN, 2004).

And although computer technology has exploded in the past 20 years, the tools created have moved us no closer to a personalized approach to learning. Schools buy the latest hardware and implement the most recent software, but the educational model is fundamentally unchanged. We continue to have for the most part what the Brazilian educator, Paulo Freire, (1996) called a banking model, one where students are seen as passive repositories where knowledge is deposited by those in control. Instead of creating a new paradigm where we can relate to one another in human-sized relationships, we create larger, so-called more productive classrooms and tout them as the next best thing that will save ourselves from irrelevance. We initiate online courses that enroll hundreds at a time. We design online degrees where one never has to meet another person. We have developed online K-12 state certifications, where a child for 12 years never has to see an instructor nor another student. We have prostituted education to support corporate greed.

---

[1] 45.8 million people in U.S. live in poverty. 19.9 percent of children go to bed hungry every night.

Yet, all is not lost and all is not terrible. The fact that I can look back and see the deficiencies of my student experience, and understand as a teacher how caught we are in a system, that by its nature de-spirits rather than inspires, means that there are gaps within that monolithic system. Crevices can open where we connect with others and raise our voices, read and write our stories, and learn from our experiences. Part of the challenge that we face is finding that wiggle room within our places of learning or employment, and do the kind of work that is invisible to most, unrewarded, and, sometimes, misconstrued—and may I say, dangerous.

Bad Advice

The greatest danger, however, is not from anything or anyone outside of ourselves. It is from within. There's no guarantee where the process of self-exploration will take us and how much it will move us away from the beaten paths expected of us by those who genuinely love us and those who don't. Both groups have very little sense of what is really going on within because they are operating in a world where those personal stories, desires, urgings, and callings are ignored or silenced. Lines from Mary Oliver's poem "The Journey" (Oliver, 1986) capture this dilemma:

One day you finally knew

what you had to do, and began,

though the voices around you

kept shouting

their bad advice—

though the whole house

began to tremble

and you felt the old tug

at your ankles (p. 38).

The bad advice is not always intended to be so. It sometimes comes from the best hearts and intentions. Everything that I have said here about schools and classrooms, though, is not meant as a condemnation of those who are in education. We are all caught one way or another in a very powerful web that wants us to stay asleep. It is a web that refuses credence to the voice within that is whispering sweet pleasure, love, and liberation. That web refuses any promise to transform our path ahead. But as Mary Oliver says in her poem, one day we finally know what we have to do. Walk away. Step outside. The house is trembling.

References

Bush, G. W. (2004). Go down to Disney World in Florida, take your families . . . Retrieved May 11, 2013 from CNN.com

Freire, P. (1996). *Pedagogy of the Oppressed,* 2nd ed. CA: Penguin Group.

hooks, bell. (1994). *Teaching to Transgress: Education as the Practice of Freedom.* New York: Routledge. p. 8.

Oliver, M. (1986). *Dream Work.* Boston, MA: Atlantic Monthly Press. p. 38.

U.S. Census Bureau (2014). Poverty. Retrieved March 15, 2015 from http://www.census.gov/hhes/www/poverty/about/overview/

The autonomy of the teacher/developer or teacher/researcher

by Mario Eraso

After teaching mathematics education courses for three years at a university in Texas, I was hired by a private middle school in south Florida to teach mathematics and robotics. During the 18 months I worked as a teacher, I saw myself as a teacher/developer, and at times desiring to mold my position into a teacher/researcher. These two terms I am referring to, a teacher who does more than just teach, were introduced to me by Bob Moses, founder and president of the Algebra Project, Inc., a national nonprofit organization that uses mathematics as an organizing tool to ensure quality public school education for every child in America. The Algebra Project is a dynamic organization that not only teaches young people math and how to be mindful citizens, but develops mathematics curriculum, engages the community to interact in classrooms, and connects and professionally develops teachers (Moses and Cobb, 2001). I believe that assuming a teacher/developer framework for my teaching roles at the middle school, allowed me to teach in a way that maximized learning.

The teacher/developer is one who continuously develops learning material for and according to the needs of the students. Because teachers are overworked by having to teach six classes, monitor homeroom sessions, manage discipline procedures, plan and grade, meet with administrators and parents, and supervise students in the hallways, cafeteria and during arrival and dismissal times, it is very tempting in today's web-based society for a teacher to use ready-made handouts available in websites. The teacher/developer is, therefore, a rare phenomenon. Only if teachers had more time for planning, the added role of developer would make sense. Now, becoming a teacher/researcher, in my opinion, requires even more time. Grounding your work on relevant background literature, choosing a methodology, analyzing data, and writing results and conclusions is clearly time consuming, even when doing action research. So, how could schools provide teachers with the possibility of practicing as a teacher/developer or researcher if there is little time for added roles in the profession? This is where the respect for the teacher as a professional and transformative education come into play.

Teaching is a complex and difficult job because it presupposes rich interactions between humans: student to student, student to teacher, and student to community. Research has shown that students have very distinct learning styles and thus teaching needs, and that the strategies to fulfill these needs vary depending on the subject. Making learning happen requires more than subject knowledge, skills, and competence. An effective teacher must be adaptable, ethical, accountable, and have the ability to assess and communicate well—all of which are characteristics of a true professional. All these teacher characteristics, that when put to use effect learning, I summarize with one word: autonomy. If a teacher has autonomy, the teacher can make decisions on selecting the appropriate methodology for a particular curriculum topic. Likewise, an autonomous teacher who is free from external control or influence can assess best her current students' needs to determine the duration of a learning unit, or whether a re-teach session is needed.

However, in the literature on teacher professionalism, teacher autonomy has been associated with a teacher's free will to decide how to teach, what to teach, and how to assess without concern to standards and often acting randomly. Autonomy has been coupled also with uniformity, a consequence of salary schedules and the credentialing process that does not let the effective teachers be differentiated from the ineffective teachers. Finally, autonomy has been associated with a teacher's lack of support. A teacher working in isolation and without assistance is said to have the autonomy of modifying the curriculum at random, for example. If we define autonomy in this manner, the term acquires a negative connotation. Rather than perceiving the autonomous teacher as someone who works separately from others, we should understand this quality of the teacher as self-directing and not subjected to the "mis-direction" by others.

Now, transformative education environments such as those created by the Algebra Project, allow the space for teachers to grow and develop professionally. It is in these environments where school-based, university-affiliated programs flourish and allow children's learning to accelerate. In these programs, teachers are part of a collaborative effort in which they interact with other teachers in the nation, with mathematics educators and mathematicians, counselors, and the community at large. Since the collaboration is intense and programmed, teachers find themselves with the ability to tap onto existing resources. Principals in the United States who see the benefits of this type of collaboration have learned from their counterparts in other countries that by allowing teachers to teach less, and plan and collaborate more, teachers can find the time to be teacher/developers or researchers, which in turn effects meaningful, deep, and long-lasting learning.

According to my definition of autonomy above, I was able to teach math and robotics autonomously at the middle school. For example, I decided to use the Geometer's Sketchpad (GSP) software as frequently as possible to teach a high school geometry course for middle school students. With this software, the static presentation of geometry given in the textbook, was supported with dynamic activities. In order to use GSP effectively, I created my own discovery activities and dynamic application projects, and rubrics, thus showing the characteristics of the teacher/developer. As a strategy for deep conceptual learning, I used classroom discussions in which students were taught explicitly how to listen to their peers and how to respond with comments or questions to other students' remarks. To insert these modules into the existing curriculum required autonomy and independence, but mostly self-determination and assurance to invest time on the prerequisite development of students' attitudes and behaviors necessary to do mathematics through communicating. I used my own criteria also to assess how to do this in the best manner. For example, I would know that a student had understood a concept if he or she could synthesize in a couple of sentences a class discussion in which at least four students participated. More importantly, I was fortunate to have the support of the principal and the friendship of the social studies teacher, a veteran with over 40 years of teaching experience, who found the time to discuss and suggest room for improvement in the different implementations I was introducing in my classes.

As in the Algebra Project's curriculum, I used drawings, icons, and symbols to support students' learning in a pre-algebra course. Specifically, I used these tools for learning integer addition and subtraction. These tools allowed me to introduce methodologies that left behind the "take away" paradigm of elementary subtraction and embraced the "compare" paradigm that leads to huge learning milestones needed in college, such as distinguishing between distance and displacement. Also, when teaching percentages, ratios, and decimals comparatively, I introduced language development strategies that I was borrowing from the Algebra Project curricular model. The idea of straitjacketing language and moving from "people talk" to "feature talk" was a particular strategy I used to assist students in learning how to communicate using scientific language (Moses and Cobb, 2001).

But it was teaching the robotics course at the middle school that most clearly exemplified my autonomy as a teacher and my role as a teacher/developer. Although for the robotics course, which was offered for one semester, there was a curriculum to follow and a methodology to be used, I let the students suggest what activities to perform, and, thereby, allowed myself to modify the curriculum. I would vet the suggestions and approve them once the students acknowledged that they had to insert certain learning objectives that I had in mind and that would align well with the original curriculum. Additionally, I used the project-based learning methodology in the robotics class because I wanted to make emphasis on students' creativity to design and program the robots. The original curriculum had several activities in which a kit of equipment and its instructions were used to build robots. In my class, every robot was different and in some way represented qualities that the students valued. For instance, one robot was slender and slow because the student wanted it to conserve energy; and another one was stocky and heavy because the student wanted it to portray power. The students designed a construction tower with three articulations, a scorpion with two claws, an elevator, a backhoe, and multiple car-like robots. It was the Heisenberg robot, inspired in the T.V. series *Breaking Bad*, that became an icon over the four semesters I taught the course. This robot was even used by the school administration during open house and parent nights to showcase the robotics course.

The students who built the Heisenberg robot started the idea when they were in level 3 during their first semester. Four of the students who wanted to repeat the course the second semester asked me if they could build a robot that would have all the sensors, switches, and attributes of all the robots they had seen their classmates design during the first semester. With the idea approved, the Heisenberg flourished as a robot with a linetracker sensor at the bottom, a distance sensor on its front, a bumper switch on its back, two articulated arms with shoulders and claws and mounted on tank tracks. The Heisenberg looked like a sphinx, the body of a sturdy tank-like robot and a human head. The students brought from home sunglasses and a black Fedora hat, and designed a goatee to decorate the head. But my friend and colleague, the social studies teacher veteran, would not be satisfied until someone could make the Heisenberg speak! The students responded to the challenge and used a phone application that would emit sound from a cell phone in the body of the robot that in turn was activated by another cell phone from where the students would speak. The Heisenberg was used also by the students in my colleague's social studies course on civics, government, and citizenship to begin a session in which the students interacted with younger elementary students promoting positive community behaviors. Even a rumor was started in the school that one day the Heisenberg would lead a daily morning session conducted at the school chapel.

During the fourth semester, a student brought from home pistons his parents had bought after the student had attended a robotics competition during a weekend fieldtrip our school organized. The student and his team members wanted to dismantle the arms of the Heisenberg and use pistons rather than articulated arms. These students learned how to program code to activate solenoid valves to control the pistons, learned about pressure units in the air chamber, and how to cut and connect pneumatic tubing. What they ended programming was the ability of the Heisenberg to jab at an opponent by inserting the pistons along the arms of the robot. My role was solely to push these students further by asking them to use what they had learned the previous semester, not necessarily to teach them anything new. I suggested that they should program jabs in a pattern that would reflect a hidden message like you do when using Morse code. So, for example, a sequence of three short, three long, and three short jabs would encode the message S.O.S. The students usually enjoyed my challenges and, as I had hoped for, were getting out of control, in the positive sense of the term. Most students who excelled exhibited positive behaviors by helping the newer students in the class. That had been the original plan of letting students retake the course. The principal and I believed that peer-to-peer role modeling was powerful and would allow us to learn from having a leadership program within the robotics class. Some of the students worked in a particular station where they kept their own materials in boxes that they found in the classroom closet. They had customized the boxes with inner compartments to store different pieces of equipment. I let them do that because it was a form of showing pride and style during the planning stages of their projects. I even put a label on the wall over the table that served as their station: Heisenberg Research Station.

Finally, my role as a teacher/developer allowed me to define and design my own levels of assessing student progress. Level 1 had the objective of programming a robot to perform a particular elementary task for a specific duration. For example, in level 1, a student could write a program to start a motor moving forward for 5 seconds, stop for 2 seconds, and move backward for 5 seconds also, but at a lower speed. Level 2 was set for students to program a robot to perform a task if a condition was met. At this level, students learned about truth tables and were able to use switches that, depending on whether they were on or off, the robot would perform one of two outcomes. Level 3 exposed students to the more complex problem of having a robot perform multiple tasks depending on setting threshold levels for several sensors.

Finally, level 4 was for the students who had decided to take the course again the following semester. In this level, robots were remotely guided with a joystick and the coding syntax and commands necessary to program the joystick were different to those of levels 1 through 3. Because of the project-based learning environment, students were encouraged to create their own activities and projects for which they had to solve problems to make the robot do exactly what was intended in the coded. The task performed by the robot, the code programmed by the student, and the words used by the student in both an oral proposal and oral evaluation needed to exactly match each other. The students went further and asked me if I could institute a fifth level of performance. Once approved, level 5 became building, wiring and programming a robot using pistons.

During the last semester, students showed me how much their interest had grown. They brought from home air pumps, pistons, arduinos, raspberry pis, miniature quadcopters, fancy keyboards with screens, and cameras. They also were approved to order internally at the school an adaptor, use an old monitor, and change the settings of a keyboard to build a computer using the raspberry pi kit a student had brought from home. The ultimate evidence of how exciting the class was for students and the community was when a parent donated to the school $1000 to buy a 3D printer. The 3D printer revamped students' interest in using Autodesk Inventor 3D software to design small objects that were later printed by the students. Their interest in the course was such that most students, about 10 of 15 in the class, had achieved the teaching assistant status after having completed the first three levels and having designed two objects in the inventor software. A student one day asked me, "Some TAs say I am not a TA. Could you print us certificates of completion?" Another student asked, "What will happen when everybody becomes a TA? Would you be interested in developing activities towards us becoming master TAs?" The original idea I had with the principal was to exhibit behaviors of leadership and mentorship, but what was also happening was that the students were becoming avid learners.

To summarize, I want to say that in my robotics class, which obviously was not mine but theirs, I exercised teacher autonomy as I have defined it in this paper. I strongly believe not even one-third of the outcomes I have described would have happened if I had not had the autonomy, principal's approval, and my friend and colleague's feedback. Teachers today, I believe, need to have more collaboration opportunities between parents and the classroom, between students, between teacher and student, should provide assessment continuity from year to year, and use multiple levels of assessment that provide students with different times for completion. So, in addition to the teacher/developer or researcher, I suggest teachers become teacher/writers as well. And I am sure many teachers already do that today and have blogs where they share their teaching successes. If a teacher can teach with autonomy and create learning excitement, why is it that society wants teachers to turn into test-driven automatons? No wonder policymakers with the perceptions that teachers should be controlled are driving talent from the profession. And some schools have clearly gone overboard in adopting "drill and kill" strategies, devaluing the teacher profession. In response to the demands of the No Child Left Behind Act, some districts have instituted "teacher proof" curricula that are scripted and, obviously, leave no room for the teacher/developer, researcher or writer. The system's oppressively rigid structures and its obsession with control of students and teachers shuts down the creativity of instructors, of students, of the entire schooling experience. Let us as teachers and learners "raise our voices in the noise of this hegemony." Let us speak for intellectual, imaginative justice inside and outside our classrooms.

Reference

Moses, R. P. & Cobb, C. (2001). *Radical Equations: Civil Rights from Mississippi to the Algebra Project.* Boston: Beacon Press.

PART 3

The spirit of agency

The spirit of agency is believing at the molecular, spiritual level that you can make a difference in the world, not by changing others, people and things, but by opening your spirit enough so that the light of others can shine through you.

—*Real World Dialogue*

Service to others matters

by Debby Wynne Kelly

"**D**addy, why are you visiting the prisoners? Mother, you are staying up so late baking for the nuns. How come? Why can't I play with the toys before you deliver them to the children, Daddy? Why don't those folks you're taking groceries to have any electricity, Mother? Why do the children have "outhouses" and no paved streets in Plunkett town, Daddy?"[1]

An inequity in the haves and have nots made my parents reel, and so they dedicated themselves to helping out in their church and surrounding community. It didn't matter that, at times, they struggled financially to make ends meet; they still reached out to others in need and shared what they had.

In the 50s and 60s, liberal thinkers were not a dime a dozen in Georgia! Maybe, even still scarce. But, that duo made up for the lack of such thinkers. Silence in the midst of racist comments was not golden. No, it meant consent to carry on with such conversation. My parents were never silent. They seemed to clearly understand MLK, Jr's message that "In the end, we will remember not the words of our enemies, but the silence of our friends" (1967). And so my Mother and Dad seemed to live what I realize now was a form of ministry and civics.

At some point I stopped asking "why" and decided to follow their example of "doing." Service, it was all about service, I realized, and then attempted to emulate their actions. First, student council in school, Girl Scout trips to hospitals, nursing homes, and Young Democrats in college to learn how the

---

[1] An African-American neighborhood in southern Atlanta, called a "slum" in "Ghettoes: a change in their outlook," *Windsor Star*, 1969; described also in Benjamin Elijah Mays, *Born to Rebel: An autobiography*, Athens, GA: The University of Georgia Press. 1971, p. 279.

political process works. And, then, I became a young parent and wanted to pass the torch of service to my children as it had been passed to my four sisters and me. Lead by example, I thought. In the cities where we have lived, Jackson, TN, Houston, TX, Boston, MA, Atlanta, GA, and Washington, DC, I have sought meaningful service in my diverse communities. Whether it was in my children's schools, church projects, education programs, or elderly care, I have tried to follow my parents' examples. For, my Dad, a huge admirer of Martin Luther King, Jr. in a segregated Atlanta, many a night at the dinner table quoted MLK's words: "Everybody can be great . . . because anybody can serve. You don't have to have a college degree to serve. You don't have to make your subject and verb agree to serve. . . . You only need a heart full of grace. A soul generated by love" (King, 1968). Love and grace and service seemed to be the lessons my parents lived. As my children have grown. I have watched them take up the torch of service over the years. Now, they are passing the torch to my grandchildren by their example.

On a recent Sunday morning, I listened intently to the homily of my rector, Rev. John Beddingfield (2015). It was all about service and ways to serve. He spoke of Quaker author, Richard Foster, who talks about service as a spiritual discipline (1988). And Foster created names for different kinds of service. One kind, he calls "hidden service," where there is only one person who knows of your service. Because it is hidden, Beddingfield explained, "Over time, there will grow within you a quality that others will begin to sense, a quality of a deeper love, a new compassion, almost a slight aura. People will notice that you are different" (Beddingfield, 2015).

And in his book about spiritual discipline, Foster, using a personal story, further explains this kind of serving. He describes an event from the most hectic and final week of finishing his doctoral dissertation, when a call from a friend who needed transportation for errands, brought him an unforeseen clarity. Worrying about the precious time he was losing by helping this friend, Foster reluctantly agreed to serve as driver. As Foster waited in the car, he pulled out Dietrich Bonhoeffer's little book, *Life Together*. We all know to have a book handy while waiting! Opening the book, Foster was struck by the words, "The . . . service one should perform for another in a Christian community is active helpfulness. This means, initially, simple assistance in trifling, external matters. . . . Nobody is too good for the meanest service. One who worries about the loss of time . . . is usually taking the importance of his own career too solemnly" (Foster, 1988). While listening to Foster's words and experience, an admonition of Pearl S. Buck came to mind. She said, "To serve is beautiful, but only if it is done with joy and a whole heart and a free mind."

One of my sisters suggests that she has witnessed Civil Rights icon, Bob Moses, never too busy to perform the "trifling, meanest service" to whomever is in need, children, parents, teachers, or colleagues. My parents delivered medicine and food to people pushed to the margins of a confederate society. My children serve in their neighborhoods, schools, and communities and sometimes global villages. Yes, service in small ways matters.

Whether you are Christian, of another religion or no religion, I do believe, you can find meaning in Beddingfield's homily, in others' modeling as well as in other people's words. But it is the small service that can fuel a grassroots movement, which can change laws, and, therefore, change lives. It does not happen in a year or even a decade, but if we keep taking those steps of service, we may, indeed, overcome.

Thank you, Mother and Daddy for teaching me at an early age that service to others matters.

References

Beddingfield, J. (2015). *Homily*. Washington, D.C.: All Souls Memorial Episcopal Church, March 8.

Buck, P. S. (1931). *The good earth*. New York, NY: Simon & Schuster.

Foster, R. J. (1988). *Celebration of discipline: The path to spiritual growth*. San Francisco: Harper Collins.

King, M. L. Jr. (1967). *The trumpet of conscience*, Steeler Lecture. November. http://forusa.org/blogs/ivan-boothe/martin-luther-king-jr-his-own-words-radical-revolutionary-opposed-war/8435

King, M. L. Jr. (1968). *Drum major instinct*. Georgia: Sermon at Ebenezer Baptist Church in Atlanta. February 4, 1968.

Where are the women?

by Joan T. Wynne

It's so clear that you have to cherish everyone. I think that's what I get from these older black women, that every soul is to be cherished, that every flower is to bloom.—Alice Walker

When I perused the list of essays for this book to organize them around possible themes of "Who speaks for justice," I sat stunningly silent. I saw not one essay, in the long list of titles, which spoke specifically to the voices of women. How had I not noticed that absence until the last moment of reading and arranging these essays? I had invited students, colleagues, activists to contribute their personal stories about justice, including the young, the elder, the male, the female, the non-gendered. Yet until this moment, did I even notice that not one piece explicitly explored justice for women or the reality of women's silenced voices.

I am a woman; in fact, I am an old woman. Where was my head? There seems no redemption for me here. Yet I continue to scratch my brain for reasons for this omission. But why bother? I guess because it's so excruciatingly painful to admit the neglect. And it does speak loudly about the dilemma of internalized sexism—that a woman who has researched, written, and spoken about issues of justice; taught students about Ella Baker, Fannie Lou Hamer, Diane Nash, Anne Braden, etc. and always remembers to talk about Helen Keller as a socialist and activist, never noticed the exclusion in this text of a story about her own gender. Nonetheless, this book cannot arrive at the publisher's door, without, at the very least, one essay that speaks directly about the woman's voice for justice.

Nonetheless, while thinking about my gross oversight, one incident from my past did bubble up inside my psyche and seemed to muddy the waters of my unconscious disregard of the particular story of women. That forgetfulness, I believe, might have begun when I was teaching in high school in the south in 1972. A white feminist came to speak to our faculty about sexism, and I told my female colleague that I wasn't interested in hearing the speaker. Of course, my colleague asked, "Why not?" And I attempted to explain that until white women stopped paying black women slave wages to clean their houses and take care of their children; stopped insisting that black women sit in kitchens instead of dining rooms to eat alone as they paused for lunch; until white women in mass hit the streets and the legislatures to fight for the rights of black women and children; and until white women quit fleeing to the suburbs so they could avoid sending their students to school with "those people's children," I wasn't really interested in anything a white woman in the south had to say about women's rights. So here I am, still stuck, reckoning with my seeming resistance to the specific plight of women.

But it is the midnight hour, and what do I do? There is so much to be said specifically about women leading for justice; women fighting for justice; women suffering across the globe because of injustice. Womanism versus Feminism. The sung and unsung she-roes who for thousands of years have advanced the cause of peace, democracy, spiritual and human rights, music and the arts, philosophy, epistemology, science, technology, and family. Certainly, at long last volumes of books are now being read and authored by and about women who have spoken for justice down the ages; though, too often, the ideas behind these books are not in the public discourse. Still, why am I, an educator, having to come to terms at this late date with my own oblivious slip?

Well, my personal neglect in this book may illumine the conundrum of another question, "With so many women teachers in public schools, where are the lives of women in our history books and all of the other textbooks?" Why, when there are 84% of us in public schools (2012), do too many of us ignore the power in our numbers to challenge the scarcity of our stories in the books we use to teach our children? No matter the research study cited, the statistics of the preponderance of male voices versus those of women in educational texts is still overwhelming. Maanvi Singh at NPR in April 2015 reported that "Gender Bias Pervades Textbooks Worldwide." Yes, another reason, beside my narcissistic need to assuage my guilt, for the necessity to include in this book a story about women who speak for justice.

Clearly not enough time remains before my deadline to develop a longer well-researched historical saga about women and justice. So, in attempting to write myself out of this blunder with any sense of respectability, I've decided to share one woman's story, the story of a young fighter for justice, extraordinare! Her name is Maisha Moses.

Born in Africa, but raised in Boston, she is a graduate of Harvard who did not leave our children behind. With Harvard's diploma and her later Master's degree in mathematics, she could now be making six figures in many arenas in this country. But she has chosen another route. She keeps intellectually alive, yet financially strapped, through her work leading the Young People's Project, an organization that develops youth as math literacy workers.

I first met her when Lisa Delpit and I created a site in Miami for the Young People's Project, a spin-off of the Algebra Project. At that time her brother, Omo Moses, was president of the Young People's Project (YPP), and Maisha was working with YPP helping to implement a competency-based Training of Trainers program that she previously had apprenticed for five years with Jim Burruss, a renowned professional development consultant. She also spearheaded a national management team to build the leadership of young people as agents of change (Profiles).

That was the beginning of my being drawn to the voice of Maisha and to her work. I often accompanied her to schools in Miami where she interacted with our children and evaluated our program, sharing her advice about how to operate and sustain our Miami YPP site. During those times, her serenity, her humility, her deep listening qualities, and her quiet leadership stilled an over-anxious, over-energetic me. Her gentle presence with everyone in the room was enough to calm my angst about the elementary children, the high school mentors, the disorder that sometimes comes with youngsters tutoring youngsters, and the schools' unconscious oppression of our children. After every meeting with her, I went home and told myself that I wanted to become Maisha.

She comes from a lineage of strong leaders and high-achieving siblings. Yet, there is a quality to her that seems almost surreal—yes, she's practical, sensible, logical—after all, she is a mathematician—but it is difficult to capture on paper her capacity to establish tranquility in the midst of chaos.

Her academic credentials, her teaching and finely honed listening and leadership skills are all sterling. But it is her continuous day-to-day struggle to "raise the floor" (Moses and Cobb, 2001) of academic achievement for the disenfranchised; to network with people across the country to support the constitutional rights of children to receive a quality education; and to use tools of graceful yet firm principle to bring people into a circle from all cultures, political persuasions, and ages, regardless of the level of their consciousness, to stand for justice. She has a way of unleashing the human spirit to speak for the good, the right, and the just.

I will end my story about Maisha Moses with her own words about her work, about how she dedicates her life and "speaks for justice":

> We ask young people to give their attention to cultivating and growing their inherent abilities to learn, lead, teach, and organize in order to work with each other and their communities to improve their mathematical literacy and to address the institutional obstacles to their success.

She further explains that the work of YPP intends to capture the imagination of the youth in accepting their unique positions as change agents in solving the problems that they and their communities face, acts often resulting in personal and communal transformations. And, as importantly, through the YPP process, she discovers that youth often "grow new approaches to the old and seemingly intractable problems they face in their schools" (Profiles).

References

Moses, R. P. & Cobb, D. (2001). *Radical equations: Civil Rights from Mississippi to the Algebra Project*. Boston: Beacon Press.

Profiles: Maisha Moses. (2006). *The Young People's Project*. Retrieved from: http://typp.org/profile/151

Singh, M. (2015). See Priya Cook: Gender bias pervades textbooks worldwide. *NPR* in April. Retrieved from http://www.npr.org/blogs/goatsandsoda/2015/04/19/400486373/see-priya-cook-gender-bias-pervades-textbooks-worldwide

Calm down, relax; it isn't that big a deal

by Sarah Schultz

I was seven. I heard thundering and the noise of large droplets of rain slashing the windows. My mother had gone to the store to buy groceries. Unlike my brother and sister, who were preoccupied with the television or computer, I peered out the window awaiting my mother's return. Thoughts began to race through my mind. *Why isn't she back yet? How many minutes does it take to get groceries? What if she got into a car accident? What would I do if my mother passed away? My father can't cook. Would he remarry?* With eyes glued to the window, I couldn't help but process the worst possible outcomes. My stomach churned and my breathing became shallow—and yet this was just a routine trip my mother made to the grocery store, each week.

But, whenever I became anxious and worried, people close to me said I was being "too sensitive." Or "It's just not that big of a deal." To me, it was a "big deal." Yet I knew something was not right. Why were other kids my age able to be unaffected by similar situations, while I couldn't purge anxiety from my brain? I wanted to tell my family how I was feeling, but I *had* to be the healthy one. My older brother had been diagnosed with Crohn's disease, and my sister had a rare form of cancer. So my parents thought they had won the genetic lottery when I was born. No visible problems. Except that I didn't wear my problems externally, but internally. I was dealing with my own raging storm. That storm was never addressed until much later in my life.

As I entered my first year of teaching in 2011, I felt an immense level of pressure from my administration, my teammates, and my students because I held myself to such high standards. Due to family expectations, I thought I had to be perfect. I often found myself worrying about what people thought of me and wondering if I were teaching the correct material. I would rerun scenarios over and over in my head and make myself feel guilty if someone was disappointed in my actions. By March of 2012, I had made myself so mentally and physically exhausted, that I finally decided to seek a professional.

Initially, I had resisted seeing a professional because I did not want to be labeled as a "crazy person." From previous personal experiences, I felt that I would be judged incompetent by others if I asked for help. I felt I would have to keep this a secret, so no one would see my "craziness." Over time, I'd noticed that there was a stigma attached to receiving mental health services, and that people who suffered mental illness typically did not seem to share their problem. According to Patrick W. Corrigan and Amy C. Watson, two researchers who have studied mental stigma, "Stigmas about mental illness seem to be widely endorsed by the Western world" (2002). Many times, my own family members and friends would tell me that I was being dramatic, and that I just needed to calm down and relax. As if it were that easy. As if I *wanted* to feel anxious.

When I became diagnosed with general Anxiety Disorder (GAD), I felt like I had finally cracked the code as to why I began each day feeling anxious and nervous. I understood why I wasn't able to let a simple mistake go, or why I felt a need to apologize profusely if I believed I had offended someone. Now, though, life started to make sense. I was taught by a therapist to evaluate my circumstances. If I felt anxious about something, I would ask myself, "Would this matter in 10 minutes? Would this matter in an hour; in a day; in a month; in a year?" I learned to practice deep breathing exercises to help alleviate the physical aspects of the anxiety. I was surprised by how much these seemingly simple things uncomplicated my world.

Being in therapy helped me to understand my thinking process, to be aware of when I was having a panic attack, and to develop some skills for how to remain calm in stressful situations. It freed my mind and opened me up to a new world of rational opportunities. I felt that my storm had finally let up, and I was able to control my anxious thoughts. I felt as though my brain could finally fight my battle of anxiety and could combat the fear and worries, so I could, for the first time, be myself. My true self. I could go to the beach on a cloudy day, without worrying if the rain would come. I learned that if the rain came, I could embrace it.

A giant leap was my becoming unashamed of seeing a therapist. Yet, when I shared my new found enlightenment with family and friends, I noticed the reaction that I actually always had been expecting. People made me feel as if I were making my symptoms too big a deal. They kept insisting that if I would just be positive, I would have the same results as therapy brought. With their negative reactions to my appreciation for therapy, I was no longer disappointed in myself, but sorely disappointed in the reactions of the people I had most trusted.

When others tend to make assumptions about issues such as anxiety, depression, schizophrenia, and bipolar disorder, it can make a person who is struggling with these conditions refuse or resist getting help. Professor of Psychiatry, Gregory K. Fritz (2007), indicated that "Most concerning for children is the fact that it leads parents to avoid seeking psychiatric treatment that could dramatically improve their child's condition" (p. 8). Fritz found that "In a recent study of 1,134 American parents, for example, about 30% said they would not want their child to become friends with a child who had depression and 25% said the same about a child with ADHD. Almost 20% of the sample even said they would not want a child with either disorder to live next door. Responses to the same question regarding a child with a physical illness such as asthma were much more generous" (p. 8).

According to the research conducted by Irene Covarrubias and Meekyung Han (2011), people with serious mental illnesses also experience decreased quality of life, fewer job opportunities, decreased opportunities for obtaining housing, decreased quality of health care, and decreased self-esteem (p. 317). Our culture too often does not tend to see mental illness as an acceptable illness; and, thus, victims of this illness are constantly experiencing prejudice and stereotyping. It is much more accepted by our culture to have something physically crippling than something that is mentally crippling.

Too often, the media has identified problems of mental health with psychopaths and criminals. Others often assume that issues with mental health are due to childlike perceptions. Or that the mentally MUST have weak characters (Corrigan and Watson, 2002). Those perceptions reinforce the stereotype that people should be afraid of anyone with mental illness. According to Social Learning theory, people who have never experienced or known anyone who has a mental illness use the television, newspaper, and other media sources to inform themselves and create perceptions according to those images (Stout et al., 2004). Unfortunately, people with mental illnesses have been portrayed in the media as violent and are, in fact, rarely represented well. In one study, Patricia A. Stout and her colleagues report that "Cultivation theory suggests that heavy exposure to consistent and recurrent messages on television will 'reiterate, confirm, and nourish' values and shape perceptions of social reality to conform to those presented on television" (Stout et al., 2004).

In the past, T. V. characters, the news stories in the media, and often movies have portrayed people with mental illness as violent, unapproachable, and untreatable. Urban educator, Lisa Delpit (Delpit, 1995) suggests in her research about power and privilege that "We do not really see through our eyes or hear through our ears, but through our beliefs." If the media is the only source we use to form our judgments of ideas and social issues, then we are doomed to lopsided perceptions of reality.

Nevertheless, besides feeling discrimination from the general population, there is also a self-stigma that looms. Researchers D. L. Stuenkel and Vivian

Wong, indicate that "Stigmatized individuals may respond to the reactions of others in a variety of ways. They are often unsure about the attitudes of others and, therefore, may feel a constant need to make a good impression. Individuals living with stigma each and every day choose to accept society's or other's views of them, or choose to reject others' discrediting viewpoints" (2009, p. 49). Many people who feel self-conscious about their mental illness use strategies such as passing, covering, disregarding, resisting, rejecting, and isolating themselves to deflect their inner feelings about their mental illness (Stuenkel & Wong, 2009). These inner feelings can limit a person from seeking help or treatment. When we label and categorize people with mental illnesses, it discourages and often thwarts their sense of being an accepted human being in their society. Such behaviors increase people's sense of shame. Societies and the media create these social constructs, and too often inhibit people from receiving the care that they need.

My research helped me understand that every brain does not function the same way. Humans are not a "cookie cutter" species. In this world, there are different intelligences, different physical abilities, different personalities, different genetic makeup, etc. People often do not understand that we have different ways of using our brains. No two brains operate the same. Not even twins (Medina, 2014).

Mental illness stigmas keep people misinformed about the preponderance of this illness in our world. Often, for parents, it is hard to admit when a child may need help. Parents may think it means that they have failed. However, researchers like Gregory Fritz suggest that parents should be praised for helping their child build self-esteem by admitting there is a problem, and that there is treatment for that problem. Otherwise, as the parents are the ones who make all of the legal decisions, children will not receive the needed social services if their parents believe in society's mental stigma and ignore their child's condition.

For teachers and parents, perception of mental health service is key. It is important to understand that many children are not getting the mental health relief that they need and deserve because of these stigmas. I know that I would have benefitted from this knowledge and treatment at a young age. As a teacher, I want to protect children who experience the same frustration. Although these children may not express their mental health issues openly, they are in many of our classrooms silently begging for help. As challenging as it was for me to deal with my own anxiety from a young age, I can only imagine how difficult it must be for this generation.

As a culture, we seem to have been sent the wrong message. Mental illness is not something to be ashamed of. Pushing away our mental health needs will not make us better, nor happier. Becoming more open with expressing our feelings and not feeling ashamed to speak about the way our minds work might anchor our imaginations in healthy contexts. There are so many beautiful things about human beings and so much each person has to offer this world. Why would we want any population to be silenced in order to conform to the social norm? Feeling shame about a chemical imbalance in our bodies seems like a throwback to unenlightened times. As Aristotle once said, "It is the mark of an educated mind to be able to entertain a thought without accepting it" (Philosoblog, 2012). Society needs to challenge the views that the media portrays about mental illness, without blind acceptance. Moreover, in schools, shouldn't we be creating spaces where all children's mental states are accepted and given healthy attention, so that they can experience a mental freedom and a relief from acute suffering.

References

Corrigan, P. & Watson, A. C. (2002). *Understanding the impact of stigma on people with mental illness.* World Psychiatry; 1 (1), 16–20.

Covarrubias, I. & Han M. (2011). Mental Health Stigma about serious mental illness among MSW students: social contact and attitude. *Social Work* 56 (4), 317+.

Delpit, L. (1995). *Other Peoples Children: Cultural Conflict in the Classroom.* New York: New Press.

Fritz, G. K. (2007, November). Stigma and childhood mental illness: Can advocates turn the tide? The Brown University Child and Adolescent Behavior Letter 23 (11), 8.

Medina, J. (2014) *Brain Rules: Wiring.* Washington, D.C.: Peer Press.

Philosoblog. (2012). It is the mark of an educated mind to be able to entertain a thought without accepting it. Retrieved from http://philosiblog. com/2012/03/07/it-is-the-mark-of-an-educated-mind-to-be-able-to-entertain-a-thought-without-accepting-it/

Stout, P. A., Villegas, J., & Jennings N. A. (2004). Images of mental illness in the media: identifying gaps in the research. *Schizophrenia Bulletin* 30 (3), 543–561.

Stuenkel D. L. & Vivian K. Wong. (2009). *Chronic illness: impact and intervention.* In: P. D. Larsen & I. M. Lubkin (Eds). *Stigma,* 7th ed. Boston: Jones and Bartlett.

Creating paradise

by Martha Barantovich

I remember the moment that changed my education philosophy and practice as though it were yesterday. It wasn't. It was in 2001. I was teaching 9th graders in an urban school setting. My course was officially titled something like, Career Exploration, or some nonsense. I was working in a newly formed "school within a school" and was part of a team of educators who were tasked with teaching the "bottom 25%" of 9th graders. Most of the students in "The Academy" were Black and/or Hispanic. I think that during our first year, we had three "White" students. On paper, our goal was to address the academic deficiencies by providing a learning environment that was contained and connected. Contained there, those 180 students were being served by six teachers. Students rotated their day with only us. We worked as a team, the six of us, and planned prior to the school year and during the school year. We met regularly to discuss concerns and issues with curriculum and behavior. We involved parents and sent out multiple reports of academic progress. We visited homes and planned events that were "rewarding" to our students.

Again, on paper, we were doing everything right. We had identified the students who "needed" to be with us by combing through pages and pages of transcripts of incoming 9th graders from all of our feeder schools. We scheduled them and looked at deficiencies. We saw what the students weren't doing: attending class on a regular basis, completing homework and classwork, performing well on standardized tests, meeting standards, behaving appropriately, being "model" citizens. To say we actually knew what we were doing in our setting would be a lie. We were just part of a system that was in the process of perpetuating the hegemonic beliefs that have existed in this country for decades. We bought into the fact that the kids were the problem. They were the ones who were creating the issues and we were there to save them. Not save in a religious sense, but save in that we were going to graduate these poor souls and send them into the workforce ready to be upholders of the norms of society. We were these poor students last great hope. As a unit, we attended a *High Schools That Work* conference to gather all the latest and greatest info on how to pigeon hole these students into the model of education that we were buying into. We had taken the cups of Kool-Aid being offered and demanded that they bring us gallons. I was so vocal when I returned to my school in the fall about how wonderful our classes were going to be and how great a system we were establishing for our students, that it never dawned on me to stop and think, instead of plowing straight ahead into all things status quo.

Never mind that there was no plan in place beyond educating these students in 9th grade in this system. Never mind that our plan was not well thought out. Never mind that our funding was tied to creating good little workers in a good little complacent society. Never mind that our philosophy of service was completely based upon Skinner-istic behaviorism and tied to punishments, not even rewards. Never mind that our little academy was only perpetuating the belief system that these students were broken. Never mind any of that. We thought, I thought, that what we were doing was just the best thing ever. I look back on that experience and am able to dig through the garbage and the mess and identify some positive outcomes. We really did create a community that was safe and protected many of our students from unfair educational practices. We did allow certain successes, academically, behaviorally, and interpersonally. I'd like to believe that we also made a difference in some of our student's lives by providing them with a safe haven.

But, really, I'm embarrassed. I'm embarrassed, because at the same time we started this program, I was enrolled in my doctoral program and was taking two courses: *Advanced Topics in Social Foundations* and *Curriculum* and *Theory and Research*. Up until that point in my doc studies, I was really just re-wetting my feet in academia. I started with a stats class because statistics is bland and unchallenging. I had been teaching for seven years and wanted to grow as a thinker. Taking these two classes together forced me into a process of thinking that I didn't know existed. I was not prepared for the amount of change I was going to move through, but I did, nonetheless. I found myself struggling through the courses and my daily life as a teacher. Not because I wasn't able or capable, but because I was a practitioner of education that I thought was effective and ideal, and I was reading about theory and philosophy that caused me to feel uncomfortable in my experiences. I was having a terrible time reconciling what I was doing and firmly believed in, and what I was reading and discussing in my courses. I was unaware, at the time, that I was beginning to undergo a transformation that forever changed how I view public education, my role in public education, the "truth" about public education systems and the like. We spent our weeks unpacking or repacking or just plain packing in the framework of philosophical belief systems that framed public education practices. On the surface, the ideology of essentialism and functionalism made me squirm. Who believed that students needed a "common core of understanding"? Who worked in settings where only certain knowledge was deemed valuable and right? As it turns out, I did. And the moment that truth came flying at me was a day that shook my "work" in public education and my purpose as a human on earth.

My professor, of course, was having us research a topic and address questions from the perspectives we were dialoguing about. I was struggling. I was overwhelmed with all that I was learning and was excited about everything. Thankfully, he had been listening to the stories I was telling and paying attention to the difficulties I was having, bridging the theory and the practical. He suggested I look into this woman, Jeannie Oakes, as she wrote about the very issues I brought up in class. I didn't know who she was. I didn't know what she did. And if I ever get a chance to meet her in person, I will tell her how much I owe her for helping me forge a new path in my career. Call it cosmic intervention; call it right time/right place; call it fate; call it whatever. But I looked up Jeannie Oakes, and I found her book, *Keeping Track*. I checked it out of the library (we were still working with floppy disks then, I couldn't overnight ship it by Amazon), went home, and started reading it. It changed my life!

"Tracking is the process whereby students are divided into categories so that they can be assigned in groups to various kinds of classes" (Oakes, 1985, p. 3). What? Huh? How? Are you serious? I couldn't read this book fast enough. As I read more and more, I found myself sinking deeper and deeper into a pit of despair. I was overcome with contempt for myself and my school and my colleagues and the system and all of the ideas that I had bought into since I had fallen in love with teaching.

How could I be a part of this system and this process that proclaimed to be doing something in the name of progress and good? Yet what I was really doing was feeding into the abyss of the idea that some people's kids are just plain better than others? How? I was devastated. I loved teaching. I loved working with high schoolers. I loved working in the school where I was. How could I have become one of them? How? Ugh. I probably spent most of that evening reading phrases and such out loud to my husband and throwing my hands up in the air in complete flabbergastedness (is that even a word?). Maybe not, but that's what I was: flabbergasted. Shocked and disappointed and sad and angry and awake. Awake for the first time that I actually had a purpose. I was now arming myself with the knowledge necessary to address the inequities that I was also an active participant in perpetuating. I woke up the next day, went to work, walked into my classroom and prepped for the day. To say that all of my lesson plans were thrown out the window is an understatement. If we had lived in the north, I probably would've set fire to all things that had been "deemed" important by the district and my colleagues.

My first class entered in only a way that 9th graders can and once we were calm and settled, I had a heart to heart with them. They all knew I was in school. They saw me reading during our "silent reading time" and would ask about what I was learning. But, in recalling that day, my speech started out something like this:

> I'm sorry. I owe you each an apology. I thought I was doing the right thing by encouraging you all to be a part of this academy, but it turns out I'm wrong. What I'm actually doing is buying into a system that doesn't think you matter. The system doesn't think you're worth pushing and educating at anything other than a basic/remedial level. The school, your teachers, we've been duped into believing that success looks like something other than you. But that's going to change. Starting right now. Starting right now, I will do everything in my power to make sure you have the same opportunities as all the other students, and I will teach you how to stand up for yourself. I can't change the system, I can't change this school, but I can change what I do to make sure you get a fairer chance at succeeding.

And I waited. I waited for the questions and the discussion and the time it was going to take us to digest what was happening. This went on all day for two days. I had three classes per day, and I taught 180 or so students with whom I needed to have this conversation. So we talked. We talked about what it meant for them to be tracked. We talked about what it meant for their life choices. We talked about what kinds of changes they wanted to see. We talked about their life outside of school. We talked about their lives in school. We used language we hadn't used and grappled with ideas we didn't understand. It was new to me. It was new to them. It was new for us. We had work to do. I had guilt I had to address. I had to learn to use the language of the thinkers to start fighting for my students, rather than use the language of the establishment to keep them in place. And it was tough.

I stayed in that system for four more years. I stayed because I knew in my heart of hearts that if *I* didn't teach "those kids" (oh, and don't get me started on the number of conversations I had with my colleagues on that phrase) that they were for sure going to become a bunch of statistics, and the narrative would never change. I stayed so that I could work with the students who had been placed into a track of education they had no control over. I stayed so that I could teach them language that would empower their experiences with adults. I spent many, many hours working with my students on how to approach the powers that be: their other teachers, the principal, the assistant principals, their coaches, neighbors, and strangers. I didn't have a language for what I was doing then, as I was a Don Quixote riding into my own set of windmills. I was alone in my school, the only one who started questioning the practices of tracking and hegemony and elitism and essentialism and the structure of the status quo. I found myself disheartened and isolated in the school and ready to make real change. So I left.

I tell this story not because I have done great work. I tell this story because now I see, as a college professor in the pre-service teacher prep courses at a large urban university, how easy it is to unconsciously mis-educate our teachers into assuming the false notion that there is a right/wrong binary set of experiences that should make up education and classroom practices. And if that's the belief, then there are right/wrong students who will continue on their chosen path and serve the system that has been created. My work now is addressing the status quo by teaching my students to develop a philosophy of education that doesn't begin with, "I believe all children can learn . . ."; rather, identifies what they believe about their pedagogy and philosophy. In addressing inequities and justice in education, my task has become narrowing the opportunity for essentialism to gain roots. I also want to expand the language that these young teachers will be using to understand what is happening in their schools. My students now are young adults who tend to believe that teaching is all about making things pretty and matching and such. And while I appreciate their effort in their belief that aesthetics matter, I'm working in earnest to address their understanding and awareness of justice and to increase their ability to have a voice. If I can help them get grounded enough so that they can speak up for themselves, it is my hope that they can transfer that same grounding to their students. This way, we can have a collective narrative that is about change and progress and justice and advancing the opportunity of all students. It wasn't until years later, when I was able to expand my understanding of critical pedagogy and inquiry as well as discover the authors and thinkers that have influenced my practices, that I ran across this quote from bell hooks, "I entered the classroom with the conviction that it was crucial for me and every other student to be an active participant, not a passive consumer . . . education as the practice of freedom . . . . education that connects the will to know with the will to become. Learning is a place where paradise can be created" (p. 14). Here's to classrooms that resemble paradise.

A sample of texts, "must-reads," for pre-service teachers, along with suggested videos

Delpit, Lisa. (1995). *Other People's Children*. New York, NY: New Press.

McIntosh, P. "White Privilege: Unpacking the invisible backpack" (1989). http://www.cirtl.net/files/PartI_CreatingAwareness_WhitePrivilege UnpackingtheInvisibleKnapsack.pdf

Oakes, J. (2010). Schools that shock the conscience. In: Theresa Perry, Bob Moses, Joan Wynne, Ernesto Cortes, Jr. and Lisa Delpit (Eds). *Quality Education as a Civil Right: Creating a grassroots movement to transform public schools* (pp. 49–69). Boston: Beacon Press.

Freire, P. (2002). *Pedagogy of the Oppressed.* New York, NY: Continuum Press.

Shor, Ira. (2000). Education is politics: Paulo Freire's critical pedagogy. In: C. Pari & Iran Shor (Eds). *Education is Politics: Critical teaching across differences.* Portsmouth, NH: Heinemann Publishing.

TED talks:

http://www.ted.com/talks/bryan_stevenson_we_need_to_talk_about_an_injustice

https://www.ted.com/talks/clint_smith_the_danger_of_silence

https://www.ted.com/talks/majora_carter_s_tale_of_urban_renewal

http://www.ted.com/talks/chimamanda_adichie_the_danger_of_a_single_story

Podcast

http://www.thisamericanlife.org/radio-archives/episode/538/is-this-working

Documentary:

Eve Ensler, Carol Jenkins, Judith Katz. (2003). *What I want my words to do to you.* PBS. http://www.pbs.org/pov/whatiwant/credits.php

References

hooks, b. (1994). *Teaching to Transgress,* NY: Routledge.

Oakes, J. (1985). *Keeping track: How schools structure inequality.* New Haven: Yale University Press.

Poetry school

by Alex Salinas

On a bone-gray concrete wall next to the Building A staircase, a chalk caricature greets Mr. Adenwalla. It's a smiling man's face wearing pink beach sunglasses, lenses flooded white as if holding intense light. "Where Are You Mi Amor?" hangs in a thought bubble. Mr. Adenwalla, on his way up the stairs to the first class of the day, smiles at the lovingly made vandalism. What is the story, he wonders.

Standing before his English Composition 1 class, whom he is meeting for the second time, he calls attendance.

"Camille DeLafuente." Mr. Adenwalla notes the lanky teenagers's face as she walks to the front of the room carrying a can of beans: the mild distress of going through a motion mysterious to her. She drops the beans in a plastic crate. "If you show up, you get ten points," announces Mr. Adenwalla, in what he thinks of as his ringmaster voice. "If you bring a canned good as a food bank donation, you get 20 points." Mr. Adenwalla asks students to make this daily offering instead of buying a textbook. He hasn't used a textbook in his classes for 10 years.

"Peter Feliu." Bemused confusion as his can drops with a hollow metal thud. The pile materializes, every day giving the learning in the room a specific heft and color with corporate touches: *Goya Beans, Campbell's Soup, Ramen Noodles.*

"Thank you," says Mr. Adenwalla.

"Nathaniel Greenfield-Baptiste." The muscled brown-skinned man in his mid-20s struts down the aisle joyfully. The nails on his left hand are painted blue, the ones on his right alternate red and silvery white. "That's what I'm talking bout, baby!" he sings. A collective chuckle breaks the solemnity of the ritual as he drops his can.

"Thank you . . . Ignacio Hurtado."

A tall figure speaks up from the back row of desks: "No! I have no can."

Mr. Adenwalla interrupts his steady intonation of names. "Even if you don't bring anything, please come up, extend your hand, make the gesture of generosity."

Ignacio laughs a mocking, attention-calling laugh. "That's kind of stupid, don't you think, making us come up like we're your little slaves or something? You really want me to come up with no can and pretend, Mr. Professor Aaa . . . whatever your name is?"

A void yawns open that everyone wants Mr. Adenwalla to fill. He allows it to suck in the space for a few seconds, then looks directly at Ignacio, drawing the whole class's gaze to him too. "Anyone who can't make the food offering can still make the gesture to earn their ten points. You don't gesture, you're not here, you get zero points."

Ignacio laughs loudly. He plods to the front of the room, quickly passes a hand over the crate like a vaudevillian magician, and smiles widely at Mr. Adenwalla, revealing a chipped front tooth nearly black with decay.

"Thank you, dear friend," announces the ringmaster with extra enthusiasm.

Ignacio remains silent until the end of the period, in conversation with only himself. He slips out at the end of the period before Mr. Adenwalla or anyone else can ask him unwelcome questions or make unwelcome eye contact. He walks through the college campus, a converted office complex of nine boxy buildings connected by a web of walkways. He's looking at the thoughts in his head rising like the spume of acid on metal. "I can't believe this is the first essay. What an idiotic assignment. Why do we have to do this? What a pain. What a pain. Who does this guy think he is? He is soft, so I'm not doing it. What is he trying to do?"

Ignacio sees himself in the classroom again, looking at his own eyes wandering around, his eyes shrunken grotesquely small, dice rolling back and forth in the sockets. He sees himself a blasted wooden doll, joints broken, puppet strings snipped, and abandoned. He feels anger and feels the word *idiot*. *You're an idiot*. He sees an axis across the classroom, with Mr. Adenwalla at one pole and himself in opposition. *Idiot*. The word and its echoing come from within like tinnitus, at times barely audible, at times rising to a screech.

Ignacio finds himself in middle of the campus. He is disoriented, trying to get out but, as it has turned out, pulled into the center. "All Your Dreams Start Here" reads a large placard with red lettering. Arrows point into the building that houses registration, financial aid, and advisement.

"I'm sorry, but I get lost easily," he tells an administrator standing behind an information table.
"Yes, I know," she says. "It can be a little overwhelming at first. Big place."
"I can't keep all these buildings straight in my head," he says. "It all looks the same."

He passes through a courtyard lined with the flags of many nations into the noisy city. He pierces the membrane between the anesthetic order of the campus into the messy ardor of the city. A car horn pierces his bubbling thoughts as he arrives at a bus bench. On the bus, he finds a seat in the back. An old woman sits next to him, asking if he knows the stop for the free clinic. Ignacio notices the plastic rosary around her neck. "I don't know," he says. "God bless you."

***

I am here
to be
with people.
Why are you making us do this?
Why should we feed the poor when the poor want to stay poor?
Why do the poor leave so much garbage on their streets?
Is this for a grade?
Why do those people's hungry children walk around their neighborhoods all alone,
uncared for, vulnerable to their own bullets?
Why do you turn us toward evil?
 Why would we spare Adam Lanza after what he did?
Why does he deserve any compassion after what he did?
Why doesn't your syllabus mention extra credit?
Who do you think you are anyway?

***

Ignacio Hurtado
1/6/14
ENC 1101
Prof. Adenwala

Diagnostic Essay: Creation Stories

Extremely Important Note: This is based just on my imagination, and I don't mean it to be the truth, I am turning this in as an exercise in creative writing according option #3 in your instructions, I prefer not to compare my "traditional" creation story to another (option #1) or to analyze what it means to me (option #2) in this environment as I feel that is totally uncalled for. Thank you and enjoy.

Revising Salvation

In this essay, I will tell a story that looks at a new version of the Christian creation story known as Genesis, which is a relationship between God and his son explaining the nature of human beings, I will attempt to interpret the Bible as well as my knowledge of Christianity that makes up my spirituality.

First of all, in the beginning, the Lord almighty was floating in the vast emptiness of space. He found the emptiness unbearable so finally squeezed it into the first word, which was love. All he wanted was love, so he made his son together they worked on creating the Earth like a jewel floating in the center of the universe.

Secondly, to make the sky the Lord asked his son to run as fast and as far as he could so the blue fields were his open heart, the sky was the first laughter. To make the ocean, the Lord brought his son into deep sleep, so the waters were those dreams then they painted the grasses and trees. They made the animals out of the mud. The land was father and son playing.

On the other hand, it was on the seventh day that we came along. The Lord wanted to rest, but the son was restless, he wanted to keep playing, he wanted to make the whole situation a simple game, he wanted to throw dice, in a fit of craziness he copied himself, however, it was a bad copy for only god is god, HE is supreme, but he was a foolish son.

Furthermore, this outrageous action enraged the Lord so he punished his son. "You are aborted, the one who makes the fatal error." Like a wrathful fist the Lord's words punched the son. His broken teeth, the blood from his mouth, his tears watered the Earth, he lay motionless on the ground with the painful anger inside his temples. The tears fell into the ground, all the poison has been soaking the ground ever since, we try to clean ourselves so that we are pure.

In conclusion, this is the big secret. There was no magic rib or fruit tree in paradise. It's us, we are the sin, the son, the same son, has been eternally walking the earth to suffer to show us our sin and wash his own from his hands. Only some of these men have been remembered, we are the mistake that comes from love, that's how I see it with my imagination in this story.

***

Nathaniel Greenfield-Baptiste bursts through the door of the classroom about halfway through the period. All the desks have been pushed to the walls, dissolving the familiar forward-facing grid ingrained by 12 years of schooling. A rope is spiraled on the opened space of the gray tile floor from the center outward. Mr. Adenwalla came to class 15 minutes early today to arrange 22 unlit candles at regular intervals along the length of the spiral.

"Oh my god, please tell me I didn't miss it!" Nathaniel says. He finds two girls who have become his desk neighbors, pecks each one on the cheek, and chortles in Gringo-accented Spanish: "Estan muy muy lindas hoy. Te quiero mucho!" Everyone, including Mr. Adenwalla, responds with an uneasy smile.

"Just in time, dear friend," Mr. Adenwalla says to Nathaniel.

Mr. Adenwalla stands at one end of the room with his students, all washed in the light of an image projected on the whiteboard. Green and red nebulas rising in cosmic blackness soften into the background for a poem:

> *Everyone*
> *Is God speaking.*
> *Why not be polite and*
> *Listen to Him?*

The ghostly digital letters seem to melt into the imperfect letters the students have brainstormed onto the board—looping or jagged letters, some stretched into hieroglyphic beauty that can carry independent meaning beyond the cribs of their native words, or shrunk into slanting illegible tracks of textual crumbs, thickets criss-crossed with paths in a wilderness.

> *Earth learns how to fly* + *rock knows how to say I love you to his children*
> *Awe? miracles? ?aliens?*
> *agua astiroids atoms*
> *Sex "invented"??? Que?*   *DNA*
> *The first cell / eye / leg* ————————> *MYSTERY*
> *ashes to ashes dust to dust*
> *Neotony*
> *baby monkeys leave the trees*
> *Africa* ————————> *all the races*

His face in dark projector light, Mr. Adenwalla reads from his smartphone

Grace Moment 1: Great Emergence. Out of the mysterious chaos some 13.8 billion years ago time, space, and energy stabilize into the gift of existence. Our Universe is born hot and tiny . . .

A woman in her sixties, the oldest student in Mr. Adenwalla's classes this semester, flits out of the cluster. "Lista!" she says, taking her place at the outermost candle. Her small, smiling face pulses with energy there. In Cuba, she worked as a Kindergarten teacher for 25 years before immigrating to the United States, and she relishes her role in this stagecraft. She's wearing a smart blue suit for the special occasion. "I believe it in the Bible, teacher," she says gravely, "but I think that can be the same with the big bang. Ok?"

She slowly bends down to light the candle. An open flame in the classroom—a violation of campus policy that Mr. Adenwalla knows can result in suspension or even termination, just like laying your head down to take a nap in your office, loaning an office key to a student, or sneaking out during the designated office hours posted on his door for a Cuban coffee boost at the cafeteria across the street.

The student lifts a poster of a black cross engendering a sky of stars, an orange sun, a gray moon. "If the big bang is the true, then who did it?" She pauses, scans faces, makes an interrogative "*aaaaaaaaah?*"

"My picture shows it that maybe it is the Christian god who made the big bang. It can be, no?"

One candle flame at a time, the students trace the history of the universe. As the dinosaurs give way to mammals, it is Ignacio Hurtado's turn to illustrate a creative grace moment: the evolution of flowers 114 million years ago. He stands before the illicit points of light. Mr. Adenwalla senses an infrared crown around Ignacio much brighter than the puny flames. "I would like to say to this whole class here, no thank you to this activity." In Ignacio's public classroom voice, the words come out at a lowered octave, pushed through a strainer. "You know, I'm really trying, but I don't agree with this. I'll just take the consequences." He stands back with his arms crossed, face tense. His neighbors inch away to make a buffer.

Mr. Adenwalla announces that if Ignacio or anyone else is interested in an alternative assignment, he doesn't mind "making a deal." In response, Ignacio walks to other end of the room, noisily dragging a desk, and sits to write. He scratches away at a furious pace, head almost pressed down to the desktop. At the end of the class, he interrupts a group of students asking Mr. Adenwalla questions to drop a folded yellow legal-paper note on the desk. "That's for you," he says blankly. "I felt I had to write it instead of doing the cosmic walk thing."

For the first time, for a split-second, Mr. Adenwalla has a close look at the tattoo on Ignacio's neck. A pink bubblegum heart with two daggers crossing it, blood dripping from the bottom, lake of fire licking upward. The imperiled heart crosses ever so slightly onto Ignacio's jaw and cheek. Such a sloppy autograph, thinks Mr. Adenwalla, on a canvas that can make such precise poetry through miniscule gestures. How much that needle must have hurt on such thin flesh!

Mr. Adenwalla puts Ignacio's note in his pocket and walks to his office, paying attention to the contact of each step on the ground, sounding the words *I'll just take the consequences* in his arboreal mind over and over. The words rustle like leaves, float down through the canopy, and fall away into groundless roots.

At his office he looks through what he tells visitors is his backward window, for it opens, incongruously, into the building rather than out to the busy streets and strip malls at the edge of the campus. He occupies an interior office that overlooks a vast computer lab with a cathedral-like ceiling. He sees the tops of dozens of heads. Students are writing school assignments, doing book reports on classic American novels, doing journals on what they learned today, doing Powerpoints for oral presentations on current events, doing what they're told, writing on *Facebook*, e-mailing distant family members, wasting state resources, applying for government assistance, pouring out love letters, hate mail, moving avatars in virtual realities, paying bills, plagiarizing and proselytizing, moving through dimensions of confusion and discovery, reading the *Miami Herald*, reading *Siddhartha*, reading *Fifty Shades of Gray*, reading *Wikipedia*.

At the top of the cathedral, through the bubble of computer noise and static electricity, a second window reveals the sky. Mr. Adenwalla must crane his neck to get just the right angle. He has been feeling the sky-like longing today. He has been spending one of his periods in the airless place within. He knows well a ripped hidden bleeding. Just before he reaches the emptiness, the emptiness about to come again, he burns a way out, engulfs the outer world, dances fire around the massive glass and steel structures sealing him in. This is his devotion, to burning.

He reaches into his pocket for Ignacio's note, feels moist contact with the paper, his sweat and his student's. Ignacio's big angular letters, the sickled spines, the square serifs feel sharp-edged in his eyes. After he reads it, he feels a great flowing within. He feels spent, parts of him breaking off like brittle paper. Words emerge. "I need to do something else," he says aloud. He closes his eyes for a few minutes, sees himself as though looking through a window. On his computer, he clicks a box indicating that Ignacio Hurtado completed his assignment with great merit today.

***

I am here
to be
with people.
Are we allowed to use I?
Are we allowed to use outside sources?
Are we allowed to listen to rap music in class with prostitutes
the f-word, the n-word, the b-word?
Why are you contradicting what they taught me in high school
Where I always hooked my reader with a question?
Are we allowed to talk about science vs. religion?
Do white people really control the world?

Is it mostly the Jews?
So who is the racist here, you or me?
So are you saying my personal American Dream is bad and dead?
Who do you think you're calling a slave?
Do corporations control the world?
When and where do these secret kings meet to rig this game of chess?

***

To: Prof. Adenwalla.
From: Ignacio Hurtado

Re: Serious Issues I'm Having with Your Class

This communication is to inform you that the topics you discuss in your class are very controversial, well, it is one month into the semester, and I do not think we should be talking about god in class, we have been talking about god or ideas about god at least a few times a week at least and I think it is controversial, have you heard about the separation of church and state? I do believe in god but I do not wish to share my god with other people. I wrote the essay about Jesus. I used all my creativity for it. It was like I was not thinking when I wrote it. The essay almost wrote itself. To be honest I felt like I did something wrong afterward. On top of all that you gave me a C+!!! I know this is not the real grade yet since this is just a practice, and we have a chance to keep working on the essay to get a real grade; but I do not feel comfortable doing it all over again. Yes I know, I have problems with my logical bridges but I am beginning to have my suspicions that you are a Muslim, therefore you have problems with my Christian faith that is the real problem! Are you a Muslim? I know I have to work on my punctuation, but a C+? That's extremely ridiculous and insulting.

Also, I still do not think it is fair that we have to bring your cans as part of our grade or be shamed if we don't. That makes me very angry and frustrated as you know that me and my mom are struggling to get jobs right now. You see the situation is I decided from the first few days of this class that you try to understand your students; you treat them as people, but the thing is, now I want to do well not like before so as you notice I'm trying my best. I'm trying to follow the rules you have about open dialogue. I know I can agree to disagree, and I know all my emotions are ok; it's about expressing them. I hope you understand that I am just trying to do what I have to do in order to get a degree and start my business. Sir with all due respect your job is just to teach us to write. Your job is just to give us the work. I am willing to make that sacrifice, but I am <u>NOT</u> willing to compromise my beliefs. Do not get me wrong, I think you are a good teacher, you create many intriguing situations, but I think you are going too far. You are making me uncomfortable. My point is that we will talk about this after class next time, that way I won't be forced to go to the higher authorities at your institution in order to rectify this situation. I apologize once again if I have upset you or your students in any way, shape, or form.

Ignacio Hurtado
ENC 1101

Ref. #938347

***

Two 13-year-old boys, apparently twins, walk through a landscape of swaying, rasping waist-high saw grass. Each step in the hot mud releases a mineral perfume. A forest of white pole-thin slash pines rises above the horizon. The sun lies low, sending the boys orange light through the swamp forest, more space than wood and leaf. The sky is rumbling, covered in clouds that seem shredded away from each other at cotton edges. The mass of gray flickers with light. The sun is suddenly gone, and the Earth becomes silent in the moonlit night.

"This is so beautiful," whispers one of the boys.

The other looks at him, annoyed. "No. This is just a walk. Get out of that cloud. Don't be an idiot. Let's hurry up and get home. It's getting dark!"

"It's not just a walk!" yells back the other. "Can't you see? This is beautiful! Stop and listen to how quiet it is!"

"You make no sense," says the twin brother. "You're going to get lost."

Mr. Adenwalla wakes from the dream, takes a journal from his nightstand, and begins writing an entry entitled "Poetry School." But, before he can really say what the words mean, he realizes he's going to be late for his first class, and starts reviewing what needs attention. Today, he realizes, he speaks with Ignacio Hurtado after class. How will he say it?

The conversation is less than 10 minutes long and almost totally one-sided. Ignacio stares at him throughout, slightly slack-jawed, offering no resistance. Obviously, no one is telling Ignacio he has to believe anything. Yes, the teacher chooses the topic, and maybe this is an unusual approach, but exploring spiritual matters can make the class more meaningful. And if the topic is triggering difficult emotions, maybe Ignacio should drop the class.

Mr. Adenwalla will help him transfer to another section. But, he emphasizes, what if he finds another difficult or, worse, a boring topic in the new course? One teacher bases a large part of her class on Shakespeare's tragedies, for example. Others on crime fiction; food ethics and trips to a community garden; apocalyptic narratives; African-American women writers, sexism and racism. Would he prefer one of those classes? Maybe, the simple yet absurd reality is that Ignacio is stuck with him, Mr. Adenwalla proposes. Maybe, he is meant to be in this class.

Mr. Adenwalla has never been this close to Ignacio for this long, and can't help, but stare at swaths of faint pockmarks rising from the nape of his neck, over the tattooed flames, up both cheeks and into his temples. He notices the contours of his thin face, eyes set in bones protruding goggle-like, cheek bones high, tight skin tapering to a small full mouth. He notices the way Ignacio's shifty caramel eyes capture yellow streaks of light. He notices the faint spicy stench of his breath and sweet traces of expensive cologne.

"You can't satisfy all of the people all of the time, dear friend," concludes Mr. Adenwalla.

"No dropping, no transfer," Ignacio says after a pause, as if trying to process a riddle. He wants to know what grade he's earned so far. Perhaps, a B, says Mr. Adenwalla, adding his customary line about grades being figments of the imagination.

"I'm going to finish what has been started," Ignacio says. He snaps his focus into Mr. Adenwalla's eyes. "Is that ok with you? Maybe this *is* meant to be."

"Ok with me, dear friend," Mr. Adenwalla says. "And by the way, I'm not a Muslim, or Hindu, or a Christian, or an atheist. Religion is a figment of the imagination too. This God the religious folks talk about might be real—not sure. I just want to learn about life."

Mr. Adenwalla is holding Ignacio's monotone and glazed look in his mind as he walks across campus to his office, deciding that truly knowing this young man is bound to his very purpose. A few students and professors are standing around his door chatting and pointing at a large sheet of paper that has been taped right under this name plate. It's a blown-up photo of a woman's curvaceous torso, cut off at the head. The bosom is wrapped in a tank top emblazoned with stars in the style of Van Gogh's famous painting. "This Is How I Want To Die?!?!" scrolls around the border, rewritten several times in thick red marker. "It seems someone wants to get our attention," he says, offering his honest assessment. He leaves the shock art on the door.

"I don't want this place to be my teaching anymore," Mr. Adenwalla says in the quiet of his office.

****

Why do I take your face and voice home with me every day?
How do I tell you what I feel as I lay under my white sheets at night?
Who are you behind these poems and lectures?
I am here
to be
with you.
You are the one.

***

Nathaniel holds the stage, reading the draft of his creation story essay to the class. His nail polish is black on one hand today, electric blue on the other. He has also taken over the white board, that canvas usually reserved for the dictums of the professor, drawing three square happy faces. Each has three eyes, the ones in the middle like breaking stitches. Mr. Adenwalla has taken his usual place during these readings in the back of the class.

"When the first consciousness came into being from the void, it suddenly realized it was all alone. I am the only I, it said, and looked at itself: It was a great fish with a hole in its head, swimming into itself, over and over again, an eternal knot, going inside of itself and coming out, looking for something although not sure what. It lived in fear until it thought, I need a friend. If I have a friend, I won't be afraid. So it cut itself in two. One side was called Fabulous, the mother energy. The other side was called Fierce, the father energy. When a bee takes pollen from one plant to another, it is Fabulous trying to reunite with Fierce. Peanut butter and jelly. Tom and Jerry. Fabulous and Fierce. *Blanco y negro*."

Nathaniel holds his blue hand before him and presses his black one into it, palm to palm, as his words unite Fabulous and Fierce. "Every being contains both Fabulous and Fierce, in different proportions . . ."

Ignacio darts up from his desk, just a few over from where Mr. Adenwalla is sitting, and moves up two rows. He begins making kissing noises and an orgasmic moan. "What is this *mariconcito* trying to say?" he yells.

Nathaniel places his pages on the teacher's table and takes a few steps forward amid alarmed "Oh my god's!"

"What are you going to do, faggot?" Ignacio howls, crossing the classroom. "I'm not afraid of you!"

"You sure you can handle all this?" Nathaniel motions his hands up and down to display his powerful physique.

Ignacio rushes at Nathaniel, reaching him in the middle of the classroom, just as Mr. Adenwalla has made his way there too. Ignacio breaks through his teacher's grasp and bear hugs Nathaniel. Unfazed, betraying no distress in the slightest twitch of face or body, Nathaniel expertly leans his cheek against Ignacio's for leverage, patiently wraps his much thicker arms around his attacker's upper torso, and interlaces his fingers at the shoulder blades. The polished tips make the supple lock beautiful. Nathaniel separates and adjusts the fingers for a moment, and they look like newly budded winglets stretching out. Ignacio lets out a plaintive moan, surrendering, head and arms falling back limply.

Nathaniel places Ignacio, who is sobbing, on the ground like a scared child. Ignacio soon catches his breath and runs out of the room.

When Mr. Adenwalla meets with his department chair later that day, they begin the logistics of expelling Ignacio Hurtado from the college. She spends an hour documenting each sign pointing to Ignacio's instability, probing what may have unhinged him and obsessing about whether Nathaniel was considering legal action. She scolds Mr. Adenwalla about not reporting the threat much earlier, and reminds him that last semester, a music professor at another campus was beaten unconscious by a masked assailant. Administrators had inside information that it was a hit, retribution for a bad grade.

"It's a dangerous world out there!" she says. "You know where we live here—open enrollment world. We're all people have, in many cases, but we have no idea where these people are coming from, what they're capable of, or how screwed up they are. We have a responsibility to keep trouble out."

"My goodness, you do like to stir things up, Mr. Adenwalla," she finally groans. "My guru! I've said it before and I'll say it again. I like some of this 'real world' stuff you do, but be careful. If you trigger people, you and I and *we* are responsible. This college is responsible."

"Why do I have the feeling you're going to get us both into big trouble one of these days? What are you doing to these people?" She is convinced that, yet again, she will need to pay special attention to Mr. Adenwalla's antics for a while.

Mr. Adenwalla is tempted for a moment, but during the conversation, he decides against sharing his vision for the coming year, the work that will, with luck, save him this time. Whatever it is, that work will happen nowhere near these nine buildings. He will do it all through his own means—no Golden Apple Innovative Teaching Grant, no collaboration with the Service-Learning and Sustainable Living Institute. Best of all, since it will not be a college-sanctioned project, he will not need anyone's permission to invite Ignacio as well as Nathaniel to participate. This is not the work of the college; it's the work of the poetry school.

"And by the way, Mr. Adenwalla," says the chair as he leaves the room. "I hope you're not forgetting to do the cognitive thing with these people. If they're not learning how to write a college essay, you're not doing your job, I'm not doing my job. *We're* not doing our job, Mr. Adenwalla. Teach the basic skills. I worry you're losing sight of that sometimes. Cognitive!"

***

I am here
to be
with people
What if they don't learn how to do language?
What if they don't practice how to solve formulas?
Where do you find the time to do this extra-curricular business?
Have you reviewed the contract recently
the manual of procedures
the student handbook?
What if they get hit by a car, or lightening, or you get hit with a lawsuit?
What if the shit hits the fan?
What will the union say then?
About getting so close to your students?

***

From: Ignacio Hurtado <belligerentwarrior2000@gmail.com>
To: Juan Adenwalla <adenwalla213@gmail.com>
Date: April 20, 2014

Subject: Mooshrooms

I'm sorry about what happened two weeks ago, I lost control of myself. I felt like hurting him, someone, anyone, and I lost control. I deserve to be expelled from school. I'm too tired anyway. I deserve the worst. I'm a danger to myself and other people, I hope this did not affect you or your class too much. I hope I didn't get anyone in trouble. Don't worry about me. I'll be fine. Thanks for everything you did. You're a good teacher. After all this happened, I noticed that I wanted to write about it. I have trouble with a lot of things, even simple things, but I see that writing is a kind of trouble that I kinda like. MY WRITING IS A MooshRoom. YES!!! Letters grow on the sad heavy world deep inside and deep outside. My writing eats what is dying, a poison that can put me outside of my own mind, I have been writing about this, and I see that my writing is smarter than me; my writing knows things I don't, and I can listen to it so I see things that broke from being in school; I feel like I came back to life in a way. I can do things, I'm not sure if that's good or not. I feel terrible, teacher. I thank you and I blame you, Mr. Professor. I know we will meet again, I know it.

PS.

Hope you don't mind if I send you some of my writing.

***

"Hello teacher," Ignacio says, walking through his former professor's door, more than four months since his ban from the campus. "Can I come in?" He closes the door before Mr. Adenwalla, who has stopped chewing on a fig cookie in disbelief, can respond.

"Of course, come in."

Mr. Adenwalla has tried to contact Ignacio several times, spoke to his mother three times, but hasn't communicated with his former student since he watched Nathaniel Greenfield-Baptiste embrace him into a sobbing heap. Ignacio has been sending Mr. Adenwalla a poem every week or two.

Ignacio takes a seat on a couch in Mr. Adenwalla's office, which he's entered for the first time. Mr. Adenwalla's desk sits before a mural on the wall recently finished by several students including Nathaniel: a red, orange and black image of an old man with long gray whiskers. He sits on a rock, dipping one toe into a lake of flowering water lilies. Calligraphic text forms the lower border of the mural: "The smallest sprout shows there is really no death." Against another wall is a stack of cans 20 deep rising halfway to the ceiling.

Ignacio has been sitting, looking for a few seconds, but stands back up to start talking. "Ok, so I heard you talked to my mom about giving me a scholarship for your poetry school thing you're trying to do. Is that true?"

"Yes, that's true."

"Why would you want me?"

"Because I see you're a poet," Mr. Adenwalla says.

Ignacio doesn't seem to register the words. They evaporate in midair. His own words are busy being born from the cooking cocoons in his brain, and they require all his attention.

Ignacio sits, leaning forward, his eyes widening. He throws a fist into a palm, quietly, with great care, with a small pop. A smile and a nod, a rare bubble of delight rising out of the hot and cold roil behind his eyes and bursting between him and his teacher.

"First of all, understand that I can't give you anything for what you're trying to give me. To hell with your invitation."

Mr. Adenwalla sits quietly.

"You hear me? You don't want to be around me. If you are, I'm going to give you a scare like you've never had before. Do you understand me? Let me know if you understand me or not."

"Yes," he says softly.

"I don't care about what you say! I don't care what anybody says. I don't think you're any good. All these idiots think you're cool, but you're not cool. I think you're just a fuck-ing do-gooder. Do you understand that? I want nothing more than to punch you in the face right now. You know why? Because you are an Arab faggot."

"Yes."

"Never call my house again, or I will come here to give you the scare of your life. I will come to this school to do something you will never ever forget." He cocks his head, eyes sparking. "God bless you, faggot."

"Really?" Mr. Adenwalla says blankly. Then with a faint glint of enthusiasm, "God bless you too! It really pains me . . ."

Before he can finish, Ignacio walks away, ignoring Mr. Adenwalla's extended hand.

***

ragin soul by ih
when i sit quiet
i can know the blown up bones
slowed up
one face at a time one eye at a time
what is inside me in billions of seconds
did i waste my billions
one breath at a time and one molecule
inside that breath one at a time so that the rage
squeezes my heavy heart like a small hand does a metal can
a rock or an iron sword
Red Rage Roars
comes up like fire!
you askin me to give something away teacher
whats the price of this real love your teachin
whats left of me
nothing but the ashes of what i learned
rainin down on the world thats makin
one last turn

just my shadow stays
burned on you so nothin is wasted

***

At dusk Mr. Adenwalla and five students sit in a circle in a great glade of saw grass. A dome of cypress trees hunches beside them. It is Saturday evening during Christmas break. Nathaniel walks into the middle of the circle and places a brown apple snail shell on a mat of hard-veined palm fronds.

"I mourn for the absence of those who can't be here," he says. "I mourn for my father who passed away last month, who never looked me in the eyes as a human being. I'm afraid for what my life will be without ever having a father, but I live it. I will live it. For all the lost family members, I mourn."

"We hear you," responds the group. After each student has spoken and left a shell, one of them, one of the most gifted writers Mr. Adenwalla has ever found in one of his courses—a dyslexic polyglot—offers the teaching. He explains that he will lead them in a song and dance. "I read about something like this in a book that the church banned," he says slyly. "It's a simple and beautiful mystery." After they learn the words to the song, the members of this gathering of the poetry school come to their feet and start whirling in the night.

"I am wounded!" cries the leader.
"And I am the one who wounds," responds the group.
"I am born," he says.
"And I give birth," responds the group.
"I am understood!"
"And I am the one who understands!"
"I am saved!"
"And I am the one who saves."

Mr. Adenwalla's offering comes at the end of class, before the students retire to their sleeping bags. He turns his head to the dome of trees behind the class and begins talking.

"This is a place where death dances with life. A long time ago, some cypress trees started growing at what is now the center of this dome. As their leaves fell, over many years, they dissolved the limestone bedrock under us. This is called a solution hole, made by the action of acid, by the process of decay. Other trees started growing around the hole. The water is deeper in the middle, so the trees grew higher, the roots broke deeper into the rock."

"The middle of this one is so deep, it couldn't hold the trees anymore, so it's avoid there, a nice water hole for the alligators to come drink in the dry season. The hole will keep eating the leaves."

Mr. Adenwalla looks deeply into the dome, opening to words for a moment. With startling clarity, he sees a figure blink into being, a fleeting spangle of white gold, a few hundred feet behind the leaves and mossy tendrils of the airplants. Something rustles, stills into Mr. Adenwalla's gaze, arresting him for a moment there, and melts away. The faceless silhouette is probably a deer, but moves with a slinking fear that reminds Mr. Adenwalla of a human being, of Ignacio Hurtado. Did he, or someone, follow them here, he wonders for a flash. Or, is this a projection beamed into the night by the lamp of his own heart.

"The trees are called the overstory," he continues. "Great name! Think about how the overstory is a mirror for the dome floor." Mr. Adenwalla keeps looking, peers through the speckled spaces of shadow between trees where consciousness flickered, looks past the space to the bruised orange-yellow of the horizon.

So many students, so many to come, thinks Mr. Adenwalla. He is with Ignacio Hurtado this night. Mr. Adenwalla reflects on his efforts to learn what became of Ignacio after the poems stopped. He found disconnected phone numbers, lapsed emails, and a series of rumors, none of which could be confirmed. He joined some family in Central America. He committed suicide in his bedroom. He's imprisoned in a different state. He's hitchhiking across the country to Alaska where a long-lost uncle lives. Or he roams the streets of the city of his birth without a home.

Debra, the essence of love in the midst of struggle

by Alyssa Hernandez

"Alyssa Hernandez . . . Your partner is Debra!" This was the moment it all began for Debbie and me. The WOW Center individuals and the Miami Dade College students sat together in the cafeteria anxiously awaiting to hear their names called. This was the day our journeys were about to kick off! After hearing Barbara, one of the staff members, call my name, I happily hurried to the front where I met Debbie. Debbie looked at me with a big old smile, and I smiled back. Full of excitement, I went straight in for a hug. Luckily she hugged me right back!

Debbie is a 36-year-old woman who has Down syndrome. She is around 5 feet tall and has straight brown hair that just barely reaches her ears, and wears red glasses with tiny green beads attached to them. You can almost always catch her with a water bottle in hand and her white vintage looking fanny pack around her waist. She lives with her boyfriend Josh in their very own apartment! She has lived in Miami all of her life. The two of them share their home with a cat named Cheeto.

While close to her mother, Debbie only sees her father occasionally on holidays or special events, like her birthday. This is something Debbie and I have in common. When she shared this information with me, I felt even more connected to her. At times, Debbie may not be easy to understand, as she often gets stuck pronouncing her words, but she is most certainly easy to talk to. She is open to conversations about almost anything. Kind and loving, she is quick to hug me when I least expect it. A genuine sweet heart she is. But Debbie can also be a little bit of a trouble maker! Luckily she has her pal Harry to keep her in check.

Harry is what she has named her right index finger, after the one and only, Harry Potter! The first time I found out about Harry was during our first group activity at the WOW Center. The MDC students were asking each of the WOW Center participants a series of simple "get-to-know" questions. On that very loud day in the cafeteria when it was my turn to interview Debbie, the first thing I did say my name. She smiled and said, "M-M-M-My name is Debbie!" As she shook my hand, I noticed she had her right index finger pointed up, slightly bent. She was smiling at me and then looking at the finger. I did not think much of it at first and went on asking the questions listed on the paper. When I asked Debbie what was her favorite movie, her face lit up as she said "Harry Potter!" and sure enough her right index finger popped out of her clutched fist. I smiled and told her how much I loved Harry Potter! I remember how excited we both were. She then looked up at me and said "his name is Harry, too!" as she then looked down at her right index finger. I said, "No way? Just like Harry Potter. Is he special like Harry Potter?" She smiled and giggled as she said, "Yes." Barbara shouted "Switch!!!" and my time was up for interviewing Debbie. After that short moment we spent together, I knew we hit it off really well and that Harry was a big part of her, but I had no idea how much so.

At first, I thought Harry was simply just an imaginary friend to Debbie, but I later learned that he is so much more than that. Intrigued to know more about Debbie's relationship with Harry, I asked again about him during one of our recent visits to the WOW Center. It was a hot sunny day as we walked to the field to play some kickball. I could tell Debbie did not like the heat, but she was still excited to be spending time together. When it was our turn to kick, Wilson, a staff member at the WOW Center, called us over from outfield.

I looked at Debbie and said, "Come on Debbie, it's our turn to make a home run!"

She looked up at me, grabbed on to my hand firmly and began to jog over to home plate. As we were making our way over, she began to speak from Harry's perspective. In a slightly deeper voice, holding her right finger in the air, she said, "Come on Debbie, h-h-hurry up! You're holding up the game!"

Once we made it to home plate, Wilson pitched the kickball over to Debbie, and she kicked it hard enough to get us safely to first. I was proud of my buddy and apparently so was Harry! Once at first base, Debbie again spoke from Harry's perspective, "Good job Debbie."

I then asked her, "Debbie what is Harry to you?"

She looked up at me with a bit of a confused face as she looked back down at Harry. She then said, "Harry makes sure Debbie behave."

I then asked her, "So is Harry like a parent?" Before she could answer, we were running again to the next base. When we caught our breath, I brought up the same question again. She then told me, "Harry is like a Dad." It then all clicked for me.

Debbie is truly a kid at heart as she is full of innocence. And maybe, she feels like she has to have someone to still keep her in check since she lives on her own. So much, so that, I believe she created Harry to be her parent, when she's not with her actual parents. It seems clear that she doesn't view herself as a complete "adult." I believe, she is aware she is still very much so a kid at heart. I also feel, there may be a relation between Harry and the fact that her Dad is in infrequent part of her life. Almost all of her comments through Harry are those that she might receive from some sort of authority. Yet through Harry, she is hard on herself. This became even more evident down the road.

A little more than half way through the semester, our journey together took a sharp turn. One afternoon at the WOW Center, I noticed Debbie was acting strange. I remember this day almost perfectly because of its magnitude. As I sat next to her in the cafeteria, I noticed she was not as cheerful. Her high spirits seemed absent that afternoon. It was as if the life had been sucked right out of her. This was a side of Debbie I previously had never witnessed. Worried about her, I quickly asked how her day was going. She raised her chin up, looked at me and then looked back down at Harry. She did not answer my question, but, oh, Harry sure did.

"Debbie's been real b-b-bad" she said, using Harry's voice.
"Why? What happened?"
"Debbie said a bad word," continuing in Harry's voice.

Debbie then suddenly smacked her own hand, the hand she uses to bring Harry to life. As I glanced down at her hand, I noticed she had tiny scratch marks along the top of her hand, specifically right near her index finger or Harry. To me, it was almost as if she was getting back at Harry for ratting her out. Before I could comment on what I had just seen and heard, Barbara was standing right in front of our table. Barbara looked at Debbie with a face of disappointment as she asked Debbie, "What are you doing here? You know you are not supposed to participate today!"

Confused with what Barbara had just said, I looked right at Debbie searching for some sort of explanation as to what was going on, but she was just as shocked as I was. Barbara then told Debbie and me to stay behind, as the rest of the group went for a walk through the park nearby. Everyone looked at us. A million thoughts raced through my head. I thought to myself, did I do or say something wrong to my buddy? Had I offended her in some way? I was so worried. As soon as the room cleared out, Barbara called the two of us over. Barbara also called Jessica over, another one of Debbie's supervisors. This made me even more worried! As the four of us stood in the cafeteria, only inches away from one another, Jessica began to speak.

She said, "Debbie why don't you tell your buddy how you have been behaving lately?" As I turned to Debbie, I noticed her face was almost pale. Debbie was so nervous and afraid. I remember feeling like a parent who had just found out her child was misbehaving in school.

Debbie did not want to answer from her perspective but instead from Harry's. Jessica and Barbara both told her how they wanted to hear from Debbie and not from Harry. Debbie took a long pause after hearing this. I could tell she was really struggling with coming to terms with what she had done. I grasped her hand and just nodded, as I looked my buddy in the eyes.

She then finally said what had happened: "I didn't want to leave computers."

Jessica elaborated on what had happened. "It was time to switch from computer class to music therapy and Debbie did not want to go. After telling her several times that it was time to leave, I said if she chose to stay, she would be choosing not to be part of the MDC program anymore. I even told her that once I leave this computer room, there was no going back. Her decision would be final. I gave her many chances, but she still chose to stay in the computer room and she cursed."

Out of the program?! I thought to myself. No they cannot do that. Can they? The semester was almost over. But, more importantly, I love Debbie. I did not want to lose the privilege of spending time with her.

I then commented, "Debbie had told me, well Harry told me, that she said a bad word, but I never heard about all of this." Barbara and Jessica then made Debbie promise me that she would behave better. Debbie squeezed my hand, looked me in the eyes, and told me, "I-I-I promise, I'll behave better because I really li-i-ike you." Her hands were sweaty and her face was full of sorrow.

I then explained to her, "Debbie, I love being your buddy, and I want us to be able to keep spending time together but you have to behave better. If not, you're going to be removed from the program." She just nodded, and said, "Yeah."

Barbara then told Debbie to go to class, and that she would not be participating in the program that afternoon. They would have to think about letting her comeback at all. Surprised and in a rage, Debbie hollered, "I don't want to go to class. I want to be in the program!" As she stomped her right foot, her head hung low. Her eyes were fixated on the ground.

I told Debbie she had to go to class.

Her response, "I'll see you next week!" as she smirked.

Puzzled, I told her, "Debbie, there may not be a next week for us if you don't start behaving better. I hope there will be, but you need to behave better."

She said, "Okay, I pr-r-omise." We said our goodbyes and she made her way to class.

I followed Barbara out of the cafeteria and into the park, where everyone else was gathered. Barbara and I began to talk. She said, "This isn't the sweet Debbie that I've known and taught for years. She is behaving very oddly, and this is not the first instance. I think she may need to be put on medication. I don't know how we're finally going to handle this situation; you might need to be assigned a new buddy."

"MEDICATION?" I thought to myself. She is just having a bad day? Are the disabled not allowed to have those? I told Barbara how I would hate to lose Debbie as a buddy, that I was already so connected to her. As I walked through the park, buddy-less, I began to reflect on everything that had just taken place. If anyone of us "abled" people did not want to leave an area for whatever reason, no one would seriously consider putting us on medication? How many times do we "abled" people curse when another cuts us off in traffic? No one tries to put us on medication for that. Why do people turn to medication as a solution for any kind of rising issue involving a disabled individual? I knew that I did not have the whole story, but my mind was racing.

Although Debbie's behavior did not improve instantly, with great effort, she did complete the program with me. It was a trying time for both of us, as our visits from there on out were chaperoned by her social worker. I saw and still see Debbie progressing remarkably. I am so proud of her. Witnessing someone you care about struggle and somehow overcome through great effort is a powerful experience.

The Friday after our last WOW visit, I received a phone call from Debbie. She was calling to let me know that she had broken our promise. A couple weeks ago, I couldn't even get her to confess to me when she was misbehaving. In the past, the only way I would ever find out was through Harry or one of her supervisors; and here she was, calling me to tell me she did something wrong. This was a courageous act of trust. I told Debbie that as long as she learned from mistakes and made efforts to improve, that it was okay.

I asked her what she was up to. She told me how she was picking up the house and going to cook later with her man. She also told me, how she really loved the stuffed animal I gave her on our last visit. When Debbie asked me what I was doing, I told her about working on some homework. Coincidentally, that homework was this essay.

"You know, I'm writing a paper on you and about the time we've spent together."

"Yea I know," she giggled as she replied.

"Is there anything you want me to include in the paper?

Her response was simple, but so very powerful: "That I love you."

Therefore, I write to you, Professor Gonzalez or to whomever else may be reading this that Debra is my friend, and she is capable of one of the most significant actions any human being can ever do—she loves unconditionally and unabashedly. She is a complete human being, struggling like all of us, yes. But she has taught me for a whole semester that magic can happen when we connect and open ourselves to love.

Grassroots leadership for the 21st Century: Leading by not leading[1]

by Joan T. Wynne

What kind of leadership does the 21st century demand? Many of us in education today realize that top-down hierarchal thinking and behaving is stultifying students' and teachers' imaginations, disenfranchising student voices, failing marginalized populations, and foiling national school reform. Asa G. Hilliard, III (1997), a decade ago, suggested that with a broken system, "revolution, not reform is needed." That revolutionary vision can be seen in a model of leadership, fully operationalized during the sixties in the Southern Freedom Movement (SFM) in the U.S.A., but honed in education during this new century by Bob Moses, founder and president of the Algebra Project, Inc. Grounded in a philosophy of empowering grassroots, bottom-up brilliance to find an equal voice alongside those in the power structure, the Movement's history did not start in the sixties. Rather, as Moses explains, it "came into existence when the first African walked off the first slave ship in chains" (Moses 2001, p 174). And though the grassroots component of the SFM model may be as old as the leadership philosophy of Lao Tsu in 700 B.C.[2], its impact on educational circles is only now being examined.

Research, sponsored by the National Science Foundation, Florida International University (FIU), and some grassroots organizations is beginning to investigate SFM's educational offspring, the Algebra Project, as a possibility

---

[1] "Grassroots Leadership for the 21st Century: Leading by Not Leading" by Joan T. Wynne from *Transformative Leadership and Educational Excellence: Learning Organizations in the Information Age* by Myint Swe Khine and Issa M. Saleh, © 2015 Sense Publishers. Reprinted by permission of the publisher.
[2] Quotation by Lao Tsu from the *Tao Te Ching* suggests the general philosophy of Movement leadership style "Go to the people. Live with them. Learn from them. Love them. Start with what they know. Build with what they have. But with the best leaders, when the work is done, the task accomplished, the people will say 'We have done this ourselves.'" While at Harvard, Moses studied the writings of Lao Tzu.

to revolutionize school reform, especially in the instruction of mathematics. Within the context of public schools, the Movement practice that seems unique in reform is its insistence on bringing together the disenfranchised into small circles to discuss, understand, and, then, demand what people say they don't want—a quality education (Moses 2001, p.16).

In this chapter, I will discuss some of the components of this transformative leadership model as I witnessed them unfold during Moses' negotiation of the leviathan obstacles that stand in his path of delivering black, brown, and poor white children from the dismal dungeons of impoverished schools. His attributes as a leader reflect not only the grassroots experiences and wisdom learned through the Southern Freedom Movement (SFM) and from his mentor Ella Baker, but also from his disciplined intention of denying any attachment to charismatic leadership. Rather, he seems committed to fostering the leadership capacity of others. Moses suggests in *Radical Equations* this distinction between the two leadership styles, charismatic versus grassroots: "My basic sense of it has always been to get people to understand that in the long run they themselves are the only protection they have against violence or injustice . . . People have to be made to understand that they cannot look for salvation anywhere but to themselves" (p. 33).

The Story

This chapter is more a narrative or portraiture than it is a research report explained through traditional reporting protocol. The story begins in 2004, when FIU invited Moses, Civil Rights legend and MacArthur Genius Fellow, to come to its campus as an Eminent Scholar in its Center for Urban Education & Innovation. He had been invited because of his 25 years of stewarding accelerated mathematics programs to disenfranchised communities across the country and because of his "focus on creative methods of teaching and learning as a strategy for empowerment and social change" (Ransby p. 252). From the first time Moses came to Miami, I have followed him into a myriad of settings from classrooms and parent meetings and academic halls of various universities to foundation board meetings and superintendent offices in Miami and other cities. As a researcher, my observing and being in those arenas alongside Moses have been both humbling and transformative. So to write this chapter as an objective eye-witness is a challenge because I was observing not just a different mode of leadership, but also witnessing what I believe to be a different way of "being" in the world. My internal question has always been how do I wrap academic words around this multi-layered, innovative yet ancient, quasi "spiritual" leadership experience?

When Cornel West wrote in 2001 that Moses is the towering activist/intellectual of his generation, he captured two of the many facets of this leadership style manifested by SMF luminaries like Ella Baker, Fannie Lou Hamer, Vincent Harding and practiced by Moses in the field of education. One of those facets is his commitment to excavate the intellectual life of students scoring at the bottom quartile of academic measures. A second is the social activism, the intention to radically change an oppressive system (Moses p.3). Moses suggests that "embedded in this work" of education and the concurrent building of a demand for positive change by people at the bottom "is the idea that if you can really bring about any kind of change at the bottom it is going to change everything" (Moses 2001, p.188). Both of these commitments are integrated into the philosophy and practice of the Algebra Project and addressed whenever Moses is in a room with other people.

While exploring the intellectual life of students or their communities, what always seems to set Moses apart from others in a room is his stillness, a quality manifested also in many SFM leaders like Baker and Harding. Such deep quiet lives in stark contrast to the monologues and directives that one often hears in classrooms, schools, or meetings with many leaders in the U.S.A. Indeed, that silence permeates Moses' teaching style and his persona in every group that he draws into a circle. It's a strategy that he often credits to the mentoring of Baker (Moses 2001, chapter 3). Though, I find Moses' profound calm so integrated into his personality, that calling it a strategy seems a misnomer, like trying to separate the dancer from the dance. Yet, at the same time, I know that this "stillness" is a quality of leadership that is more powerful than any of the others I will write about, and one I believe necessary to emulate in the hyper-sensory-stimulated twenty-first century. Though other cultures may manifest this quality more widely, the fast-paced, efficiency driven American culture is not known for it.

You must enter into the small silences (Moffitt 1961)

Several incidences of this disciplined quiet stand out in my research notes as strong demonstrations not only of its unique nature amidst hierarchal institutions in America, but also of the positive outcomes resulting from its practice. The first example is a meeting with Moses and a group of faculty who had been invited by the Executive Director of the Center, Lisa Delpit, to dialogue with the newly recruited Eminent Scholar. The dean's conference room was filled with about 26 faculty members. All seemed eager to meet and hear from this highly respected and reputed urban leader. After Delpit

introduced Moses and asked the faculty to introduce themselves, Moses quietly asked "What is it that you would like to accomplish in these next two
hours?" After the question, silence filled the room. Moses didn't speak. The
professors didn't speak. People began to shift in their seats, either looking
down or looking around for someone to speak. Approximately four or five
minutes passed, which at the time seemed longer, and Moses remained still,
looking straight at his audience, and seemed the only one in the room comfortable with the absence of words.

Professors are often wedded to fixed agendas, expectations of leader-domi-
nated lectures, or pre-determined formats for discussions. Thus, being in the
room with a leader, who believed that the wisdom needed for any effort lived
within the people in the room and had to unfold with "leaderless" dialogue,
seemed to bring this set of professors to palpable discomfort. They had come
to hear his wisdom, not to be participants in the excavation of their own.
Eventually, a professor broke the silence with a question which later gave way
to a group decision of an open conversation about the challenges of being a
college of education in the midst of the fourth largest school district in the
nation. Later, after the meeting, one of my colleagues asked me, "Is that
silence a strategy of Moses? I've never experienced that in an academic
setting."

In the classroom with a cohort of 9th grade Algebra Project students and at
a church basement where Moses led adult mathematics literacy workshops, I
experienced that same quality as a means of allowing learners the space and
time to answer their own questions about solving mathematical concepts,
permitting them to dig deeper into their own reasoning for solving a problem. His pedagogy, a framework designed to develop conceptual knowledge,
not rote formulaic answers, intends to build student confidence so that they
and their small groups can probe within themselves for answers.

However, it was at our first parent-student meeting where Moses was beginning to organize the parents to support their students' new foray into the
world of higher level mathematical thinking, that his stillness was again palpable and resourceful. Four professors, some from FIU and some from
Miami Dade College, accompanied me to that meeting to become a part of
this effort to sustain an AP site in Miami, where students performing in the
bottom-quartile of academic measures were being offered an accelerated
mathematics program. Moses and this team plan to shepherd these students
from the 9th grade through the 12th grade, preparing them for access to and
success in college.

At this parent meeting, where also some brothers and sisters, aunts and
uncles came, Moses formed us into a circle, explained to the parents the
scope of the project and then asked the question, "What steps do you want

to take next to support your students on this four year journey?" Again, like the meeting with the college professors, an uncomfortable hush crept in. Moses sat quite still and never took his eyes away from the circle. Many, if not most, of these parents had never been asked what they thought or wanted to do about their children's education. The room remained quiet for what seemed again like a very long time. Even the professors wiggled a bit in their chairs, wondering if anything could be ushered in from this silence. Finally, one parent spoke, then another, then another and before the end of the night, the participants had planned the dates, the agenda, and a cross-cultural menu for subsequent meetings, as well as a commitment letter of support drafted by the parents to pledge their family's support for the work of the Algebra Project. After the meeting, in the parking lot, the professors and I confessed to each other our own discomfort with Moses' long silences while marveling at its brilliance, admitting that this had allowed the participants to find their way into shaping their own dialogue, strategies, and interventions to push their students toward college.

At another parent/student meeting, we watched as Moses sat quietly allowing students fifteen to twenty minutes to debate what time they wanted their classes to begin each morning at an upcoming summer institute. Later each of us professors, who had sat in the same circle, admitted that we would, heretofore, have impatiently intervened and made the decision for the students, unwittingly squashing their initiative and their ownership of the process. We, too, were learning from Moses' leadership.

Possibly, the most memorable example, though, of this quality unfolded the first day of a six-week residential summer academic institute that AP and FIU operated for this newly formed ninth grade cohort and for twenty-two students from another high school in the city. None of these students had ever been away from their parents for this length of time. Some had never been away from home. The students came from two rival schools where fear of one another surfaced at the parent/student information meetings held separately at both schools prior to this first day. Suddenly forty, fourteen-year old rivals arrived at the front door of a residence hall meeting space, disembarked from two separate buses, carrying their belongings and entered into a large meeting room in the hall. Some were driven there by their parents who also came into the meeting.

I welcomed the group who sat noisily in chairs and sofas, telling them how excited we were to have them at FIU, how long and with what enthusiasm the staff had planned for making their stay on campus a good experience, and, then, introduced their instructors, their college chaperones, and the other staff who would be working with them for the six weeks. The students listened yet chattered and sometimes giggled during introductions and comments from professors and staff. When everyone else had been presented, I, then, introduced Moses whom the 22 non-cohort students never before had met. After the introduction, Moses stood before them and said nothing. He stood looking at the students and their parents. Some of the students continued to chatter. Moses stood silent. Students began to hush other students. Moses stood silent. Some students then began to nervously giggle at the ensuing quiet. Professors shifted from foot to foot. The discomfort swelled.

For several minutes, Moses stood silent, looking at everyone there. I had never before experienced this kind of patient waiting for a room full of anxious strangers and giggling teenagers, staring back, to settle into a respectful calm. The room became motionless and soundless, and, then, his quiet, calm voice began to tell the history and purpose behind the effort to bring them all together in this place at this time. He spoke of their obligation to bring the best they had to offer to the summer experience, not just for their own success, but to help build a movement to secure the rights of all students to a quality education. He, then, asked them to immediately decide if they were ready to make a serious commitment to the goals of the institute. If they were not ready, he indicated, there was no shame attached to leaving. He again insisted that if not eager then for rigorous academic pursuit, they might consider coming to a subsequent institute. He continued, saying that no one was forced to be there; that it was their choice, and they should not make that choice lightly. He paused and gave students the opportunity to leave. No one left. The rest of the day proceeded. I still remember standing there in awe of the courage and confidence to hold oneself silent and present to each moment and person for such a long time. The incident also reminded me of a description of Moses in *Parting the Waters* when Taylor Branch cites the first meeting between Martin Luther King, Jr. and Moses, who was then only twenty-five: "Moses carried about him the strong presence of an Eastern mystic. There was something odd about him, yet he also managed to communicate a soothing, spiritual depth" (Branch, 1988, p. 325).

Slow the Bus Down

Moses used similar acts of patience with me. Often before or after sessions at workshops with adults or young people, I would proffer an idea about some content or pedagogy or activity that we might bring the next time we met with the group; and Moses, each time I asked, would suggest to me that we should wait for the group to decide what they needed or wanted. But on later occasions, because I was on such a steep learning curve about grassroots organizing and leadership, I would forget and ask the same question. Moses, as though it were the first time he had heard me ask the question, patiently gave the same answer. After one of these moments, I realized again the depth of the generosity that Moses, and people in the Movement trained by Baker, bring to any dialogue, and the huge philosophical shift this kind of leadership reveals. I had grown up in an Anglo-American world where a typical metaphor for describing most processes, especially in education, was "Hurry up and get on the train; it is leaving the station, and you will be left behind." But Moses kept gently reminding me to, "Slow the bus down so the people can get on." His patient stillness in all of these instances made possible the gift of slowing the bus down so that everyone's talents and wisdom had time to emerge and to join the ride toward creative revolution.

In addition, this quality, the use of "small silences," demonstrates a profound faith in the wisdom of those living on the margins, "Black, Latino, and poor white students who are trapped at the bottom with prisons as their plantations" (Moses, p. 12). The silence, patience, and calm create a luxury of space and time for people to find their authentic voices in the midst of chaos, of confusion, of struggle, of discomfort; time to dig for their words, their ideas, their insights; space to piece them together so they can own and use them to invent their own solutions to the sometimes daunting realities they face and the educational monstrosities they suffer.

Baker, too, believed that the people at the bottom of society's hierarchal ladder often offered the most ingenious ideas (Ransby 2007). In an unwelcoming culture, as academe typically is for disenfranchised people, creating a safe container for them to let their ideas percolate is mutually beneficial for the institution and the people it serves. Indeed, such mutuality demands and shapes institutional change. As Moses explains it, "A network, a tradition like this, involving teachers, students, schools, and community, is not established in one fell swoop. You go around it and around it, and you keep going around it and deepening it. You keep returning to it until all the implications of what you are doing become clear and sink in." (Moses p. 188)

Helping to Create the Demand

Leading by not leading might be another way to describe the qualities that surfaced as I followed Moses into diverse arenas. That component, in fact, is what first drew me to Moses and his Algebra Project work. I had been immersed in urban school reform since the 1970's and had become discouraged, always working for sweeping reform, but in three decades witnessing "so much reform, so little change" (Payne, 2007) in schools. Yet I know, as educators, most of us have desperately wanted to be co-creators of a democratic, quality educational experience for all of America's children, not just for the elite—as Moses puts it, "to recognize that all of the children *in* the nation are children *of* the nation." (Center 2004). In hopes of accomplishing this, we educators have changed our curriculum, our pedagogy, our leadership styles, our textbooks, and our management systems. We have made large schools into groupings of small academies. We have promoted teacher leadership, shared governance, collaboration, rigorous professional development, reflective practice, and learning communities—yet still the majority of urban schools in every city continue to deliver inferior education to black, brown, and poor white children (Dropout factories 2007).

After reading in 2001, *Radical Equations: Civil Rights from Mississippi to the Algebra Project*, however, I began to understand the missing piece of all of these reform efforts. That piece is the "demand side" of the work, or what Moses also calls "earned insurgency." Helping to develop that component within any group is the transformative leadership piece that too many of us don't' quite understand, or don't value, or don't feel we have the time or skill to cultivate. It's the knowledge that Moses learned in the sixties with the sharecroppers. While then the group was sacrificing for the constitutional right to vote, and in the present century, we struggle for the constitutional right of a quality education for *all* children, that same quality of leading without leading is vital. Moses often reminds us that now, as then, there is a place for advocates of all kinds—educators, lawyers, foundations, civic leaders, churches, businesses, community agencies—to push for democratic rights. But "the only ones who can really demand the kind of education they need and the kind of changes needed to get it are the students, their parents, and their community, which largely remain silent on issues like this." (Moses, p.151)

For, in the absence of the community's demand, the country insists and teachers believe that black, Latino, poor white students and their parents do not value education and/or don't have the capacity to achieve academic excellence. Thus, they become the scapegoats for low performance, a belief system that allows the nation to resist holding itself accountable for delivering "first class" instruction to all. The Algebra Project's insistence on building a base of student and parent demand for superior curriculum and pedagogy is a commitment and skill vital for all educational leaders, whether serving in colleges, universities, or public schools. But "leading without leading," an integral part of building a grassroots' demand is a painstakingly disciplined, back and forth process, that many leaders have little patience for.

Moses' shifting lately of the language from "demand" to "earned insurgency" (PBS) indicates his insight that students must make sacrifices for their education as did "sharecroppers" who made sacrifices (risking their jobs, homes, and often their lives) to demand their right to vote. If today's students are to demand a quality education from the nation, they, Moses often explains, must be willing to take mathematics for 90 minutes every day for four years; sacrifice time at home to study; and devote time in their communities as math literacy workers. Moses' and the Algebra Project's demand on the students to pursue academic excellence, not mediocrity, is as deliberate as its demand on the nation to deliver quality education.

Leadership Lessons Learned

When I think about my journey of being like an intern, shadowing a leader, gathering data, attempting to see the patterns of leadership, the nuances and the directions, I'm reminded of Harding's, *Hope and History*. In the book, Harding, while explaining "the transformative uses of biography," describes his encounter with a youngster caught up in a drug and gang world, a young man who speaks with "unconventional wisdom." Harding relates that after his lengthy exchange of dialogues with this young man, he began to recognize the need for young people to have "human signposts" who can help point them toward healthy visions and transformation (Harding, 1990). "They need to see and know the lives of women and men who provide intimations of our human grandeur, who open doors beyond darkness and invite us all toward the magnificent light of our own best possibilities, as mature, compassionate, evolving human beings" (p. 16).

In these dark times in urban education where the statistics of failure can overwhelm us, in a nation where all the old paradigms of social and economic polices have recently collapsed, I believe that knowing the success story of leadership demonstrated by Moses is especially valuable. Knowing that his qualities evolved through a crucible of darker times, fashioned by men and women like Amzie Moore, E. W. Steptoe and Fannie Lou Hamer, people pushed to the very bottom of society's rung deep in the Mississippi delta, yet who drew upon a vast, historic, and collective Movement wisdom to mount the struggle against racism, power, and privilege—and won, then, maybe we can unearth those qualities within ourselves to transform not only education, but also the nation.

So what are those qualities that I witnessed that seem the most relevant to a transformational leadership that might dig us out of the quagmire of inadequate public education, out of the vast inequities in urban and rural schools, and out of elite education that keeps the children of the wealthy lost in a sea of moral morass?

The practice of silence: Harding suggests that Bob Moses calls it "the work of 'internal organizing' for anyone who seeks to work at serious reorganization of the world around us" (Harding p. 24). It might unfold from a practice in yoga, or meditation, or simply developing a comfort with stillness. When witnessed, it is a potent force.

The discipline of patience: A sense that the task is never complete so the need to rush becomes irrelevant and often counterproductive. If as Hamer suggested, "Freedom is a constant struggle; make a joyful noise," (Roberts, 2004) then there is always time to sink into the silences and wait for "the people" to lead their own struggle toward intellectual engagement and restorative justice. Moses, like Hamer, sees his work as a lifelong journey. Once when I was attempting to persuade him to accept a tenured position at the university, he asked what that would mean. I told him that for one thing, it would mean a retirement pension and benefits. He quickly informed me that neither would be necessary as he had every intention of "dying with his boots on." Moreover, with Moses the destination of the struggle seems integral to the careful attention to each moment in the journey, and the moment is met with complete integrity, like a doctor listening for the rhythms of a heartbeat.

The belief in the small and the intimate in life: Mother Theresa said, "We can do no great things, only small things with great love." Moses consistently manifests a belief that creating small groups with intimate connection to each other around a shared vision builds strong and bold movements. He did this kind of work in Mississippi; and, though, he has become what Dave Lawrence, a civic leader in Miami, calls a national treasure, Moses continues to spend time in the classroom working with one cohort at a time for four years at a time, teaching mathematics to keep the movement alive in the young while testing out theories of accelerated curriculum and pedagogy. His belief in the intimate of life seems counter to the typical national demand for grandiose schemes; its rush to "scale up" reform; its lust for big numbers to guide and shape us; its demand for answers without being willing to live the question; and its distaste for the prolonged struggle toward radical change. There is an organic nature to the leadership and work of Moses and the Algebra Project. He insists that AP "is a process, not an event" (p. 18). And he never seems to rush the process to grow it big—to force feed its success—his product is never a hot-house plant. Like a small farmer he knows the seasons of change. He knows that when rushed, when grown too fast or too big, ideas and practices like plants can become toxic or void of any nutrient or meaningful content. For over thirty years, Moses has taken the Algebra Project step by step toward success. He's watched as young people grabbed hold of AP in Mississippi and spun it off into a different direction into a Young People's Project (YPP), managed by young people for young people, learning mathematics as they serve their communities as math literacy workers in after-school programs. Like Baker, though, Moses resists manipulating YPP to resemble his vision, but has stepped aside for it to organically grow its own leadership, directions, and intellectual base. After ten years of growth, YPP, too, now has a large National Science Foundation award and is developing new sites around the country.

The personal connection: Moses consistently in Miami demonstrates a belief in personally connecting with whomever he works. When he was first forming the 9th grade cohort, he visited the homes of each student. Often the school had incorrect addresses for students; Moses kept at it until he found the home of every student. He visited those homes on multiple occasions as well as met parents and relatives at the school several times a year for brainstorming sessions. He visits sick students when they are stuck at home; he takes students to the doctor; he brings them groceries. This is the man who, President Barrack Obama, in an interview with a journalist, called his "role model" (Lizza 2007, p. 3).

In his book, Moses says that connecting is an essential part of the work of the Algebra Project: "The first thing you have to do is make a personal connection. You have to find out who it is you are working with. All across the South you could see that in grassroots rural people. That was their style. Miss Baker took this style to a sophisticated level of political work" (Moses p. 32).

Giving voice to the voiceless: Moses reminds us that "Young people finding their voice instead of being spoken for is a crucial part of the process" (Moses p.19). Consequently, he creates opportunities at conferences, university classrooms, and diverse meeting halls where his high school students can tell their stories and share their mathematical knowledge across the country. Learning from Baker and his experiences in the SFM, he also insists that leadership "should emerge from the community and be helped in its growth by grassroots organizers" (Moses, p. 34).

With Moses, leadership itself seems a co-creative process, always moving, never culminating, a procession of people and ideas changing places in a circle, not a triangle. Resisting any attempts at making the national Algebra Project a center of power, Moses continuously pushes power into the hands of the local sites. He seeks, and sometimes helps to create, local grassroots cadres to develop a consciousness that nothing will be sustained without their owning personal leadership, without constantly re-evaluating successes and failures to keep their efforts fluid and responsive to the environment in which they live and the people with whom they work. Like a jazz musician who "modifies a musical rhythm by shifting the accent to a weak beat of the bar," Moses places his attention on the weakest voices in society and helps them find their song—and, like Hamer, together, they make a "joyful noise."

He orchestrated that "jazz" again in August of 2008 when a newly assigned principal at the local high school was considering closing the Algebra Project site. To counter her attempt, I suggested that Bob, I, and others might meet with the principal and extol the virtues of the project. Bob quietly said, "No." The students and parents, he suggested, should write a letter about their experiences in the project and then meet with the principal to share the letter. They did, and they alone persuaded the principal to maintain the project at their school. Moses' two years of work with these students, building them as a cohort and a community, produced a desire and a confidence in them to demand what they needed. They had earned their insurgency.

A profound capacity to listen deeply and well: I have yet to find anyone who has not felt deeply heard after walking away from a meeting with Moses. Whether he agrees or not, he listens intently to whomever is speaking. He asks penetrating questions and waits patiently for others to digest the words and respond from their own experiences. Without taking the first note in most meetings, months later he can repeat who said what when. His capacity, though, to listen, really listen, to the young is remarkable to experience. His proclivity for prolonged silence with them and his honest curiosity to know their thinking allow them to push that thinking in new directions. Whether in the classroom or in sessions with students planning events, Moses consistently models this profound respect for what young people are saying. He explains that, "It is the voices of the young people I hear every day, more than anything, that gives me hope" (Moses p. 191).

Historian, Charles Payne, suggests this quality of careful listening as one that Moses early in his life projected: "The broad outlines of the Mississippi movement of the sixties had been laid out, primarily between an older warrior [Amzie Moore] with little formal education but years of experience fighting Mississippi and a younger man [Bob Moses] with sense enough to listen, Harvard notwithstanding" (Payne p. 106-107). In most arenas, leaders who listen well are treasured.

Building the network of relationships in communities and across the nation

Moses since the sixties, as a field secretary for the Student Non-violent Coordinating Committee (SNCC), has learned the necessity of always widening the web of the network both locally and nationally to support his work. In Mississippi, he, along with local insurgent leaders, organized the sharecroppers, young people in the towns, thousands of white students from Northern universities, federal prosecutors, doctors, teachers, preachers, politicians and other social justice groups beyond SNCC around the issue of voting rights. This network proved invaluable, for as Moses puts it: "When Mississippi locked us up, the Feds could set us free" (Moses 2009).

In the Algebra Project, he started in a classroom with his children, teaching them algebra, then other people's children in that same classroom, then organized other parents, former SFM activists, teachers across the country, elite mathematics researchers from Cornell, Kent State, the Mathematics and Science Research Institute (MSRI), foundations like MacArthur, Lilly, Open Society, the National Science Foundation, the Children's Trust, universities, professors and graduate students, lawyers, school board members, unions like the Industrial Areas Foundation (IAF), politicians, journalists and thousands of young people around the issue of delivering accelerated academic education to the nation's bottom quartile and creating a movement for Quality Education as a Constitutional Right. His circle spreads across the nation from Los Angeles to Miami: "The question of how we all learn to work across several arenas is unsolved. Those arenas are large and complicated . . . . Really working in all these arenas will require that many people adopt a more holistic outlook than they have ever done before" (Moses 2001, p. 16). Moses nurtures this complex network while at the same time spending 3 days a week teaching mathematics to his local AP cohort. And always, living the words of Baker to bring the family along, Moses' circle includes his family, his wife, his two sons and two daughters in the work.

Reaching for strategies to move forward, instead of getting stuck in a search for blame. Moses' rapid movement from problem to strategies for addressing thorny issues is often demonstrated with staff, circles of supporters, parents, and students. I have often observed and silently approved his response to students who might misbehave. At those times, like most "good" teachers, he moves immediately to discovering the reason behind the behavior instead of locking into ideas of punishment; he elicits student engagement in finding the root and the solution, not only in mathematics but also in their lives.

Recently, though, his propensity to move instantly from problem toward strategy stood in stark contrast to my own. He walked into my office immediately after a meeting where expected support was suddenly withdrawn. After he reported to me the outcome of the meeting, I instantly protested, "Why would they do that? How can they do that? How short-sighted." Without entertaining my outburst, Moses asked "What do you think are some strategies to now keep our work going in Miami?" My brain had shut down with the shock of the bad news, while Moses had already begun sharing ideas for garnering other support. Wallowing in blame is just not part of Moses' psyche. His intellect and imagination seem always in gear for moving creatively toward the next step. Yet, at the same time, he can surrender to the ideas of any group at hand, especially the young, if those ideas are congruent with the gestalt of the vision.

Work within and against various structures: Within most public school systems there are structures in place which might seem to enhance the system, yet often damage the humans within that system. Wise leaders recognize those structures and understand the need to work against them when they stifle the creativity and relationship building of the system's participants. While working in urban and rural systems, Moses, like many of us, has suffered arcane public school protocols and processes. The bigger the system, the more rigid and unimaginative the rules—and the more unconscious the intimidation of the people it is supposed to serve. Against these monolithic systems, Moses' organic sense of life, learning, and leadership stands in stark and elegant relief. His refusal to replicate yet one more hierarchal, one-size-fits-all instructional and organizational model, though, is often misunderstood as unrealistic or somehow incomplete.

Nevertheless, during strategy sessions, Moses has often explained that we must continue to go up and down the hierarchy of the system, the chain of command, to keep the support alive for the students' intellectual development, and that we should maneuver around those structures we cannot change and create our own system for who contacts whom on each level of authority:

> It is a little bit like guerrilla warfare. You're striking. You're pulling back. You're looking at where you are. You're striking again. You're looking for an opening. You're looking for a soft spot, trying to find out where you can penetrate. And you are working with and against various structures. You're in them, but you're working against them at various levels. (p. 17)

Yet always Moses reminds us that the students and parents must be the driving force behind the survival of the project's vision of "facing a system that does not lend itself to your needs and devising means by which you change that system" (p. 19). Though Moses continually attempts to build consensus and networks among diverse advocacy groups, the radical change needed, he insists, will result ultimately from disenfranchised communities pushing against the system, not from the well-meaning advocacy of outside agents.

When I get disheartened by the harsh realities and inequities in the public school system (Orfield, 2004) and the dearth of leaders with a vision, I think about Moses' almost fifty years of quiet revolution. I think of his front-line participation in the Southern Freedom Movement; of the times he was beaten and shot at; of the times he spent in jail when Civil Rights Attorney, John Doar came from D. C. to get Moses out of those southern jails and prisons. I think also about Ella Baker and Fannie Lou Hamer and Amzie Moore and the thousands of Harding's "human signposts" who changed the south forever and who changed the nation's political system so that a Barrack Obama could become President of the United States of America. And, then,

I go and sit with Moses' Algebra Project students and listen to them talk. That's when I sense that the system is not impenetrable, and that if I have the patience and the stillness, I will hear the strong shifting musical rhythm that comes from the "accent on a weak beat of the bar." Then I know we're closer to public schools making freedom's "joyful noise."

References

Branch, T. (1988). *Parting the waters: America in the King years 1954-63*. New York: Simon and Schuster.

Center for Urban Education & Innovation (2004). "Interview with Bob Moses." Promotional DVD. Miami, FL: Florida International University.

Harding, V. (1990). *Hope and history: Why we must share the Movement*. Maryland: Orbis Books.

Henry A. & Curry, C. (2000). *Aaron Henry: The fire ever burning*. Jackson, Mississippi: University of Mississippi Press.

Hilliard, Asa G., III (1997), "The structure of valid staff development." *Journal of Staff Development*. Spring, Vol.18, No.2.

Lizza, R. (2007). Barack Obama's unlikely political education. *The Agitator*. (http://www. tnr.com/doc.mhtml?i=20070319&s=lizza031907)

Moffitt, J. (1961) "To look at anything." *The Living Seed*. New York: Harcourt Brace & Co.

Moses, R. & Cobb, C. (2001), *Radical equations: Civil rights from Mississippi to the Algebra Project*. Beacon Press: Boston, MA.

Moses, (2009) "Constitutional Property versus Constitutional People." In Perry, T., Delpit, L., Moses, R, & Wynne, J. eds. *Quality Education as a Constitutional Right*. Boston: Beacon Press. (due in fall '09)

Orfield, G., Losen, D., Wald, J. & Swanson, C. B. (2004). Losing our future: How minority yourth are being left behind by the graduation rate crisis. Urban Institute, available at http://www.urban.org/UplaodedPDF/410936_LosingOurFuture.pdf

Payne, C. (1995). *I've Got the Light of Freedom: The organizing tradition and the Mississippi freedom struggle*. Berkeley: University of California Press.

Payne, C. (2008). So much reform, so little change: The persistence of failure in urban schools. Cambridge, MASS: Harvard Education Press.

Ransby, B. (2003). *Ella Baker & the Black Freedom Movement: A radical Democratic vision.* Chapel Hill, The University of North Carolina Press.

Roberts, Wally. (2004). E-mail sharing his experience living one summer in Fannie Lou Hamer's home.

Think Exist.Com. Quotations from Lao Tzu. http://thinkexist.com/quotation/go-to-the-people-live-with-them-learn-from-them/348565.html

PART 4

The world in language

The world is richer than it is possible to express in any single language.

—Ilya Prigogine

The lost voice of a spic

by Gerson Sanchez

"I need some roofing done, how much would you charge me for that?"
"You Mexicans work so hard; you never get tired!"
"So when you graduate from high school, are you going to work in construction or gardening?"
"That's all these damn spics are good for!"

I can still hear the echoes of these racist notions hurled in the hallways of Walter Hines Page High School. On a daily basis, denigrating jokes and comments like the ones quoted above, were promoted by my white peers and, consequently, internalized by my fellow Latino brothers and sisters. The demeaning opinions voiced by my classmates during this preadolescent stage began to create an emotion of inferiority within me. William Cross's model of black identity development (Cross, et al., 1996) states that black children who constantly see patterns of negativity being demonstrated toward themselves or others who are black, are likely to develop a sense of internalized racism. If these assumptions are not challenged, as children reach the adolescent stage, racist and negative self-concepts will most likely be strengthened (Evans et al., 2010).

Even though I am not black, I am a person of color. More specifically, I am the son of Nicaraguan immigrants, and, therefore, Cross's theory seems applicable to me. The constant xenophobic comments and jokes of bigotry voiced by my classmates served as an impetus to deracinate dreams of higher education from the young minds of my Latino brothers and sisters, and me; and, thus, further reminding us that our sole purpose as Latinos was to only do menial labor. Higher education, once a dream, had now become arcane and unattainable in our young minds. Experiences such as these remained throughout my undergraduate years and have now brought my life to a menacing implosion. The vestiges of that implosion have caused me to reflect and ask: What can I accomplish as a Latino? What is my purpose in life? Am I capable? Is the American Dream a reality? Or is it called the American Dream, because you have to be asleep to believe it (Widmann, 2015)?

Reflecting on my dilemma of wrestling with the dominant culture's perception of me, and the impact on my psyche of that battle between who I am and who they think I am, I began to form a question about accountability. Who is responsible for my identity dilemma? Who needs to protect students from faulty notions of their place in the world? Do teachers have a civic duty to their students to openly discuss and combat faulty notions of "White Supremacy," no matter how often or where those ideas rear their ugly head? These questions have led me to research various scholars and practitioners such as Alicia Carrol, Lisa Delpit, Patricia Gandara, Bob Moses, Jennifer Simpson, Joan Wynne. My research has also led me to dig deeply into concepts of integrity, truth, and justice; especially how these ideals should be interpreted in the classroom and what they mean to students of color, in this case, Latino students.

The experiences I endured in that small high school of Greensboro, North Carolina caused me to question the integrity of my teachers. How could my teachers hear these daily condescending comments of their student in their classrooms and do nothing about it? In the words of the eminent scholar and activist, Cornel West, "The condition of truth is allowing suffering to speak regardless of popularity, where is your integrity?" (West, 2014) Did my teachers even have any integrity? Was this integrity/or lack of, exemplified by teachers, also hindering my peers and me from receiving a quality education? Why were they not addressing the suffering, happening before their very eyes? Where was the justice that I was longing for?

Throughout high school, questions such as these circulated in my head and further ingrained a sense of self-lament. The combination of constant noxious statements, as well as my parent's divorce, resulted in the continuous ebb of my grades. My minimum wage job of scooping ice cream became my safe haven, a place where I could temporarily forget school and home. In the eyes of my teachers, it may have appeared that my comportment was apathetic or lethargic toward my studies, but that was not the case. I did care; I just did not know how to succeed in a place that seemed to not care about their Latino students. They made assumptions without asking questions, which, I believe, mirrored their apathy and lethargy toward me. Did they think I was dumb? Did they think of my accent or my baggy clothes as a nuisance? Why did they treat me as a walking set of deficiencies (Nieto, 2010)? More importantly, did they think I had nothing to offer? Borrowing a metaphor from Robert Moses, Why didn't they "slow the bus down" so that my talents and wisdom had time to flourish (Wynne, 2009)? Had they slowed the bus down, they would have realized that I had been playing piano since the age of five; or that I was a person of ethics and integrity; or that I was already part of America's workforce at the age of 16; or that my parent's immigrated to this country due to the civil war in Nicaragua; and, thus, I brought a different perspective to the classroom that might further enrich my fellow peers. But my teachers never slowed that bus so they could get to know me.

In order to better understand my brown perspective, it is imperative to address the demographic of my institution. Half of the school was white, with middle-upper class students, and the other half was composed of poor white, black, Latino, and Montagnard students. Additionally, we had a small population of poor immigrant students. From a geographic standpoint, the structure of the building separated the wealthy side and the poor side of Greensboro. The more affluent part of Greensboro was on the west side of the school facing lush greenery. The eastern side of the building, which housed the courses for the poor students, faced a palpable decay of businesses and housing infrastructures. I remember my senior class had to visit a school for autistic children that was on the east side of the school; however, none of the white students knew its location, but all the students of color knew exactly where it was. The dichotomy between the white students and the students of color was clearly and physically evident. Despite the fact that many of us were raised in Greensboro, we all understood and interpreted the city in different ways.

The school reflected the divisions that often occur in cities and towns with a growing Latino demographic. During the 1990s in North Carolina, as in many southern states, Latino populations grew by more than 300 percent. Specifically, the population of foreign-born Latinos grew by 1050 percent in North Carolina (Winders, 2005). If we are the fastest growing ethnic minority group in the United States (Gandara & Contreras, 2009), why do we not have a higher number of Latinos graduating from high schools and attending institutions of higher education? The sad and harsh reality is that about half of Latino students fail to attain a high school diploma. Other ethnic minorities, including African-Americans have seen increases in college graduation rates, but my Latino brothers and sisters have yet to see such progress in the past 30 years (Gandara & Contreras, 2009). Understanding these realities allows me to ask once again, if my teachers heard the vehemently pernicious comments aimed at my Latino brothers and sisters, why did they not say anything? What was their duty as teachers when they saw the brown kids not returning to school the following day? What was their role as educators in those specific moments?

Urban educator, Joan Wynne (2012), explains what seems to be not only North Carolina's school dilemma, but also that of the nation. She explains that "Approximately 84% of teachers in public schools are white and mostly female. With all of this power and access to public education, why have we failed to effectively educate black and brown children, especially those forced to live in poverty, including the white poor?" She questions white educators' resistance to challenge those who "make tons of money from a school-to-prison pipeline?" Wynne also confronts the failure of teachers to instruct "white children about their civic responsibility to become agents of social justice and equity?" (p. 6)

This indictment of schools, taken from Wynne's book, *Confessions of a White Educator: Stories in Search of Justice and Diversity*, suggests that same call for justice that I have longed for since I was 12 years-old. She speaks from the perspective of a white teacher who was raised in the southern state of Georgia, and her premise is simple, where is the justice?

Not only has my story led me to interrogate the notion of justice, but it has also pushed me to meditate on the insidious actions of institutional racism that thwarts the everyday lives of the disenfranchised. Were my teachers being racist or were they just blind to what was happening? I remember one of the few times someone brought up the issue of racism in class, the teacher brushed it off. She said, "I don't see color, and neither should you. We should all be color blind." Was she right? Should my high school classmates and I have embraced color blindness?

From the perspective of Critical Race Theory (CRT), racism is regarded as normal and ordinary, not aberrational. CRT scholars understand that racism is a pervasive part of the U.S. culture and is so engrained in the body politic that it seems invisible to anyone who isn't victimized by it. From that stance, the reason racism is not redressed in society is because it is not acknowledged. Therefore, even though color blindness can sound ostensibly good, it also can be egregious when it stands in the way of "taking account of difference in order to help those in need" (Delgado & Stefancic (Eds), 2012, p. 26). By definition, it wants to blot out difference, making sameness superior to diversity. Color blindness, unconsciously or not, tries to make the visible invisible. Thus, Black, Brown, Red, and Yellow children would become invisible to a dominant culture.

So it's been a long journey to learn that my teacher was doing me and my peers a disservice by attempting to persuade us to be color blind. But, just as big an issue within that framework, is that whites who embrace color blindness, when faced with evidence of discrimination, "acknowledge its occurrence but label the episodes as 'isolated incidents' and proceed to blame minorities for playing the 'race card'" (Bonilla-Silva, 2014, p. 303). A study, conducted in North Carolina in an effort to analyze how school actors construct and respond to racism, nailed this propensity to label racism as an aberration or to ignore it altogether (Hardie & Tyson, 2013). Looking at different racial tensions between black and white students at a local high school, the researchers found that despite all the racial issues and riots occurring in the high school, teachers and administrators did not discuss the issues in their class. In fact, "Teachers appeared reluctant to discuss the incident in front of students" (Hardie & Tyson, 2013, p. 92).

As happened in my high school, these teachers resisted addressing the issue of racism, but instead unconsciously promoted color blindness. In her book, *Why Are All the Black Kids Sitting Together in the Cafeteria*, Beverly Daniel Tatum (1997) addressed issues such as self-segregation in schools and how we as educators can get past our reluctance to address racism. In Tate's experience, students have come into her classroom having learned that there is a taboo against speaking about issues of race, especially when in ethnic or racially mixed settings. Therefore, she believes that one of her duties as a teacher, although it may be challenging, is to create a safe environment in her class-room to overcome that taboo. In her book, she relates times where she has heard white students refer to someone as black in hushed tones, whispering to each other as to not be heard. In her words, "When I detect this behavior, I like to point it out, saying it is not an insult to identify a Black person as Black" (Tatum, 1997, p. 37). She embraced these opportunities to eradicate the taboo of explicitly recognizing color, of speaking about race in class-rooms. That, she believed, was her civic duty as a teacher. Believing that her responsibility is not to keep quiet, but to speak openly about these issues that affect all students, not just students of color. After all, racism is a disease that impacts the victim and the perpetrator in a multicultural nation and world. As Sonia Nieto (2010) said, "Multicultural education is not about political correctness, sensitivity training or ethnic cheerleading. It is primarily about social justice" (p. 270).

As I look back at my story, I acknowledge that my life has been influenced and affected by poverty, inability to speak the dominant language of the United States, discrimination, and by a myriad of other factors. However, those other factors also include love, mentors, and prayers from friends and family. Borrowing the words of Cornel West, "I am who I am because someone loved me" (West, 2014). Nevertheless, the lack of justice and integrity exemplified by my teachers in high school and college, along with the condescending epithets directed at my Latino brothers and sisters, contributed to my development as an individual. The seeds of the imposter syndrome, an identity as a fraud, that often marginalized high achievers internalize (Parkman & Beard, 2008, p. 32), were first sewn in me upon my arrival in high school and have lingered. Even though, I am now pursuing a

Master's degree and currently exploring possibilities to enroll in an eminent doctoral program, the syndrome is still deeply rooted in me. Although my friends and family congratulate me on my zealous drive, unfortunately, the memories of an arduous journey inflicted by hegemonic teaching are still enmeshed in my mind.

Malcolm X once said, "Tomorrow belongs only to the people who prepare for it today" (Shabazz, 1970), and that is what I aspire to do. Today, I am preparing for tomorrow because I understand that the knowledge I seek needs to be mobilized to eradicate the insularity of marginalized people. I hope to seem not cantankerous or divisive, but to provide insight from a first-hand perspective on a harsh reality that many of our children face due to educational hegemony, a societal abuse that has left many of us mentally exhausted and scarred. The unjust, pernicious, and dominating system that has led to the physical, mental, and spiritual demise of too many of our children can no longer be tolerated. As the novelist James Baldwin said, "Everything now, we must assume, is in our hands; we have no right to assume otherwise" (West, 1993, p. XXIII).

References

Bonilla-Silva, E. (2014). *Racism without racists: Color-blind racism and the persistence of racial inequality in America,* 4th ed. Lanham, MD: Rowman & Littlefield.

Cross, W., et al. (1996). Fhagen-Smith, Peony Pedersen, Paul B.; Draguns, Juris G.; Lonner, Walter J., Trimble, Joseph E. Nigrescence and ego identity development: Accounting for differential Black identity patterns. *Counseling across cultures,* 4th ed. Thousand Oaks, CA, US: Sage Publications, Inc., pp. 108–123, xvii, 373.

Delgado, R., & Stefancic, J. (Eds). (2012). *Critical race theory an introduction,* 2nd ed. New York: New York University Press.

Evans, N. E., Forney, D. S., Guido, F. M., Patton, L. D., & Renn, K. A. (Eds). (2010). *Student development in college: Theory, research, and practice,* 2nd ed. San Francisco: Jossey-Bass.

Gandara, P., & Contreras, F. (2009). *The Latino education crisis: The consequences of failed social policies.* Cambridge, Mass.: Harvard University Press.

Hardie, J. H., & Tyson, K. (2013). Other people's racism: Race, rednecks, and riots in a Southern high school. *Sociology of Education* 86 (1), 83–102.

Nieto, S. (2010). *Language, culture, and teaching: Critical perspectives,* 2nd ed. New York: Routledge.

Parkman, A., & Beard, R. (2008). Succession Planning and the Imposter Phenomenon in Higher Education. *CUPA-HR Journal*, 59 (2), 29–36.

Shabazz, B. (1970). *By any means necessary: Speeches, interviews, and a letter by Malcolm X*. New York: Pathfinder Press.

Tatum, B. (1997). *Why are all the black kids sitting together in the cafeteria*. New York: Basic Books.

West, C. (1993). *Race matters*. Boston: Beacon Press.

West, C. (2014). *Black prophetic fire*. Retrieved from https://www.youtube.com/watch?v=5LhmQ-DwLTU

Widmann, J. (2015, March 10). Manufacturing apathy: Education's role in providing what the owners want. *Truthout*. Retrieved from: http://truth-out.org/

Winders, J. (2005). Changing politics of race and region: Latino migration to the US South. *Progress in Human Geography* **29** (6), 683–699.

Wynne, J. (2009). Grassroots leadership for the 21st century: Leading by not leading. In: Khine, M. S. & Saleh, M. I. (Eds). *Transformative leadership and educational excellence: Learning organizations in the information age*. Rotterdam, The Netherlands: Sense Publishers. pp. 88–100.

Wynne, J. T., Delpit, L., & Miles, R. E. (2012). *Confessions of a white educator: Stories in search of justice and diversity*. Dubuque, IA: Kendall Hunt.

Naming, walking, and magic

by Carlos Gonzalez

The words you speak become the house you live in.—Hafiz (Ladinsky, 1999, p. 281)

Brazilian lyricist and novelist, Paulo Coelho, says that magic is a kind of bridge between the visible and invisible (2014). My work as a teacher and my students' experiences in the learning spaces I help create sometimes reflect Coelho's definition. In class, I often make the argument that language is the ultimate form of magic. Without it we don't really understand the world about us. It is that bridge between what is known and what wants to be known or is currently invisible.

In our sessions, because most of my students are familiar with and culturally rooted in the Bible, I mention a passage where God tells Adam to name the animals in the Garden of Eden. For me, this story works as a powerful reminder that the impulse to name is an integral part of what it means to be human. The naming of the animals implies that the way we relate to the world has something to do with our ability to name what is in front of us.

The challenge comes when we don't have language for what we are confronting. In such instances, our names or vocabulary often fails us. Over the past 13 years or so, we have collectively struggled to properly name the violence that flows from the margins and often hits the very centers of power that we think are immune to challenge. Personally, naming is especially difficult when it comes to matters of the heart. Sometimes during times of testing, we are left speechless and voiceless, confronted with what at the moment is nameless and terrifying. At these times, it is the role of the magician to name, particularly in these times of uncertainty and gloom. Proper naming can open possibilities other than fatalistic violence.

But not everyone is interested in magic. For some there's little interest in exploring the unknown or invisible world. The dark crannies of our lives, the marginal parts of ourselves and communities, for some, are better left off reach. The reasons for this are many. There may be a vested interest in keeping the terror of the nameless alive. Terror sells all sorts of things, makes marketing destruction more palatable. And some are scared of naming for fear of what may become visible. The bottom line is that it seems to take energy, effort, skill, and most of all, courage to live a magical life.

But there are some who thrive when walking to the edge and groping for the name of that which at the moment is nameless. The people who do this well are the poets, scientists, and mystics. How they do this is an amazing process. It seems that it often comes in a moment of quick realization. But frequently, the breakthrough in naming comes as a result of a lifetime of arduous exploration, experimentation, and perseverance. While saying this, I also want to point out that before you and I cede our rightful desire to name to only the few, it's important to remember that we each can develop or grow a bit of the poet, scientist, and mystic in us. That's what most of us were before we started kindergarten. Just pay attention to children playing and interacting with one another, and you can see that the inhibitions that come with a desire to look and sound just right and professional are not there. Children are fantastic magicians. By the way, they are also excellent teachers. If we want to rediscover our magical abilities, we should spend some time with four-year-olds!

As I write this, I realize that my class can be an opportunity to see how close we can come to the edge, how willing we are to explore and to name what we don't know, and play with the possibility of co-creating the reality we want to live. This sounds like a huge undertaking, but when we look at it carefully, we see that it's what we do on a daily basis but just don't notice. Unfortunately, I don't have the kinds of magical powers that can make any of us want to move in this direction. All I can do is invite and entice. It's up to each of us to want to move closer into the shadows and begin our own apprenticeship with intentionally naming.

I ask my students early in the semester to begin writing their first set of essays for the term. These first texts may start with what they can see easily. Over time, students may become aware that the themes they chose to write about may move closer to the shadows, those places where it's not completely clear what they are exploring or knowing. Before that happens, they will need to grow courage and also curiosity. Maybe the word curiosity is not the right one here. The association of curiosity and cats is an unfortunate one. I think the word I'm looking for is something like wonder.

To live in wonder and in awe is a stance that draws us from the familiar and seemingly safe to the place where we contact mystery. I can't forget Rabbi

Abraham Joshua Heschel's dictum regarding this stance: "Wonder rather than doubt is the root of all knowledge" (1976, p. 11). Heschel helps us understand that what often happens to both students and teachers as they walk into the classroom is quite the opposite of wonder. Students get discouraged by what feels like, and often is, meaningless work. Educators lose their courage, become disheartened, when what they offer students is superficially acknowledged and not seriously explored, and all too often we focus on the institutional requirements and ignore or suppress the possibility before us, the opportunity to do magic, make and walk bridges.

The Classroom as a Magical Arena

At our best, you and I, student and teacher, we work creating bridges every time we enter a classroom. There, when I'm at my best, I invite and nudge students into that place where they can tap into their innate wonder and desire to know what is at the moment not seen. I never quite know how to do this. I don't have access to an easy formula. The intention itself is an invitation for me to come to my own edge and rummage for what creates the bridge.

Fortunately, the kind of teaching I do has to do with language. I and most of my students are bi-lingual Spanish/English speakers. Magic seems to be an ingrained part of the curriculum. As a teacher of that curriculum, I often need to work through some of the barriers that we each bring; otherwise, we may not see the potential of our time and work. For many students, writing is seen as a one way mode of communication: writer to reader. What may not be so obvious is that writing is also a means of personal exploration, of figuring out, of knowing. We write to name what we don't know. (This is happening in this short reflection right now.)

I've meandered through the question of agreeing or not with Coelho's definition of magic. This meandering has allowed me to hear his voice anew, to see his words paint new dimensions to the teacher/learner process. By taking the time to wonder and wander through his words and definitions, my sense of what I try to do in the classroom crystallized. I am an alchemist, a magician, and bridge maker in training. Though, I am not the only one with this identity. I envision my students as alchemists, magicians, and bridge makers. Together we often co-reveal what, at the moment, seems invisible; and we do so in the common day-in and day-out of conversation, learning logs, essays, and Twitter updates. Alone or together, we interrogate our individual views of magic. As we examine texts, we sometimes build together the bridges that are pure magic.

References

Coelho, P. (2014). The Alchemy of Pilgrimage. *On being with Krista Tippet* (Ed.). Retrieved April 21, 2015. http://www.onbeing.org/program/paulo-coelho-the-alchemy-of-pilgrimage/6639

Heschel, A. (1976). *Man Is Not Alone: A Philosophy of Religion.* New York, NY: Farar, Straus, and Giroux Publishing. p. 11.

Ladinsky, D. (1999). *The Gift: Poems by the Great Sufi Master.* New York, NY: Arcana Publishing Co. p. 281.

My English isn't too good-looking

by Pamela Hernandez

I have always embraced my language incorrectness and took pleasure in slang words and the use of Ebonics—"you feel me?" It's not because I'm ignorant or without education, it's because I offer my truest self when I am able to express my ideas freely. I communicate successfully using double negatives and Hialeah street jargon, *oye asere que bola*. I celebrate my bilingual tongue, and practice code switching as well. I can speak Spanish, English, Ebonics, Standard English, Spanglish, and at the Cuban Café I speak *café con leche and pan con biste*.

Today in the school where I work, I heard a teacher tell her students that they "don't talk right." Last week it was red slashes on a paper, tearing through the student's diction. What is proper English and who determines who is speaking "right" or "wrong?" Why do the hegemonic language police get to decide that using "standard English?" is the best way of communicating or holding ordinary conversations? The Hispanic or Latino population in the United States is young and growing quickly, due to immigration and higher birth rates. Our country is becoming more and more multicultural and with the arrival of new-comers, new customs, cultures, traditions, and also come new languages, accents, dialects, and slang. In order to accommodate and communicate effectively with the growing majority of this country, the hegemonic "Standard English" language just won't do the trick. Having said this, I fully understand that it is imperative that we begin to cultivate a generation of successful and effective communicators who do know "standard English," but we must also respect students' home languages in the classroom and require our students to learn different languages and dialects.

Effective communicators also can be bilingual and bi-dialectal. For this reason, educators must refrain from telling students "They don't talk right" or "This isn't proper English," or reprimanding students for speaking their native languages in class (Wynne, 2002). Instead, we should teach our students how important it is to be bilingual, bi-dialectal, and even trilingual. This does not mean that I recommend that students only speak an entirely new language. Rather, it means preserving a student's natural language and explaining that moving forward in the world requires them to practice code switching.We should understand and teach our students their use of Ebonics or Spanglish, etc. is colorful and lively and shouldn't be condemned; instead kept in their back pockets and used whenever necessary. As an educator in an urban, low-income community, I have witnessed an emphasis placed on Spanish speaking students to learn to speak only English. While I agree being fluent in Standard English is imperative in this society, we should not limit students'use of any other language or dialect. We must cultivate a generation where bilingualism is the norm, and where students and children are being taught multicultural education, and intercultural competency through language acquisition.

Our country's main language has been the hegemonic English language; however, in central cities and states all over this country, that reality is changing. In 2013, the U.S. census estimated the nation's population was 316.5 million. The same U.S. census estimated the population of Hispanic and Latino people made up 65.6 percent of the population in the city, where I live. The Hispanic/Latino population is one of the largest minority populations in the country, and the numbers of Hispanics/Latino people continue to grow around the United States. According to the Pew Research Center, in California, Whites made up 38.8 percent of the population. In contrast, Hispanics made up the majorityof the population with 39.0 percent. According to The Henry J. Kaiser Family Foundation in 2015, whites made up 62 percent and the second largest population being Hispanics, made up 17 percent. These statistics show that with the increasing number of Hispanics and Latinos, the Spanish language and the Spanglish dialect are a force to be reckoned with. According to Jennifer Ortman and Christine Guarneri and their research in the U.S. Population Projections from 2000 to 2050 (2009), the Hispanic population is going to continue to grow through the years, meaning that the Hispanic/Latino people will continue to bring more multicultural children into this world, more Mexican Americans, Dominican Americans, Cuban Americans, etc. America won't be just for "Anglo-Americans" any more, America will be for the multiculturalist.

In many schools around my city, Spanish speaking students are expected to learn and perfect in the English language, a reasonable goal. However, I believe that giving students the opportunity to learn another language in all public schools also should be a requirement. Many cities like Miami, FL and San Andres, CA have a rapidly growing Hispanic population. It would be especially beneficial for students and people in those cities to learn multiple languages and among those, of course, Spanish might prove to be very advantageous.

My experience in teaching in an urban school that requires only Spanish speaking students to learn English, while not requiring English speaking students to learn Spanish, has made many students feel that their home country is inferior, and that their Spanish language is inferior to the English language. However, the census statistics may suggest that people who only know English will be at a disadvantage in the years to come. For example, in cities like Miami, where there is a large population of Hispanic/Latino and Caribbean populations that will continue to grow, employers will probably seek out employees who are bilingual, who can speak both Spanish and English, or Creole and English, since these are two dominant minority languages in the city and county. Bilingual students may become more attractive as applicants because they can communicate more effectively with all people. Learning different languages is vital. Therefore, encouraging students to learn different languages including Spanish seems a reasonable educational proposition. Therefore, doesn't it make sense to explore the benefit for our schools to place English speaking students in a "Spanish class for English speakers"?

In the world today, over 5,000 languages are spoken, as well as several varieties of languages (Ramirez 2005). However, as language scholar, David Ramirez claims, "Those varieties with higher status are called languages, and those with lesser status are usually called dialects" (2005, p. 3). Because Spanglish and Ebonics are often spoken by Spanish and African-American students, these students are typically portrayed as inferior people when compared to White Americans. According to my current urban school district's statistical report, from Pre-Kindergarten through 12th grade, there are 239,681 students who identify with being Hispanic (District Report, 2014). Latino and Hispanic students make up the majority of the public schools here. However, "Because many educators view language varieties of the home and community as deficient, they do not believe that children should have a right to their own language (Ramirez et al., 2005)." If our students don't have the right to their own language, then who does? We must become radical in our teaching, in our schools, in our homes; and we must fight to preserve our children's identities and cultures. Too many schools just want our students to "shut up and sit down" and "write like this," and "talk like that," but our Spanish, Arabic, Creole speaking students, and all of our urban students should have the right to their own language, and be able to express themselves in a variety of ways, not just in stubborn standard English.

In my own experience working in a large urban public school, with ESOL students (English for speakers of other languages), a lot of those students have labeled themselves as ESOL, instead of just students. Their Spanish language has turned into something of ridicule and lower class status.

"Ms. Hernandez, I can't do this, I'm ESOL" is a typical comment I have heard throughout this year. Since the students' first language is Spanish, and they are placed in a class that doesn't value the diversity of languages or culture, one that is focused only on teaching these students the English language with no respect for the home language, the students associate their ethnicity and first language with being less intelligent than a student whose first language is English. Furthermore, Ramirez et al. (2005) explains that several varieties of language spoken by students have not been raised to the status of school languages. Why not? Because what would happen if privileged students were required to learn Ebonics, the same way that minority students are forced to learn Standard English? We might begin to bridge the gap between privileged students in upper and middle class and urban students in poor communities. That may be a scary thought for the hegemonic English Gods sitting on their thrones of grammar, punctuation, and regulation.

Once, when standing in line at the Racetrack gas station, my Spanglish was put to the test. I was waiting in line to pay for gas, and I overheard a conflict occurring between a Spanish customer and an American cashier. "How much gas do you want" the cashier repeated into the man's blank stares. "*Queiro gasolina*" the man repeated. The empty exchange of words continued, and the conversation was going nowhere. "How much *tu le queire poner*" I asked the man. "*Vente*" the man answered. I turned to the cashier, "He'd like twenty on pump six please." In my city, this happens every day, because of the lack of bilingualism. The use of the Spanglish dialect would have allowed these two people to communicate more effectively. The term Spanglish "indiscriminately refers to the incursion of English words, meanings, and forms of expression into Spanish… and to alternate between Spanish and English phrases and classes, as in classic, intra-sentential code switching (Banks, 2012). If the cashier could just have said one word, "quanto," meaning how much, the customer would have understood the question. If the customer had known the English number system, he would have been able to tell her twenty. In this case, fluency in both Spanish and English isn't needed. However, a tolerance for Spanglish would have proven to be effective. These two simple words, "quanto" and "twenty," represent how important and useful the Spanglish dialect can be, in an ever increasing Spanish America.

The struggle with Hispanics and Latinos, and their language mirrors the issues that African-Americans have always faced with Black English and/or Ebonics. In December 18, 1996 the issue of Ebonics and education became public. The Oakland School Board argued that Ebonics is a "language distinct from English that should be recognized, tolerated, and, otherwise, accounted for in the instruction" (Blommaert, 1999). For them it only made sense since a majority of the students were African-Americans who typically spoke Ebonics. This would have been a grand opportunity to teach students about the history of their dialect, and encourage students to appreciate their culture, and feel proud to be studying a language that African-Americans invented and still use today, instead, though, speaking Ebonics is considered shameful.

In my city, the majority of students in public schools are Hispanics and Latinos (239,681). Similar to the argument of the Oakland School Board and Ebonics, Spanglish, I believe, should be tolerated and recognized as a way to communicate, especially in a primarily Hispanic public school system. Some of the issues the Oakland School Board faced were the questioning of what it would mean for the students if Ebonics was introduced into the curriculum. "Would recognizing and allowing for minority speech patterns improve students' performance, or would it 'ghettoize' the schools (Blommaert, 1999)." Many scholars (Delpit, Kilgour-Dowdy, Ladson-Billings, Nieto, Wynne) agree that not only does respect for students' home language improve performance, but, most importantly, it gives students a more positive self-image. As educators, we should not only aim to teach our students material for tests, but we also should be developing our students as well rounded individuals who are comfortable in their own skins. Language is one way the guardians of the hegemonic English language keep minorities suppressed. They want to convince people that it would be an injustice for minority dialects to be accepted in schools; they fear it might "ghettoize" the students. Yet, the possibility also exists that by introducing Ebonics or Spanglish into the classroom, teachers can educate students on how to code switch. By teaching our students to code switch, a teacher indicates that both forms of languages have a place and a value in this world. For our students, these minority dialects seem imperative for communicating with family members and surviving in an urban, minority community.

The real injustice, it seems to me, is presenting English or Standard English as the most important language, in and outside of the classroom. If we consider Black English to be "learned as the native language variety of 60 percent of the more than 35 million persons of African-American descent in the United States, then there are probably more than 20 million people for whom this is the 'first dialect'" (Blommaert, 1999). If the majority of the population in a school speaks Black English or Ebonics, then suppressing that group of students by demonizing their native language would be destructive (Wynne, 2002). Urban educational expert, Lisa Delpit in the preface of her book, *The Skin That We Speak*, shares the thoughts of one of the contributors of the volume, Asa G. Hilliard III. "He knew the forces aligned against our youth: those who would tell them that they were not smart enough; those who would say that they did not speak 'right'; those who would cause them to question their own worth and thus stunt their growth; those who would suggest that they are anything other than phenomenal" (2002, p. ix).

Many of my students live in poverty and attend the urban school where I work, and for several reasons, they feel like they aren't smart enough.

- They are constantly told that they don't talk right, even though they can communicate perfectly fine with their family members, friends, and me. Sure, they don't use standardized-test English, and I don't need them to when they are just trying to tell me about their day, or how their parents are migrant workers, and that they will have to switch schools yet again.
- They don't think they are smart enough because they can't understand everything the standardized question is asking them. In their language, in their country, they haven't seen words like this, or the word means something different in their native language.
- They don't think they are good enough because they are Mexican, Cuban, Dominican, Haitian, Jamaican, Chinese, or Indian, and they don't speak English like Americans do.
- They don't learn about their history in America and the world—they learn about White American History. In our school, their culture is not taught or encouraged.

My students' identities are at risk. I would never want my student or my own child to feel like they are valued any less than a wealthy American-born person. The total number of Hispanic students (239,681) in public schools in my city stands as an outlier, compared to other ethnic groups in my city. The U.S. educational standard seems less prepared to allow minority students to inject their urban culture and languages. In The Silenced Dialogue, Delpit (1988), cautions us that children and students have a right to their own language and they have a right to their own culture. She insists that we contest cultural hegemony and that fight the system. This task requires for parents, teachers, and students themselves to speak out and declare that students be permitted to express themselves in their own language style, regardless of its dialect or slang. Moreover, she goes on to say that it is not the students who need to change, but the schools, and forcing students to do anything else, she says, is short of condemnatory and unreasonable.

The approval of different languages and dialects within the school house could be very impactful for both students and teachers. The students can develop a more positive self-identity and learn about code switching. However, perhaps, most importantly, teachers will have the opportunity to educate students on different cultures and ethnic groups, who identify with a particular language or dialect. Multiculturalist, Kenneth Cushner and Jennifer Mahon agree that "Developing the intercultural competence of young people, both in the domestic context as well as in the international sphere, requires a core of teachers and teacher educators who have not only attained this sensitivity and skill themselves but are also able to transmit this to young people in their charge" (2009, p. 304). Intercultural competence is defined by some, as the ability to communicate successfully and appropriately with people who have different cultures. Today, our youth are entering aprogressively interconnected society, which demands they attain intercultural competence. It's not enough to understand the density of global problems. Our students must also develop the capability to collaborate with others in the resolution of those problems. Yet, Cushner and Mahon claim that "Schooling as we know it today is not socializing students sufficiently for a global context, in part because many say it is beyond the scope of U.S. educational standards" (2009, p. 315).

Finally, in the concluding hours of the dominance of the hegemonic English language, I urge parents, students, teachers, and friends to advocate for a better universal education system that requires all students to be bilingual. Being fluent in more than one language is vital for living in a country, where there are so many different languages and dialects spoken. Increasing our students' knowledge of different languages and cultures will allow them to effectively communicate with people from diverse cultures as well as increase their opportunities for procuring jobs both locally and internationally. Let's fight for our students to learn different languages, for both teachers and students to become global citizens, and to take another step toward celebrating language diversity.

References

Banks. J. A. (Ed.). (2012). *Encyclopedia of Diversity in Education.* Thousand Oaks, CA: Sage Publications Inc. pp. 447–448.

Blommaert. J. (Ed.). (1999). *Language Ideological Debates.* Berlin, NY: Walter de Gruyter. pp. 202–204.

Cushner. K. & Mahon. J. (2009). *Intercultural Competence in Teacher Education: Developing the Intercultural Competence of Educators and Their Students.* D. K. Derla (Ed.). Thousand Oaks, CA: Sage Publications, Inc.

Delpit, L. D. (Aug 1988). The silenced dialogue: Power and pedagogy in educating other people's children. *Harvard Educational Review,* **58**, 3; Research Library.

Delpit, L. & Kilgour-Dowdy, J. (Eds.) (2002) *The skin that we speak: Thoughts on language and culture in the classroom.* New York, NY: The New Press.

Ladson-Billings, G. (2002). I ain't writin' nuttin': Permissions to fail and demands to succeed in urban classrooms. Lisa Delpit & Joanne K. Dowdy (Eds.). *The skin that we speak: Thoughts on language and culture in the classroom.* New York, NY: The New Press. pp. 107–120.

Nieto, S. (2012) Good teachers in difficult times. Keynote: College of Education, Florida International University, Miami, FL.

Ortman J. M. & Guarneri. C. E. (2009). *United States Population Projections: 2000 to 2050*. Retrieved from https://www.census.gov/population/projections/files/analytical-document09.pdf

Ramirez, D. J., Terrence W. J., Gerda. K., Enid. L., & Wayne. W. E. (Eds.). (2005). *Ebonics*. Tonawanda, NY: Cromwell Press Ltd. pp. 3–4.

The Henry J. Kaiser Family Foundation. (2015). *Population Distribution by Race/Ethnicity*.Retrievedfromhttp://kff.org/other/state-indicator/distribution-by-raceethnicity/

United States Census Bureau. (n.d.). *United States 2013 Population Estimate*. Retrieved from http://www.census.gov/search-results.html?q=population&

Wynne, J. (2002). Who talks right? L. Delpit & J. K. Dowdy (Eds.). *The skin that we speak: Thoughts on language and culture in the classroom*. New York, NY: The New Press. pp. 203–219.

Wynne, J. (2012). Introduction. J. Wynne, L. Delpit, and R. Miles (Eds.). *Confessions of a white educator: Stories in search of justice and diversity*. Dubuque, IA: Kendall Hunt Publishing Co.

PART 5

The problem is cultural

I still believe the problem is cultural, but it is larger than
the children or their teachers . . . the cultural framework of
our country has, almost since its inception, dictated
that "black" is bad and less than and in all arenas "white"
is good and superior. This perspective is so ingrained
and so normalized that we all stumble through our days
with eyes closed to avoid seeing it. We miss the pain in
our children's eyes when they have internalized
the societal belief that they are dumb, unmotivated,
and dispensable.

—Lisa Delpit, *Multiplication is for
white people: Raising the expectations
for other people's children*

Dealing with whiteness to empower students to fight for common good

by Mary Alison Burger

> The collective struggle presupposes collective responsibility . . . Yes, every-
> body will have to be compromised in the fight for common good . . . there
> are no innocents and no onlookers. We all have dirty hands; we are all soiling
> them in the swamps of our country and in the terrifying emptiness of our
> brains. Every onlooker is either a coward or a traitor (Fanon, 1968, p. 199).

I am an upper-middle-class, college-educated white woman. I say that first because it is a vitally important signifier when discussing issues regarding race, class, and gender. It is important because it frames my entire reality. It is important because it requires a constant, tireless vigilance, to check, and recheck my privilege, my perspective, and my input on issues that do not affect me directly. It is vital to make sure that I am not engaging in the very oppression I am trying to oppose. I am an upper-middle-class, college-educated white woman, and I am doing the best that I can to combat, as an educator, what critical educational scholar, Joan Wynne (2012), identifies as the "isms," of sexism, racism, and classism, through a tireless advocacy for an "anti-oppressive" education (Shim, 2012).

If I ever encounter a person of my ethnicity claiming to be completely void of racism, I am immediately suspicious of them because I believe it is not possible. It is not possible because the entire premise of our U.S. history is constructed around the ideas of white male privilege, imperialism, and a "pernicious" white hegemonic dominance that is pervasive in every corner of our existence, particularly in that of education (Castagno 2013). It is not possible, because as a white person, I am bombarded with both active and passive racist messages, suggestions, and acculturation from the moment I am born. I am surrounded by encryptions of racism in day-to-day life that encourage me to keep in place institutional structures that, every day, limit people of color's upward mobility and civic participation in a social environment. Jenna Shim. in her article

"Pierre Bourdieu and intercultural education: It is not just about lack of knowledge about others," (2012) notes "We are not the sole authors of our perceptions, thoughts, and (re)actions because we are all inescapably constituted within a variety of historically constituted social and political discourses (p. 213)." As extensions of a past full of slavery, oppression, Jim Crow and segregation, we are *all* agents in the *habitus* (p. 213) of racism. It is hardwired into our history, so, it seems to me that probably no white person can *truly* be "above" racism. There is no such thing. So what now?

Coming to terms with my role in the African-American liberation movement has garnered some honest and challenging questions: What can I do? Where does a young white woman fit in this struggle for equity? What can I *truly* do to join my black brothers and sisters in this fight to free America from racism, without getting in their way? Wynne perfectly captures and identifies the "schizophrenic conundrum," of being a white antiracist, trying to, as she aptly puts, "finding-while-fighting my place in the national scheme of white supremacy—snarled in the web of veiled utterances that protect it" (p. xiii). She asks a question I have asked myself over and over. "How do I disentangle my tongue twisted for decades in making sounds sustained for hundreds of years in the dismissive dominant discourse?" (p. xiii). I believe the answer to her question is an intensely complicated one beyond the scope of this essay, but there are two simple things that I *do* know that have led me to some form of action—first and foremost, racism is a white issue, and what I mean by this is, it is an issue of white people, either blatantly ignoring, or lacking knowledge and sensitivity to the historical mistreatment, discrimination, oppression, liberation, rebellions, and triumphs of African-Americans that are still pervasive today.

Secondly, as a white woman I have white privilege, a tool that I can use to my advantage, as it grants me the accessibility to talk to other white people about these issues. Knowing these things, I've developed a boundless sense of personal responsibility, to use my accumulated knowledge as tools to attempt to break down these hegemonic structures, and an understanding that it is my duty to use my privilege as a platform for advocacy rather than one of oppression. I feel that the most sinister acts of racism are not those enacted out of ignorance, but out of knowing better, and opting instead to stay silent and allow injustices to continue. As Frantz Fanon's quote in the heading states *"Every onlooker is either a coward or a traitor."*

I feel my role in this struggle is to do what my brothers and sisters of color might not do, for fear of being type-cast as the social trope of "the angry black individual" (vis-à-vis the symbolism of Richard Wright's (2005) character of Bigger Thomas in *Native Son*). It is my position to be as belligerent and vocal about these issues as possible, to speak out, and speak up, and to interrupt the cultural pervasiveness of racism at every opportunity that I can.

Naturally learning to be an antiracist is not an overnight metamorphosis, but a constant and ongoing learning process that requires a large degree of patience, listening, and humility. There is an important and necessary amount of research and background knowledge that must be in place, in order to be an effective agent for change. Avoiding neo-liberalism, paternalism, projection, and being prepared to own up to an error is a studious and ongoing practice.

I was fortunate enough to have been raised by a mother who encouraged me from the moment I had a blood-beating heart that every human life is of equal value irrespective of any kind of "difference" they may have. Although this ideological and egalitarian belief was certainly over simplistic and lacking critical finesse, as my mother was not an academic, she was the catalyst that ultimately ignited, in me, an overwhelming and powerful indignation for bigotry of any kind that followed me into adulthood.

Still though, I have stumbled along throughout my own journey, misspoken, misunderstood, and made embarrassing mistakes. As an undergraduate, I entered into the University of Florida, staunchly vocal about my opposition to any form of discrimination, and quickly began to recognize that my passion and outspokenness for social justice issues sacrificed my likability among my white peers. Because of this, I began to gravitate to the black community, sharing a situation similar to the one Dr. Joan Wynne (2012) explains in her Introduction to *Confessions of a White Educator: Stories in search of justice and diversity*:

> Because my parents philosophically stood against racism and segregation, as a family we lived in contradiction to the society we were born into. No one . . . seemed to share the same world view. Although my white skin advantaged and protected me, I became accustomed to feeling intellectually and politically alienated . . . only in the black community could I have possibly found a large number of like-minded people (p. xi).

As a voracious reader and writer, whose very soul resides in literature, I eventually found myself in a performance poetry organization, to which I was the only white member. Sharing an equal love for language, the members became not just my close friends but my family. We performed not only on campus, but within the Gainesville community, almost always at all African-American events. I entered these situations with a common, misguided belief that many young white people harbor, that being an anti-racist means being "color blind," an ignorant and naïve concept that if we ignore race altogether, ergo racism will vanish with it. Oftentimes, this subject would come up at length, and I was frequently confronted with discussions, exchanges, questions, and sometimes outright confrontations about race. I was blessed to receive tutelage from several African-American mentors willing to explain to me, at length, the things that, as a white woman, I just could never understand. It became obvious to me quickly that race was not something that one could just "ignore" and that my concept of colorblind sameness was just as damaging, if not more so, than the acts of blatant racism to which I was so opposed.

So I listened. I listened and I learned. I didn't know it at the time, but these conversations would become the cornerstone of a platform for equity that I would carry with me for life. One that recognized that colorblind sameness was not preventing racism, but promoting it, by pretending it does not happen; something I could opt to do as a white person, but someone of color cannot. One that recognized a glaring characteristic of privilege, a blindness to itself; and one that recognized that a truly equitable world is not one of homogeneousness and uniformity, or colorblind sameness, but one that embraces all cultural identities, while granting them equity and opportunity in every conceivable way. These were all powerful lessons, ones that I owe my deepest gratitude to my friends for having the patience to share with me. It illustrates that the knowledge that I hold so dear is not information that I have come upon by accident and demonstrates the necessity of listening and learning in order to truly operate as an agent for change. But even now I am still learning. This essay itself is a careful reflection and amassment of all I have learned so far, and I am not nearly done, I will never be done.

To me, it is a devastating injustice that amongst white communities, our environment is so saturated in discriminatory practice that consciousness is more elusive than ignorance. It is a loathsome truth that I did not have to directly address race or its social consequences until I chose to do so. I feel that this is a gross reflection of negligence that permeates how we are educating our young people. So I have decided that a second component and responsibility to my role as a white antiracist, is to work towards, as Shim (2012) puts, an "anti-oppressive" education, or one geared towards deconstructing these damaging narratives.

While I acknowledged above that racism is a "white" issue, and that it is important as a white anti-racist to continually reach out to white people, I also feel that another area where I need to explore is why we are consistently failing our black and brown youth in our schools. So I want to teach, and I want to teach the disenfranchised. I want to teach NOT because I want to "save people." I am not a moral imperialist; I am not "the white savior," and this is not a *Freedom Writers'* essay. Those notions, I believe, are paternalistic. I want to teach because I want young people to have the education they deserve. I want to teach because I have an understanding that education will inspire young people to demand change where it needs to happen and because this kind of educational foundation should be mandatory for all students. I want to teach because as Shim (2012) states "The field of education functions in such a way as to reproduce and legitimize class/racial inequalities and maintain status quo since the educational credentials are held mostly by those already in dominant positions (p. 214)."

It is my belief that for students to be successful, they need an educator sensitive to the obstacles they face. Students need more teachers that understand fully the societal barriers that are preventing youth from reaching their potential. There is a desperate need for educators who have a detailed comprehension of these barriers and an understanding of strategies to overcome them. I believe in exploring research and practice that provide me with the skillset to guarantee the success of my students, not only scholastically, but intellectually, and professionally. I am convinced that remaining on a personal and intellectual learning curve, I will be able to enhance students' ability to self-actualize and overcome systemic limitations through consciousness. I hope that, through my own modeling of life-long learning, I can inspire a passion for learning in other students of life and academics that will arm them for success for the rest of their lives. As my hero, and favorite author, Fanon (1968) stated in his famous canonical work, *Wretched of the Earth*:

> To educate the masses politically does not mean, cannot mean, making a political speech. What it means is to try, relentlessly and passionately, to teach the masses that everything depends on them; that if we stagnate it is their responsibility, and that if we go forward, it is due to them too . . . that there is no famous man who will take the responsibility for everything . . . the magic hands are finally only the hands of the people (p. 197).

Holding a similar philosophy as Fanon, Civil Rights icon and President of the Algebra Project, Bob Moses, encourages grassroots people, students, parents, and teachers to make a demand on schools and society to deliver quality education to every mother's child (2001). Again, like Fanon, Moses (2001) insists "that in the long run they themselves are the only protection they have against violence or injustice . . . they cannot look for salvation anywhere but to themselves" (p. 33). I will be using my summer to study, research, and work with local youth in the Algebra Project because I want to learn how to empower myself and others to raise our voices and actions, to work our "magic hands," and to demand justice in a society that still sees "constitutional people as constitutional property!" (Moses 2010).

References

Castagno, A. E. (2013). Multicultural education and the protection of whiteness. *American Journal of Education,* 120 (1), 101.

Fanon, F. (1968). *The wretched of the earth.* New York: Grove Press.

Moses, R. & Charlie Cobb (2001). *Radical equations: Civil Rights from Mississippi to the Algebra Project.* Boston: Beacon Press.

Moses, R. (2010). Constitutional property v. constitutional people. *Quality education as a constitutional right: Creating a grassroots movement to reform public education.* Perry, T. et al. (eds). Boston: Beacon Press. pp. 70–92.

Shim, J. M. (2012). Pierre Bourdieu and intercultural education: It is not just about lack of knowledge about others. *Intercultural Education* 23 (3), 209.

Wright, R. (2005). *Native son* (1st Perennial Classics ed.). New York: Harper Perennial Modern Classics.

Wynne, J., Delpit, L. & Miles, R. (eds.) (2012). Introduction. *Confessions of a white educator: Stories in search of justice and diversity.* Dubuque, Iowa: Kendall Hunt Publishing Co. pp. xi–xxiii.

Listening to students: Stories from the Education Effect

by Maria Lovett

As the Preface of this book requests, let me begin by being *specific*—I have so much to learn. Each day I unpack my own white obliviousness, question my privileges and also attempt to, as Bob Moses, Civil Rights icon and founder of the Algebra Project says, "keep on pushin" in the struggle against hegemony. I am part of the Education Effect, a university community school partnership in Promise City[1] Unpacking my privilege is wrapped tightly to the story of being schooled by the brilliant young minds I have been so fortunate to work with, come to know and learn from.

October 2013. It was a few days before the ribbon cutting of our new Aquaponics Lab and Organic Garden—what we now refer to as the "Living Classroom"; and the students were busy planting trees, bushes and vegetables, feeding the fish and testing the alkaline levels of the water. One of the high school students explained to me how the system works, as I, a professor in education, had no clue. He explained:

> Aquaponics is the combination of aquaculture, growing fish, and hydroponics, the soilless growing of plants. We are raising 250 tilapia in each tank, and the waste from the fish is filtered through the system and fertilizes the large crop of herbs and vegetables growing above. We test the water quality checking Ph and carbon dioxide levels and monitor the nitrogen cycle to insure the fish live and the plants grow.

We then walked through the garden of over 100 plants representing 13 different species native to Florida. "This is cluisa—also called the autograph tree because you can write your name on the leaves, this is moringa, a highly nutritious plant native to Florida, that we call a super food," another student explained. Two butterflies zipped by and a bee landed on my sleeve. "You

---

[1] All names of locations and individuals have been changed except for Bob Moses.

know that bee wouldn't have been here a few weeks ago—the butterflies either. There were no bees or butterflies around here. They are here now because we planted that milkweed over there. And the lemon grass. . ."

  "Things are changing?" I asked.
  "Yep. Promise City won't be a food desert for long," a student chimed in.

The back yard of the school—what once was an empty lot, occupied by dilapidated portable classrooms and cars lined up for sports practice—was transforming—and so were we all.

I am not an agroecologist or environmentalist and until this program and these students I had never heard of "aquaponics." Three and a half years ago, I became the director of the Education Effect—my university's university community school partnership with a local high school in a neighborhood, forced to live in poverty, in an urban city of America. Collaborating with the community, schools, students, and parents, the partnership aligns university resources and opportunities to address the pressing educational and social needs of students at the high school and its feeder schools. The Education Effect resonates with the mutual understanding that our university's future and the future of school district's disenfranchised communities and schools are connected.

The goal of the partnership is to support 100 percent student graduation from high school and see every student ready to be successful in college and pursue careers of their choice. While it is understood that not every student may wish to pursue college or university, this should be a result of individual choice—not institutional barriers. To achieve our goals—we believe, as the story above shares, the work often involves us adults stepping aside, and becoming students to such brilliant young people.

Inequity in our public education system is evident and pervasive. Access to resources, high quality instruction, a safe and inspiring learning environment is not equally accessible for all our children (Wynne & Giles, 2010). Low-income students are more likely than middle and high-income students to fall behind in academics, score low on standardized tests and drop out of school. In addition, poor students are more likely to attend schools that have significantly less academic support and per pupil funding (Southern Education Foundation, 2013). According to a 40-year study by the Southern Education Foundation, in 1970, 40 percent of students from the highest income quartile graduated from college. In 2012, it was roughly 80 percent. For students in the bottom income quartile in 1970, 7 percent graduated with a B.A. In 2012, it was only 9 percent. In other words, as Bob Moses (2014) stated, for poor students, it hasn't budged.

In our state, 56 percent of public school children qualify for free or reduced lunch, 74 percent in our county, in the community where our partnership began it is 90 percent, and at our high school it is even higher (SEF 2013, district data). When we began the Education Effect in 2011, the graduation rate at the school was 64 percent; it now hovers at 80 percent. An accomplishment yes, but our students still struggle to graduate "college ready" (prepared to meet standard admission requirements for college acceptance without remediation). While 75 percent of students are now "college ready" in reading (up from 52 percent in 2012), only 35 percent of students graduate "college ready" in math. Both reading and math scores are requisites for college admission.

The Education Effect partnership had been in place for five months when I began. Working with disenfranchised students struggling in a broken system on a daily basis made it impossible to deny that indeed Jim Crow was alive and flourishing. In less than one week on the job, I was acutely aware that this work would transform *me*, and that I had much to learn; but what could be achieved for the students was so uncertain when the institutional barriers were so high and the smog of hegemony so thick. Early on, issues of concern included the metaphors we were using and the language we were speaking such as "addressing the achievement gap" and "transforming the community." There wasn't an achievement gap; there was an opportunity gap. Or more accurately, let's stop talking about gaps, and as Moses (2001) has indicated, change the metaphor all together, and talk about "raising the floor" for all children to succeed.

Typical thinking around university engagement too often reflects the propensity to lead community engagement. Instead, the emphasis should be on allowing the community, the students in these schools to lead, asking them to pose the questions and seek the solutions. I understood we could transform ourselves, but is it our role to transform or suggest that we are the agents in transforming others? Paolo Freire (1970) speaks to transforming *our* world, not *theirs*. In the Education Effect, we needed a serious shift in our thinking if we thought our goal was to change the school, the community. Learning from the Southern Freedom Movement's grassroots organizing tradition (Moses, 2001), I began to understand that not only is this view self-righteous, but it objectifies the work already happening. So I started looking deeper, opening myself up to learning from the students on the ground, in the school.

In January 2012, my first week, a colleague and I were asked to cover a dual enrollment class (where high school students take college courses in high school for college credit) in public speaking. The disconnect between the university academic calendar and the district's schedule left these students in limbo for three weeks. So my colleague and I volunteered to substitute for the remaining weeks, and framed the content of our mini unit around Bob Moses' call for a campaign to guarantee quality education as a constitutional right for all children. After I explained an activity and the students moved into their groups, Matthew, a senior in the class came up to me and said, with courtesy, "With all due respect, this is a public speaking class, and I just want to point out that you say 'um' a lot. Not sure if you noticed that so I thought I would let you know."

"I didn't realize that actually, thanks," I answered, and I am sure, blushed. As I left that class I thought, "Wow, I am about to be the student to these high school kids and I have so much to learn! I've been working on my "ums" in my public speaking ever since. Lesson #1.

It was not long before I realized what was missing in the partnership's discourse, in its praxis. We were ignoring the "elephant in the classroom," or in this case, "the elephant" in our university community school partnership (Wynne, 2005). Frankly, the demon in the room that wasn't being named was institutionalized racism. As a white educator, I echo the sentiments of Joan Wynne in *Confessions of a white educator* (2012), that we have an obligation and responsibility as white reformers and researchers to name the demon of race and racism, and not expect black people to do this. We need to name the hegemonic structures that form institutionalized racism, which cripples these communities and our kids (Wynne, 2012). If you don't name it, don't face it, you can't change it, including the changes that need to happen within ourselves.

In an interview with *The Real News* program *Reality Asserts Itself*, Bob Moses explained: "The Civil Rights movement of the 60's got Jim Crow out of three areas: public accommodation, the right to vote and the national democratic party structure . . . but we didn't get it out of education" (2014). If, indeed, the new Jim Crow is alive and flourishing, and we were to implement a partnership called the "education *effect*," we needed a very different approach than just making connections between the university resources and the community/school needs and vice versa. To be successful, we needed to reflect the urgency of educational inequality and inequity in this historic community. We needed to adopt processes that would strategically address the needs of all children, particularly those most often pushed to the bottom. "I think the strongest political idea embedded in this work is the idea that if you can really bring about any kind of change at the bottom, it is going to change everything" (Moses, 2001, p. 188). We learned from Moses that the fight for quality education for all our children is the constitutional and civil rights issue of our time. Thus, as we began to implement the Education Effect we adapted our model to reflect the grassroots approach offered by Ella Baker, Moses, and the organizing tradition of the Southern Freedom Movement.

Although not funded by the seed investment to the Education Effect, we leveraged the partnership; and in 2012, the district and the high school Principal committed to build upon the eight-year partnership of the local College of Education with the Algebra Project (AP) by creating a new AP site at the high school with a cohort of 34 in-coming ninth graders, all of whom were low performers. In fall, 2013, the high school added three more ninth-grade AP cohorts and in 2014, an additional three cohorts. Because, AP in cities as diverse as Los Angeles to Ypsilanti, Michigan, has a 30-year success rate with students caught at the bottom of academic achievement (NSF report), our coalition agreed that expanding the university/AP collaborative would be a win-win for Promise City. AP's insistence on "serving up accelerated mathematics and experiential pedagogy to struggling students, instruction typically reserved for 'gifted" programs' (Wynne, 2010), caught the imagination of the Principal for the students. That insistence is congruent with the Education Effect's mission to co-create and give the best to those who previously have been denied academic quality.

Furthermore, AP's commitment to engage parents and the community in the education of their children is totally consistent with our partnership's vision of engagement. And, of course, the Algebra Project's insistence that they are getting youth ready, not just to graduate from high school, but also to be ready to do college math for college credit (PBS, 2006) echoes our desire to propel our community's students toward academic excellence. But collaborating with and learning from the Algebra Project, pedagogy and Bob Moses gave the Education Effect much more than just the AP program. Moses' ideas gave us a philosophical framework and tangible concepts to inform all aspects of the Education Effect. Thus, the implementation of our work was guided in particular by the following principles: (1) High quality, equitable, and equal access to education is the constitutional and civil rights issue of our time. (2) Students are at the center, making "the demand" for their own quality, equitable education. (3) The work is a process, not an event (Moses, 2001). (4) Students are positioned as "knowledge workers" and adopting the "Each One Teach One" (2001) pedagogy, instruction that is essential throughout all our initiatives.

Quality Education as a Constitutional Right

I was driving with a student to a community meeting about a proposal for a Wi-Fi program in the largest public housing development in the state, located across the street from the high school. James is a high school senior and lives in the neighborhood. He is very vocal about the need for access to the Internet and technology and the impact the so-called digital divide or more accurately the "digital desert" has on his education. He was attending the community meeting to speak on behalf of students. As we waited at the traffic light, we were stopped by a convoy of trucks, the SWAT team, and over a dozen officers in full riot gear.

"Geeze, this is just like a page out of *The New Jim Crow by Michelle Alexander*," I muttered to John.

"I'm not sure what you mean by that, but they are about to go bust down some doors," John said.

"This happen often?" I asked.

"Yep . . . (He laughed, I assumed, at my naiveté).

"The use of the police as a military force in communities like Promise City was created due to the War on Drugs. See that book I am reading? It is highlighted right there," I said, pointing to the book.

John read the passage. "Dr. Lovett, this isn't new to me, I could have told you that myself."

"Yep," I thought, "You live it. I read it in books."

High quality, equitable, and equal access to education is the constitutional and civil rights issue of our time. Education is a right, not a privilege and a sense of urgency and attention to this macro-narrative drives our work. This framework and understanding speaks deeply to the contemporary crisis of what is so often referred to as "the school to prison pipeline." Moses refers to today's education as sharecropper education (2001). Poor youth and youth of color are given an education that is equivalent to an eighth grade education. This prevents access to college and to economic stability. He sees a parallel with registering sharecroppers to vote in the 1960s with young people today. In an interview with NPR Moses asks:

> . . . Who are the constitutional people in the country? Over the course of 2 and ¼ centuries, we have managed in spite or ourselves, to extend the reach of that concept to larger and larger classes of adults. What we haven't figured out is how to extend that to the youth of our country. These kids spend most of their time in school. So this is how they relate to the country. So the country needs to figure out how it relates to them . . . The sharecroppers we worked with were the serfs of the industrial age. So, if we are turning kids out of high schools that have the equivalent of an 8th grade education, then in effect we are setting them up for the serfdom of the information age. Those people in the plantations, they were hidden, out of sight, and they suffered quietly. These kids will not suffer quietly (O'Connor, 2014).

If the Education Effect intended to focus its mission on a commitment to seeing youth as constitutional people, with the right to a quality education, we had to ask ourselves what does that look like? This led us to interrogate the next principle: Young people making the demand.

The Demand

According to Moses, young people have to work the demand. Students are at the center. Our goal is to raise the voices of the heretofore silenced and to amplify students' own language (Wynne, 2012). "Young people finding their voice instead of being spoken for is a crucial part of the process... We believe the kind of systemic change necessary to prepare our young people for the demands of the twenty-first century requires young people to take the lead in changing it" (Moses, 2001, p. 19). To support "the demand," the Education Effect shifted from being advocates *for* the students. Rather, we sought to facilitate spaces and opportunities where the youth could be positioned to make this demand themselves. Students began to see themselves as a part of something bigger, demanding the ability to obtain a high quality education not just for themselves, but to serve their community.

> Shanika: I am the first person in my family to attend college. Because of The Education Effect, you see kids talking about college, talking about being ready to go and start a new life. It's really touching because a lot of people are like: 'Oh you're not going to be anything, look at where you are from.' And to change that misconception is really, really good. Now, walking the streets of [the community] and my neighborhood where I grew up, I realize that I am the future of [the city] (personal interview, The Education Effect video).

Clearly for her, it is not about getting out. It is about being a part of the change that young people want to see in their community.

Working the demand is probably the most essential aspect of the work, and it is also the most challenging. Here, the pollution of hegemony and power dynamics in the schools, in society; are obstacles for students. For example, there was recent chatter about gang activity in the community that was impacting the ninth graders. The kids knew about it. Many wanted help. Some kids were even getting into fights because their names were being attached to a group they were not a part of. But, when a teacher asked why they didn't tell the administration at the school, the students said, "Ah no, then *we* might get suspended." Whether that is true or not, that is the perception of the students. The school system is not a safe space. The popular rhetoric is that the students are afraid of "snitching." However, maybe, it isn't about snitching. Possibly, once again, it is we adults who are letting the students down. Not providing the safe space, not listening deeply, so that students can advocate and make the demand for safety, for an education, for the pursuit of happiness.

> Everyone said sharecroppers were apathetic until we got them demanding to vote. That finally got attention. Here, where kids are failing wholesale through the cracks or chasms; dropping out of sight; becoming fodder for jails; people say they do not want to learn. The only ones who can dispel that notion are

the kids themselves. They, like Mrs. Hamer, Mrs. Devine, E. W. Steptoe, and others who changed the political face of Mississippi in the 1960s, have to demand what everyone says they don't want (Moses, 2001, p. 17).

I was reminded of Moses sharecropper analogy one morning at the high school when the ninth-grade Algebra Project teacher asked if I was available for lunch. Travis, a student in her third block had requested a meeting. "Sure," I said, "What's it about?"

The teacher answered, "He has some concerns with the class and wants to talk about it."

I went to McDonald's (per his request) to pick up lunch, and we met in my office. Travis, a small skinny 14-year-old didn't say much at first. Nor did he touch his lunch. Anxious about his silence, I asked, "So we are here to discuss some things happening in the class? What is upsetting you?"

Finally he said, it's Ms. K. (Ms. K. is a part of a service corps organization that places young adults in urban schools as mentors and teacher assistants.) The Algebra Project teacher indicated that Ms. K and Travis had some confrontations in the class.

"She's always 'agging on me. . . and gets too close, and asks me a question and won't even give me time to answer. I need a minute okay?'" he blurted out.

It was important to Travis to explain to his teacher why he "was acting up" in class. But, he demanded that his side be heard too. He reflected on what might make the relationship work better. "Maybe if she knew more about me," he offered. "But she has to be more patient too. It's not like I always have to share my story, you know?"

The teacher and Travis came up with a plan to address his needs. Travis took his lunch and headed back to the courtyard for the end of the lunch period. "How come he didn't eat his lunch?" I asked the teacher. She replied, "Because he wanted to find his sister and split it with her." I am the learner, again,

The Work is Process Based, Not Event Based

"Ella Baker spent her entire life trying to 'change the system.' Somewhere along the way she recognized that her goal was not a single 'end' but rather an ongoing 'means,' that is a process. Radical change for Ella Baker was about a persistent and protracted process of discourse, debate, consensus, reflection, and struggle" (Ransby, 2003, p. 1). In a national, local, school and university world that emphasizes metrics and outcomes, it is hard not to be distracted by focusing on "the event." But heeding the works of Baker and Moses, our project emphasized that this is a collaborative partnership that fluctuates to meet the ever-changing needs of our students and the community. It is simultaneously addressing both personal experiences and systemic change. The processes are illustrated not in rhetoric, but in action. And, despite pacing guides and measurable outcomes, as Moses says, sometimes you have to "slow the bus down" (Wynne, 2009, p. 92) so everyone can get on board.

One of the best examples of understanding the concept of the work as a process, not an event, includes involving parents. I'm pretty certain that every education program has something written about "increasing parental engagement." But, what does that look like? As an educator working with both pre-service and current teachers, I am frequently frustrated by the repeated banter of "blaming the parents." As we strive to recognize the brilliance and experience of our students, are we doing the same to recognize the gifts our parents bring to the process? Do we honor their lived experience, so often struggling against social and economic barriers that prevent what hegemonic institutions typically define as "involvement?" Do we pause, make space, and provide opportunities to learn from our parents? Do we visit them in their communities or do we demand that they come to the school?

Schools host parent "events" throughout the year, but they are hardly engaging. Outside of "Back to School Night" where parents meet with their child's teachers, parent nights typically consist of mandatory meetings held in an auditorium where parents sign in and watch a prescriptive PowerPoint on what it takes for their students to graduate, be successful, and so on. In true hegemonic fashion, parents and their children are talked to, not with, and little space for dialogue is included. Do we ever ask parents "what they thought or wanted to do about their children's education?" (Wynne p. 230). Typically, no, and after the last slide, everyone scurries out the door; another parent night, check.

At our high school, we tried some alternative methods such as a family night in the garden, where the school jazz band played; the culinary program cooked a meal based on ingredients from the garden; and students, demonstrating their knowledge, led the guests through the Aquaponics labs. We were gathering enthusiasm; the attendance was growing. They were nice events. But that was the problem, they were just events. And only nice. We weren't really making progress on equity in education, on collaboration, on engagement, on talking about the tough stuff that impacted their children. We weren't creating opportunities to learn from the parents.

We managed to experience small successes with the Algebra Project. We were preparing for our third cohort of students. It was the spring of 2014, and we collaborated with the principal of the Middle School to host an Algebra Project information night for parents and students. Under Moses's direction, we soon realized that we were not going to host an information session; rather, students would demonstrate the information. About 10 current

Algebra Project students set up workstations around the school's media center. Immediately, before there was a "welcome" or "introductions" or anything else typically found on an agenda, the guests, parents, and students, were greeted by an AP student at the door and were given an explanation of what was happening around the room. The parents and the students were led to individual stations where they engaged in the math lesson (height charters, polynomials, road coloring, graphing calculators, etc.) taught by one of the current 9th or 10th grade AP students. It was miraculous. Parents asked probing questions to the students and made comments such as: "Wish I had learned math this way." Or "You really know and understand what you are talking about don't you?" The event was a success. Over 40 parents, students, community members, and teachers attended.

But, we missed the mark again. We didn't embrace the principle that this is a process not an event. We had hoped to use this "event" as an opportunity to recruit a new in-coming ninth grade cohort to participate in our summer induction program. We made phone calls, sent flyers, and visited homes asking students to participate in our Algebra Project summer induction program. That included facilitation from Moses, the new AP math teacher, six visiting teachers from Ireland who were interested in learning more about the Algebra Project and FIU graduate students who would facilitate lessons on science and civics. Despite all, our efforts and what we thought sounded like a great program, despite many enthusiastic responses to our invitation, on the first day participation was minimal. We were missing the parent advocate.

Enter Angela Mays. While we have been blessed to know and work with Ms. Mays for the last few years, it was in the summer of 2014, when she met Bob Moses that our relationship with her became a game changer. When we began the 2014 summer induction program for our third cohort of Algebra Project students, only five kids showed up. Moses and Mays hit the streets, making home visits, and spending time in the community with students and families. By the end of the week, we had 25 in-coming ninth graders (20 boys and 5 girls) showing up every day, on time, even early and engaged. Angela Mays is our city's Fannie Lou Hammer. Mays is a resident of the historical Black community we serve and grew up in both that community as well as the oldest Black community in the city. She is a mother, grandmother, and auntie to almost every child in the community. Mays is the founder of a community wide parental engagement organization, and she graciously taught us that, "It's on us to get to know parents." By the end of the week, we had parents volunteering in the class and asking the football coach to require their football-playing son to come to the summer institute before attending practice. So, yes, it is a process not an event that will make the change we want to see in the world.

Students as knowledge workers +
"Each One Teach One"

Positioning students as knowledge workers, employed as often as possible, for using their knowledge guided the project's work. Students engaged in the "each one teach one" model, originally designed by AP and the Young People's Project, where youth teach their peers, younger students, even parents and other adults. It became the signature of the Education Effects philosophy. Applying this principle contributed to the exponential growth and reach of our Aquaponics Lab and Organic Garden. Supporting students' interest and mastery in sciences and bringing the classroom "to life," we established the most comprehensive Aquaponics Lab in the county; positioning students as action researchers addressing urgent issues around health, food justice, and sustainability.

Camilla, a recent graduate of the school, who is now studying bioengineering at another university reported:

> We would come across plant problems such as nematodes, which destroyed our tomatoes. So, we planted a counter plant [so the tomatoes could grow]. I went to New Mexico to attend the Rooted in Community Conference, where I learned skills and concepts about food justice and protesting, along with the intergenerational richness in education [Referring here to The Rooted Conference's involvement in conversations and collaborations with Native American elders in the community]. We want to see changes in our community, and we desire to have the necessary skills to do so (personal correspondence).

The lab and garden have become a centerpiece for experiential learning across a variety of disciplines including science, art, and design, culinary arts and civic engagement. A science teacher wrote:

> Students have taken ownership of their projects . . . Parents come up to me and say, 'I know exactly what my son learned today because he came home and told me all about it and now we are growing our own herbs.' They are not just leaving their knowledge at the school; they have been bringing it home with them to their community and have spread the knowledge they have obtained (personal correspondence).

Jermaine, a recent graduate from our high school who now is employed as the coordinator for the lab and garden explained:

> The opportunity to work at the garden has expanded my knowledge and passion. It has given me a chance to reflect on my community and life. How can I make a difference in this garden? My co-workers have been an

incredible team who have worked hard and with love. And that is reflected in the outstanding growth of every plant and tree in our beautiful garden.

As knowledge workers, our students are leading the way in challenging the crippling representations and misrepresentations of their community (Lovett and Squier, 2010). "The activities gave our school a name for itself. Proving for a fact that we are more than the stereotype of violence and lack of education," said Anthony (personal correspondence).

Students like Anthony made me aware that confronting those misrepresentations do not only take place in the realm of media or the greater community, they also take place in the classroom. As, I was preparing for our presentation at a national conference with two ninth-grade Algebra Project students, Alvin, a quiet thoughtful young man with a grin that covers his whole face, when you are fortunate enough to catch it, was very hesitant to speak. His best friend, Terrell, was trying to encourage him to get over his shyness. "Listen, when I was in elementary, I wouldn't speak up either. Even if I knew the answer, and usually I did, I just didn't want to say anything. Then, I don't know, in middle school, I just realized I had to show 'em'." While the purpose of his words was to encourage his friend, once again, it was I who learned. Terrell, who is 16 and in ninth grade had been held back twice. As I heard his story, I thought: that is why he was held back, not because he didn't know, but because we, educators in his path, didn't listen. We did not deeply listen to his silence; open ourselves to learning from him.

When it came time for the students to speak in the conference, I was nervous. Actually, I was nervous the whole time, I always am when I present. Did I say "um" a lot? I think of Matthew. Terrell knew this about me and from his place in the front row, kept giving me the "thumbs up" sign of encouragement. So, when it was time for the students to speak, I wondered if they were nervous too. I didn't want our kids to feel put on the spot. Most of the other students participating in the conference were seniors in high school or in college or a university. Our kids were in ninth grade. Yet without hesitation, when I paused, Terrell stood up. Terrell, at over 6 feet tall and 200 pounds and a star on the football team, which is what he is "known for" in the school, said:

> This work has given me the opportunity to show what I know. To be in the Algebra Project class and talk about the math; to learn and show what I am learning and what I know. And help my classmates. It's given me confidence to speak up. That's made a big difference in my life.

When we were heading home from the conference, I asked Terrell what he liked most from the weekend. The weekend was filled with workshops on hip hop, athletics, dinners out, time spent with his mentor, and his first time on an airplane. "My favorite part was our speech in the presentation," he said.

It's not what I expected him to say. And that's the point about my being *specific*; I keep on pushin' but mostly, I keep on learning.

I end with one last story. One afternoon, in their closing circle, the Algebra Project teacher was leading the "shout outs." One student next to me asked, "Where is Mr. Bob? Where did Mr. Bob go?" The AP teacher explained that he was preparing for a talk to be given in a few hours, and he would be back tomorrow. Students proclaimed: "Shout out for Mr. Bob! For being here and teaching with us." Later that evening, I shared the story with Moses: "They missed me, huh? That's nice." He smiled big. A big quiet, smile like Alvin shares.

Like Moses, I too, feel that "It is the voices of the young people I hear every day, more than anything, that give me hope" (Moses in Wynne p. 236, 2012). Those voices, along with our teachers' voices, now, give the Education Effect hope too. If that hope becomes a reality, then, we will be effective after all.

References

Freire, P. (1970). *Pedagogy of the Oppressed.* New York: Herder and Herder.

Jay, P. (Senior Editor). (June 20, 2014). *News Program.* Baltimore: Real News. *The Mississippi Freedom Summer – Bob Moses on Reality Asserts Itself.* http://therealnews.com/t2/index.php?option=com_content&task=view&id=31&Iemid=74&jumival=12034

Lovett, M. and Squier, J. (2010). Writing with video. In Cope, B. and Kalantzis, M. (Eds.). *Ubiquitous Learning.* Urbana, IL: University of Illinois Press.

Moses, R. P. (2010). Constitutional Property v. Constitutional People. In Perry, T. Moses, R. P., Wynne, J. T., Cortez, E., and Delpit, L. (Eds.). *Quality Education as a Constitutional Right: Creating a Grassroots Movement to Transform Public Schools.*

Moses, R. P. (2014). Keynote address. Educational Testing Service: Institute for Student Achievement, Summer Institute. Princeton.

Moses, R. P. and Cobb, C. E. Jr. (2001). *Radical Equations: Civil Rights from Mississippi to the Algebra Project.* Boston: Beacon Press.

O'Connor, J. (Host). (2014, July 28). State Impact: A Q & A With Activist And AlgebraProject Founder Bob Moses [Radio broadcast episode]. http://stateimpact.npr.org/florida/2014/07/28/a-q-a-with-activist-and-algebraproject-founder-bob-moses/

Moses R. & The Algebra Project. (July 15, 2007). *NOW with David Brancaccio.* New York: PBS.

Ransby, B. (2003). *Ella Baker & the Black Freedom Movement: A radical democratic vision.* Chapel Hill, NC: The University of North Carolina Press.

Southern Education Foundation (2013). A New Majority, Low Income Students in theSouth and the Nation. October 2013.

West, M. (2012) The Algebra Project cohort assessment. National Science Foundation Report (NSF/DRK12).

Wynne, J. T. (2005). The Elephant in the Classroom: Racism in School Reform. In Dowdy, J. K. and Wynne, J. T. (Eds.). *Racism, Research, & Educational Reform: Voices from the City.* New York: Peter Lang Publishing, Inc. pp. 58–88.

Wynne, J. (2009). Grassroots leadership for the 21st century: Leading by not leading. In I. M. Selah & M. S Khine (Eds.). *Transformative leadership and educational excellence: Learning organizations in the information age.* The Netherlands: Sense Publications.

Wynne, J. (2012). Introduction. In: Wynne, J., Delpit, L., and Miles, R. (Eds.). *Confessions of a White Educator: Stories in Search of Justice and Diversity.* Dubuque, IA: Kendall Hunt.

Wynne, J. T. and Giles, J. (2010). Stories of collaboration and research within an Algebra Project context: Offering quality education to students pushed to the bottom of academic achievement. In Perry, T., Moses, R. P., Wynne, J. T., Cortés, E. Jr., and Delpit, L. (Eds.). *Quality Education as a Constitutional Right: Creating a Grassroots Movement to Transform Public Schools.* Boston: Beacon Press. pp. 146–166.

Living with the tensions of hope and despair

by Joan T. Wynne

"The United States is a racist country and because of that, I, as a White person, am the beneficiary of power and privileges that have an adverse effect on citizens of color" (2014, p. 10). I have begun opening presentations I make to any audience, at national conferences or in university classes, with that sentence, one that a young writer for *The Nation*, Mychal Denzel Smith, has persuaded me is a necessary starting place for any White person who wants to unravel racism in our society.

Because of my life-long journey of "un-learning" racism, I find his sentence to be essential and pertinent also to my writing for this book. The sentence reminds me that a southern White woman, creating a chapter on the impact of racism on the college experience of Black students seems arrogant and a bit preposterous. So before I can address the topic, I must admit that anything I say comes tempered by the reality that I can never fully understand the impact of racism on these students. I can read and cite the research about it. I can do my own research about it. I can observe it in my classrooms; but, because of my unearned power and privilege, I can never really know it as my African-American and Black students do. In this chapter, though, I will describe what I do know in hopes it might be valuable to practitioners, especially to people who look like me and who care about eliminating racism—not only to better teach Black students, but also to rid ourselves of the pathology that we, not African-Americans, have carried within our national DNA for centuries.

The late singer and stalwart activist, Pete Seeger, once said in an interview that "The key to the future of the world is finding the optimistic stories and letting them be known" (2014, p. A20). I intend to do just that. Yet, before telling those stories, I'm driven to depict another facet of our dilemma as activists. That dilemma seems to demand a recognition of the tension between the hopeful and the discouraging. For, to fully understand the optimistic stories, we, first, must wrestle with the difficult and sometimes sinister things that confront us all in a hegemonic world. Thus, the beginning of this chapter addresses my observations of the negative consequences of the dominant culture's institutions on Black students. Later, the optimistic stories emerge illustrating the philosophy and pedagogy that can be effective in creating environments that support the intellectual achievements of Black students, stories that also include the wisdom of students (Focus, 2014) who have informed my exploration of the dilemma.

The Ominous

Because I now live in Florida where within an 18 month span, two unarmed Black teenage boys were murdered—one, Trayvon Martin (Robles 2012 p. A2), for walking while Black in a mostly all-White neighborhood, and another, Jordan Davis (Hsieh, 2014), for playing loud music in a car—I am more dedicated than ever to understanding how racism plays a part not only in the mis-education of our African-American children, but in the mis-education of our Anglo children who are schooled to become adults who can "stand their ground" to murder Black boys or who can serve as masters of judicial systems that legitimize these murders.

What kind of schooling is needed for White Americans to stand up for protecting the lives of all children? Racism is a blight on this nation, and a blight on any intellectual who sits silently as her Black students' very lives are daily threatened. That threat never seems more clearly stated than in the words of Ella Baker, who said: "We who believe in freedom cannot rest, until the killing of Black men, Black mothers' sons is as important as the killing of White men, White mothers' sons" (Ransby 2003, p. 335). Those words constantly challenge me to dig deeper, to explore abusive schooling more urgently, whenever I write about the education of Black students, and, indeed, about the education of any mother's child. For, all of our children are at stake at different levels—those who are being victimized by demoralizing education and violence, and the integrity of those whose education is so severely distorted that many later become either the perpetrators or the protectors of violence against Black children. If not addressed in the classroom, the tentacles of White Supremacy, that strangle the K-16 system of public and private education, leave no one undiminished by the destructive powers of the dominant culture. And the dearth of disciplined discussion about it allows and encourages a divisive nation.

Civil Rights icon and President of The Algebra Project, Bob Moses, in a keynote address at a public forum explained the dire consequences of bad education for our Black, Brown, and White, poor children. During his address, Moses reported,

> The Southern Educational Fund looked at a 40-year period from 1970 to 2010 and asked the question who gets a B.A.? Not who goes to college, but who gets a B.A.? They answered it in terms of the quartiles, the top economic quartile and the bottom economic quartile. In 1970, 40% of the top economic quartile got their B.A.s. Forty years later 80% received it. It doubled over this 40-year period. In 1970, 7% of the bottom quartile got B.A.s. *Forty years later in 2010, only 9% of the bottom quartile graduated from college* (Moses, 2014).

With that grim 40 year record of sorry education delivered to our students at the bottom, can we continue to pretend that we are a democratic nation who offers quality education to all its people? Or will we continue to blame the victims for this travesty of unequal opportunity?

In other chapters of this book, K-12 racist realities are addressed, especially the horrific criminalizing of our young children, paving the way for a corporate school-to-prison pipeline. So my chapter is not intended to address K-12 schooling. Yet, I must share here one of the more shocking statistics, that I only recently discovered. A Department of Education report in March, 2014 declared that "Black children represent 18 percent of preschool enrollment, but 42 percent of the preschool children suspended once, and 48 percent of the preschool children suspended more than once" (Civil Rights Data 2014). Really? Suspending virtual toddlers? What is wrong with a nation that cannot deal with three to five year olds? And what kind of nation keeps the doors open to pre-schools that don't know how to nurture or discipline children who not too long ago have just learned to talk and walk? But still a stunning silence exists in mainstream corridors of this country about the exploitation of our children of color.

With these kinds of child abuse, institutionalized racism is crucial to any legitimate study of quality education for all children. Moreover, these debacles in K-12 severely impact the opportunities for African-American students to attend and succeed in college, long before they are of age to enroll. Recently, California published a snapshot of their state's manifestations of systemic racism on Black students in their universities (Rivera 2013):

- Blacks have the lowest completion rates for freshman and transfer students at all three higher education segments: community colleges, California State University and the University of California.
- Black students are more likely than any other group to attend college without ever earning a degree.
- The achievement gap between Blacks and Whites earning a bachelor's degree or higher has narrowed by only a percentage point over the last decade. In 2011, about 24% of Black adults had obtained a bachelor's compared with 41% of Whites. [Opportunity gap, not achievement gap, probably more aptly describes this dilemma.]

- Black students appear to have been disproportionately affected by policy decisions such as the state ban on affirmative action in education and budget cuts in recent years that resulted in significant declines in enrollment at community colleges and Cal State campuses.

- Reluctance on the part of policy makers and educators to tackle racial disparities head-on is one factor in the persistent gaps, said Michele Siqueiros, executive director of the Campaign for College Opportunity.

- "I've come to be more convinced of an inability to really address these issues more openly in a way that forces state policy makers to come up with ideas and colleges to find solutions," Siqueiros said. "Especially after the ban on affirmative action, we don't feel comfortable talking about race and nothing really happens."

So where do we go from here? How do we more effectively consider the difficult issues in order to integrate our sense of humanity into the optimistic and the hopeful?

Focus Groups

Thinking about that challenge propelled me to first elicit the wisdom of my Black students, to include their voices in the publication. Sixty-seven percent of the students in the university where I now teach are Hispanic/Latino students. But many of my Black students come from the Caribbean Islands—Cuba, Trinidad, Jamaica, Haiti. Some are African-American. However, because of scheduling conflicts, (two months to finalize respondents' available dates) and because of a fear by some students that this confidential conversation might somehow, by some participant, be revealed, only seven students joined the focus groups. Their fear of disclosure reminded me of the treacherous terrain that many of our students travel. Finally, though, four of the seven students who were able to participate in focus groups were Black students from the Caribbean and three identified themselves as African-American. Some were still attending my present university; some had attended Primarily White Universities (PWI) in other parts of the state.

James Baldwin once insisted that ". . . while the tale of how we suffer and how we are delighted and how we triumph is never new, it must be heard. There isn't any other tale to tell, it's the only light we've got in all this darkness" (1995). Guided by his perspective, I invited the focus students to share their stories of navigating the university system. I wanted to hear their insights about the challenges of dealing with covert and/or overt racist behavior and attitudes while attempting academic success in a PWI. Though this university is considered a minority institution, the majority of its Hispanic/Latino population describe themselves as White Hispanic and in the particular city where most of them live, they hold power and privilege that doesn't exist for them elsewhere in the state. Therefore, many of the Hispanics in classroom discussions originally report that they never think about themselves as victims of racism.

Though, like Beverly Tatum (1997), President of Spelman College, I believe the darkness of racism and its consequences in schools is all around us. It's the elephant in the classroom that no one wants to talk about out loud. And, like Baldwin, I think the stories of those who suffer racism in our schools must be heard. They must be heard over and over until the nation commits to reckoning with its 400 unrelenting years of bloody, racist history. As a developing democracy, to move forward from the darkness of that history into the light of liberation may lie in our willingness to listen deeply and well and to learn from the collective stories of "suffering, delight, and triumph."

Therefore, my goals for initiating these focus groups were:

1. To explore the dynamic of and discoveries from intentional conversations among those who have experienced overt and/or covert racism in schools and universities.

2. To listen for any mention of schisms that often occur between African-Americans and Caribbean Blacks in my classroom and in many U.S. urban universities.

3. To learn from students' stories of specific challenges they have faced that I may not have recognized as a professor from the dominant culture.

Conversations involving the two focus groups began with the same guiding question: Can you describe any specific challenges that you faced because of overt or covert racism in your university experience?

Emergent Themes

Four themes seemed to evolve throughout the dialogue among respondents in both groups: Isolation; Struggles to name racism; Exhaustion from playing expected roles; and Schisms between Black cultures.

I. Isolation

Often, the sense of isolation was addressed, an isolation that Black students felt as a consequence of being in a PWI, where no one, professors nor students, assumed a responsibility to reach out to them. As one respondent explained about the classroom, "And so it seemed like you were just kind of by yourself, just doing your own thing. Everybody would kind of group up together, people that weren't Black or whatever, and you would just kind of be sitting there on your own."

One of the doctoral candidates told the story of attending an educational conference, sitting in a restaurant talking to two White female participants. While she sat with them, a White male later joined their table, spoke and looked directly at the other women, yet never acknowledged her presence, as though she were invisible. The other women shifted their attention to him and never again spoke to her. Similar stories were cited by all seven focus participants, describing this isolation in classrooms, in cafeterias, at social events, at professional meetings, etc. However, their stories of determination to forge ahead and, indeed, achieve, might startle those who see these students only as victims, or incapable of academic achievement, or too sensitive about racism, or worse, somehow guilty for the nation's institutionalized racism.

II. Struggles to Name It

Yet, in the opening of each dialogue, an unexpected response emerged in the group. The respondents seemed initially somewhat unconscious of racist attitudes or behaviors at the university. It took the telling of many stories among them to unravel the obvious. As one student explained, "Because it hasn't been so overt, it is hard for me to think of an incident." When stories began to unfold in the conversation about specific encounters they had experienced when relating to White professors and students or White Hispanic/Latinos either at the university or at their employment, all respondents initially used expressions like "I don't think this was racist; it may have just been ignorance."

One of the students' reflections of an experience during her undergraduate program explained her struggle to understand the motivation of the advice of her Anglo professor/advisor:

> For the dietitian program you put in bids for an internship . . . So you pick your three and you pray that you get into one of those three. Okay. And so to the professor, I was like well this place gives a voucher so you get a certain amount of money every month. She kept saying, "No, no, don't pick that one. . . .You're definitely not going to get into that one." Okay. Well, what about this one? "No, no, no don't do that one." And you know you're thinking that the professor knows best but then kind of in the back of your head you're like is she being racist? You're not really sure because this is a person that's above you . . . your professor that you've been with for the last year. So you're like well, I guess I'm just going to pick these three that she thinks are the only ones I can do—not really knowing if, maybe, I could have done one of my first three choices. . . . Maybe it was racism. Maybe it's not. I still really don't know. I kind of feel like maybe it was though.

Another student told a story about White students from her high school whom she knew well, but who once on the same PWI campus with her, went their separate ways and never befriended her again. She commented that she didn't "know if this would be called racism, but I never had any White friends approach me in college." Later she told a story of being one of three Black students in a majority "White Hispanics" graduate course, where students were encouraged to complete research projects with others who were interested in the same research topic. She said that the three Black students remained alone in their group with no one else gravitating toward their research. Again, she said she assumed the Cuban Americans still were uncomfortable working alongside Black students, but insisted it might have been for other reasons. She seemed unwilling to suggest that the reason could be an unconscious undercurrent of racist "othering" by those students.

Her ambiguity about how to describe a reality that society denies exists, echoed previous comments from other Black students in my classrooms after they finish reading, *Other People's Children* (Delpit 1995). In the 16 years I've been using that book in courses, most of my Black students react similarly to it. Each, using different words or phrases, confirms what one Ph.D. student succinctly remarked, with tears rolling down her cheeks, "I thought I was crazy until I read her book. She says what I have been feeling all of my life, but I thought I was crazy." The waltz forced on Black students to dance around covert racist attitudes and behaviors sometimes makes them feel schizophrenic. They want to achieve in college. Indeed, their families expect them to. Yet these barriers to experiencing a "typical college life" often makes Black students question their judgment of reality; sometimes making them feel "crazy."

One respondent explained, "You don't know what that is so you question yourself. . . .you've come from a school where everyone is Black and all of the teachers around you are Black, and the administration is Black. So you don't know what racism is. You've seen it on TV. You've heard about it before but to actually experience it in a White college. . ."

A graduate student suggested, "There's an undercurrent working behind the scenes all of the time that we have kind of figured out it's there. We don't see it exactly but we also know that you have to do certain things when you navigate that current. So even if you don't see the current happening . . . you know you've got to perform better. You have to be sure everything is on the up and up."

In one group session, respondents discussed how they often ignore or mentally question assumptions that other cultures make about them, whenever Black students are in a room with predominantly White people. One Ph.D. student/respondent suggested:

And it's more micro aggressive, I guess. . . . Not only am I here for some of my degree, but I'm working here. And a lot of times I walk into a room, and I just feel this automatic assumption arises that "you don't know as much as we do." And I look around as to who else is in the same position as I am, and I think I can count on one hand how many Black descended individuals who are ITs [Instructional Technicians]. So I just wonder a lot of times with them, are you presuming that I don't know this because I'm Black? Or are you just presuming I don't know this because I don't know it . . . I look at my resume and I'm like, well, I think I pretty much accounted for what I know. And, I think, you guys have tested me enough by now. You still shouldn't be looking at me and wondering those types of things as to what it is I'm capable of. So I experienced more that than anything else on this campus.

Another respondent, who also works at the university, explained a further dimension of work experiences for Blacks in a White environment:

. . . . I probably wouldn't call some of the things that I've experienced racism per se. . . . What I think in terms of experience here, what I've noticed for myself, my assistant is Hispanic, White Hispanic. And I know whenever we go out together if we have an appointment to go someplace to a meeting they assume she is Dr. _____. Or if we're both in my office and we're expecting someone to come in, they assume that she is Dr. _____, although I'm behind the desk, and she's sitting in front of me. So I find it very interesting.

Her comment suggests the convolutions that students mentally juggle as they try to navigate a system where institutional racism pervades, yet is always masked as the victim's problem, not an institutional structural trap.

Nevertheless, in both focus groups, as the conversations evolved, tales of overt racism unfolded, but most were instances that had happened at PWI's that they had previously attended in another part of the state. One respondent mentioned, "And so the newspaper there, the cartoonist did this little cartoon with Condoleezza Rice and Kanye West and basically painted them monkeys." Another student reported the unabashed and pervasive flying of Confederate flags on homes and cars in another city in the state. Many, however, cited instances of racist pictures or discussions on *Facebook* pages of White students with whom they now attend classes. Several mentioned their surprise when their White peers "befriended" them on Facebook yet sooner or later posted unmistakable, racist comments: "Sally is always nice to me and stuff. But then I look on her Facebook page and she's got some racist monkey picture of Obama and I'm like, 'Man, I never would have thought Sally was thinking like that.'" Another respondent commented, "I don't know. It seems like social media to me is helping to refuel racism."

Nevertheless, in an e-mail, sent after her participation in the focus group, a respondent unknowingly corroborated my observation of the respondents' struggles to clearly identify racism. She remarked that "Throughout the conversation we reflected on multiple incidents and wrestled with being able to say it was covert, overt or simply racism at all. As college students we experienced both types of racism, weathered all of the side effects and still could not name or simply call it out. If we can't name it, how can we change it?"

III. Exhaustion from Playing the Role of Hostess

In one focus group, the metaphor of hostess, one also introduced in bell hooks' text,[14] emerged as a thread to explain the mainstream culture's implicit expectation of the chief role of Black students, and Black people in general, whenever they are in the room with White Americans.

Respondent A: But that every time you go to a new group there is that constant need to prove yourself. . . . Yeah, it does a toll emotionally as far as being tiring because then once you realize ain't nobody else hosting. Nobody else cares about what they say to people around here why should I care about what I say?

Respondent B: Right. And it's tiring, right . . . the fact that sometimes you're put in the position to make people comfortable. Yeah, it is like being the hostess. I have to make you comfortable so you can be comfortable with me. That's tiring. So it's like you're at a party and you have to host everybody. That would be tiring. I mean you want to be a guest. You want to be a guest. So that sometimes you do and sometimes you don't, I'm not tired today. Other times I'm tired, but I'm not doing it today, so I'm not hosting, I'm a guest.

Respondent A: And that's when problems usually start.

Respondent B: Right. Who does she think she is? She thinks she belongs. I mean no one is saying this, but the look is like, 'Oh she looks comfortable here. Why is she so comfortable here?' Because you know what, I'm a guest today. I'm not hosting.

(Group Laughter)

Respondent C: I'm telling you we can't have a day off.

Respondent B: No. And then people wonder why people are so comfortable, and they let their hair down with people from their own cultures— because [when you're with your own culture] you don't have to host. We all are guests. But we need to be able to intermingle with other cultures as guests, not a host and a guest, a host and a guest, a host and a guest.

Respondent A: How can we all get invited to the party? ... And leave somebody else to host? Or why have a host at all? Let's just all show up.

The act of hosting, (a flip of the use of the metaphor by hooks) of having to make everyone else feel comfortable in a room, seemed to speak to the mainstream notion that Blacks should not show competence nor aloofness, irritation, and certainly, not anger. To the contrary, the unspoken and maybe unconscious notion is that Blacks should continue to take care of people, as they for centuries in the south were demanded to do. This unconscious yet structural racist belief system continues to wear many Black students down; to make them "tired."

IV. Schisms between Black Cultures

During the focus groups, subtle tensions surfaced between those who identified more with African-American culture versus those who identified primarily with a Caribbean Island culture. In each group, students acknowledged those tensions existed at the university and in the city. Exploring some of the assumptions that created the divisions shaped a great deal of the conversation. At Morehouse College, I had noticed the same division between African-American students and students and professors from various countries in Africa. In her book, *Teaching Community: A Pedagogy of Hope*, hooks explains: "Dominator culture has tried to keep us all afraid, to make us choose safety instead of risk, sameness instead of diversity" (2003, p. 33). That fear and practice bubbled up in each focus group around attitudes of Caribbean and African-Americans toward each other.

An African-American student explained: "That's kind of what we were talking about earlier about Caribbean's not associating themselves with African-Americans. Like oh, no I'm not African-American, I'm Haitian. I'm not African-American, I'm Jamaican. So it's like still separating ourselves while we should be cohesive."

One respondent explained her epiphany as a Jamaican-born student who attended K-16 schools in Florida:

> My family is Jamaican and I was taught you are not African-American and neither do you want to be African-American. You want to make sure that folks know that you're Caribbean; you're Jamaican; you're other. And, of course, I think going to ___ U definitely snapped it out of me because when people looked at me and they left two seats empty they weren't saying, 'Oh there's the Jamaican girl.' No, they're thinking, 'Oh she's Black. She's got a big afro; we don't want to sit next to her'. . . . . . that's a conversation on a whole that we need to have more as a people and what does it mean to actually be Black in America period. Like I said, after seeing myself for 12 years

of schooling here as a Jamaican, and socializing only with Jamaicans, I experienced a rude awakening when I attended ___ U. That's when I began to identify myself differently, as a Black woman . . . devoted to the struggle.

In the other focus group, a Caribbean student explained, "You hear all of the bad things about African-Americans, they're lazy. They don't want to work. They use public assistance, blah, blah, blah. I'm going to be honest with you, we come with those thoughts. We come with those thoughts . . . What we didn't understand is the structure of racism, because we didn't have a structure of racism where we came from that impeded our development. So we didn't get it. And I didn't get it either . . . I don't think my parents even got it yet.

Later, the same respondent commented, "Yes, sometimes between African-American and immigrant Blacks there's some kind of division . . . . Like we're potentially better or we think we're better than other Blacks, especially African-Americans, right. But I think it's not about being better. I think it's just the fact that we're coming from an environment that's all about you ethnically. You've seen everyone who is powerful, doctors, lawyers, nurses, everybody is Black, and I really don't see that in this country. So [unlike African-Americans] I'm not yearning to see it because I've seen it before."

Several respondents suggested that student clubs that designated themselves as a specific ethnic culture such as Jamaican or African-American or Bahamian, etc. further complicated this issue of separation among Black students.

Yet, during these portions of the conversations, everyone seemed baffled by the oppressive behavior of White Hispanics/Latinos when interacting with Black students. All respondents insisted that whether they were from the islands or from America, if they were Black, the Hispanic culture did not accept nor befriend them. Whenever sharing scenarios about the deliberate choice of "White" Hispanic/Latino peers or professors to avoid them, the Black students all seemed to wonder what one respondent voiced, "How could you be participating in the very thing that other people are imposing on you?" Many insisted that they had heard Hispanic/Latino peers mention the shock of oppressive attitudes and behaviors they experienced when travelling outside the city into other parts of the state. The respondents suggested that the city seemed to provide a protective cocoon for its Hispanic/Latino population, and unless White Hispanics travelled beyond the city's boundaries, they were unable to see themselves as caught in the vice of hegemony. One of the focus participants insisted, "If they could just understand that if we all stood together, stood united, we could seriously change this system that oppresses all of us."

The Optimistic Stories

A week after the dialogue, a couple of respondents, when seeing me in the elevator, mentioned that they had continued to talk about the conversations from the focus group. They asked if we might reconvene, maybe meet with other students, and continue the conversation. They also mentioned that they had experienced a few epiphanies as a result of the dialogue about racism. We agreed to meet during the fall semester and talk again about how we might fit future dialogues into their busy university schedules. I also asked if they might e-mail a sentence or two describing those epiphanies. The following are their e-mailed responses:

Epiphanies

E-mail Respondent 1: A dialogue about racism can be difficult to have, considering in America we live in it constantly. It is often such a complex issue that it cannot be separated from everyday life. It can be blatant and obvious, but most of the time it is subtle and unclear. From the discussions I began to understand more about how I navigate the world—I recognize covert racist actions may be happening around me, but I do not give it much thought. If I do, it is often in the form of counter narrative stories that I run down as a list of why this action may have occurred. Often after reviewing the counter narratives list, it does come back down to "probably because I am Black." The dialogue discussion also provided me, a Black American, with some of the perspectives of Caribbean Blacks living in the U.S. The notion of cultural capital that Caribbean people gain from growing up in a society that is predominantly Black helped me understand what is often perceived by Black Americans as a "better than you" persona; it is simply a greater amount of cultural capital they are ingrained with from living in a society where they are not told they are "less than."

E-mail Respondent 2: Basically, the dialogue reminded me how "targeted" my social identities (race, gender, etc.) are here . . . and how psychologically exhausting it is to be a Black-female-professional or simply a human being in the U.S. This exhaustion, I think results in racial/ethnic minorities becoming hypersensitive to their environment, as a defense mechanism, to combat this racial-psychological warfare that exists in the U.S.

E-mail Respondent 3: . . . because of the dialogue I did remind myself that I have a voice; that I do not have to be bound by the contingencies or the constructs that others create for me. Nor do I need to subject myself to the one I created for myself. So, for that . . . I sincerely thank you!

These comments as well as the dialogue in both focus groups seemed to echo the concerns of many of my African-American and Black students during the 12 years of teaching at the present university. Re-reading the transcripts from this dialogue has helped me rethink my pedagogy and assumptions about tensions between students here. Reading the respondent's e-mails reminded me that, as Baldwin suggests, having space and time to tell the "tales" of struggle and triumphs around the issues of racism might be a necessary journey for many of our Black students at the university. And because such a space and time happens so rarely in classrooms, I've committed to co-create with interested students a professional learning community, where Black students can come together once or twice a month and address these issues by telling their stories.

Yet, having worked with Black students at a number of universities, the conversations during the focus groups offered no surprises about the racist culture in PWIs. Except when teaching at Morehouse, I have witnessed institutionalized racism on every plantation where I have taught. The surprise for me at PWIs has always been, not the abuse of students of color, but mainstream professors' unconsciousness of that abuse and of the hegemonic structures that undergird their own university life. My students have consistently validated this observation when they, during and at the end of my courses, challenge the nature of their college education with comments such as, "Why am I a graduating senior, and I have never engaged in conversations about racism and classism in any other courses?" or "I'm at the end of my Master's Program, and no other class has ever addressed issues of justice."

Thus, the dialogue with the focus groups seemed an affirmation of the practices and curriculum used in my classrooms. Both investigate the impact of institutionalized racism, classism, sexism, homophobia, etc. on education. Like Paulo Freire (2001), I believe that education is never politically neutral; it either supports the status quo or encourages transformation of our worlds. Included in that belief is the notion that anything we want to change must be addressed intentionally and directly within the classroom. If we don't name it, it sits there in defiance. Moreover, confronting justice issues can lead toward eliminating the structures that diminish our marginalized students and that also trap mainstream students into destructive notions of White Supremacy, mocking the nation's dreams of democracy.

Due largely to my experiences at Morehouse College and to my African-American mentors, who have over 30 years modeled for me a different way of being and of teaching in a compromised world, I have over the last 30 years developed course content and practices that many students have evaluated as successful. They claim the curriculum and the pedagogy have raised their consciousness about hegemony and have paved a road for them to become better teachers in their public school classrooms. Like bell hooks, I believe that "Moving through fear, finding out what connects us, revelling in our differences; this is the process that brings us closer, that gives us a world of shared values, of meaningful community" (2003, p. 197).

One of the college's Cuban-American graduate students, who was graduating from her Master's program at the university that semester, when responding to an assigned reading in one of my courses, posted the following on the on-line discussion site:

> ... the process of unlearning racism is a mind blowing experience. From the readings I've begun to realize the hidden truths about the way I treat some of my students. I had never considered myself racist in the past and yet like the teachers from this article, I would have never known the harm I was causing without taking a course like this and realizing I had to take a deeper look at my actions and thoughts. I know I still have a lot to learn but I have begun to see a change in my attitude towards my students and parents. I think that all teachers' especially new teachers coming into the classroom should be required to take a course like this. . . teachers are never truly prepared of how to deal with our underlying attitudes about students and parents. . . . I have lived it as a teacher in an urban school. In a city like _____where almost all the schools have such diverse populations of students, why is it that undergraduate students are not required to take an Urban education course? The article also states, "The teacher loses sight of her own power to teach all children, and she, unconsciously, sends messages to her students that they are unteachable". . . as an experienced teacher, I have been there as well and these types of courses are the ones that readjust our thinking and remind us that we are not "just" teachers . . .

Her comment is typical of other student responses about awakenings in these courses versus their disappointments in the curriculum of other college courses. However, I take little credit for these transformations because my content and practices come not from my own wisdom but the wisdom of my African-American mentors. They have deeply influenced my research and teaching.

Because of Asa G. Hilliard, III's work (Hilliard, 1995, 1998, 2014, pp. 25–38) and mentoring, I began to consider that no matter what I taught, I must address the hegemonic structures, policies, and practices of schooling; that it was not enough for me to discuss with my pre-service and in-service students the "how" of teaching, but I must also consider the "what" of teaching. Consequently, I integrate into all of my courses an historical perspective of how race was and is still being lived in America in order to invite my students into the struggle to liberate themselves and their students from the destruction of hegemonic systems.

From Lisa Delpit (1995, 2012; 2002), I learned the language to address issues of power and privilege that manifest themselves in schools and that cripple the achievement of our Black, Brown, and poor students in K-16 public and private schools. From observing her leadership style, I learned the value of deep listening to the "other"; of believing in the brilliance of every mother's child; of exposing White students to the reality that White Supremacy diminishes us all; of how to turn my anger toward racism into more creative, exploratory conversations; of understanding the value of humor and laughter while resisting hegemony; of taking no one too seriously, especially myself.

From Bob Moses (Moses, 2001; Wynne, 2012), I discovered the value of investigating the nation's historical records and the organizing tools of the Southern Freedom Movement (Harding, 1990; Wynne 2002, pp. 215–216) to teach the power and intellectual capacity of the people pushed to the bottom of society's academic and economic ladder. Through him, I learned the wisdom of Ella Baker and Fannie Lou Hamer, who believed that the people at the bottom often offered the most ingenious ideas (Ransby 2003). And through Moses, I realized that my responsibility included teaching teachers how to allow space and time for students at the bottom-quartile to wrestle with abstractions and to use their language, not their oppressor's, to demystify mathematical and interdisciplinary concepts, process, and design. From Moses, I also learned the "demand" side of education—that the children at the bottom, through disciplined study, must earn their right to become insurgents, to demand what the country says they don't want, a quality education; that advocacy is useful, but ultimately, significant change will only come when those at the bottom demand their constitutional rights as "constitutional people" (Moses 2014).

From Theresa Perry, I learned the imperative of teaching the "counter-narrative" to the nation's story of the history and education of African-Americans (Perry, 2004). Because of her retelling the history of African-Americans' passion for education, I began to flip the image of African-Americans from victims to liberators, engaged in a 400 year old struggle to educate themselves and to free the nation from oppressive policies and practices. Teaching that historical context in classrooms seems to create possibilities for a liberation journey for the teachers I teach and for the students they teach.

Pedagogy

For decades, I have designed practices that can mirror anti-hegemonic content. Instead of a "sage-on-stage" methodology, my courses offer student-centered, participatory engagement with each other, with me, and with the content. These practices are validated in most research about sound pedagogy for the teaching and learning of new ideas and skills (Weimer, 2002; Moffett, 1988; Becvar, 1997; Palmer, 2007). Nevertheless, these strategies primarily interest me as an intentional challenge to that which buoys authoritarian power in the classroom. Yet, at the same time, I insist that no one is force-fed any belief system or ideology, most especially my own. Refuting hegemony demands a delicate and disciplined dance of avoiding proselytizing and of honoring the organic nature of individual intellectual discovery. It demands a tolerance for ambiguity, for nuance, for living the question instead of the answer.

Circles as the Primary Instructional Structures

Typically at the university, most classrooms are set up with rows of desks facing the front of the room. On the first day of every class, before I introduce myself, I ask if anyone has ever heard the word "hegemony." Most often the collective answer is "No." After I explain what the word means, we explore the alignment of their desks as a hegemonic structure. Then, we, move the desks into a circle, while discussing the issues of power that the two distinct physical structures symbolize.

Afterwards, we introduce ourselves as peers in the teaching/learning process. Though, I admit during this portion that the power of the letter grade demanded by the university, students, and parents, hands the professor an unequal tool of power (Later in the course, we explore how to banish or transform this evaluative, subjective "sorting" tool.) We continue by discussing mutual course expectations; what we each hope to learn; what must happen in the class for them and me to feel that the class time has been well spent.

Collaborative learning and teaching

To counteract institutionalized isolation, self-aggrandizement, unhealthy competition, I introduce the value of collaboration in intellectual explorations. Time is spent inviting students to complete a Group Process form that addresses their past experience with groups; their frustrations; the expectations for each members' participation; the strengths each brings to the group; and what must happen for the group experience to be valuable for them? After completing the form, students create groups of 5, charged to include people from unfamiliar cultures. Groups then are asked to go anywhere inside or outside the classroom for 20 minutes and discuss their questionnaires and create a group name. Afterwards, groups report their experiences to the class, discussing roles that can lead to high performing teams.

Because in most cultures, "breaking bread" together is a sacred ritual that helps create community, an out-of-class assignment is to dine together with their small group, while discussing the theme of their collaborative research projects, data collection and analysis, and responsibilities of each researcher. Also because I believe this ritual is significant for creating community, I bring food to share each session. Our last class is spent sharing dinner at my home.

Written Responses to Selected Readings

The content of the course is partially grounded in the readings that require written responses posted on an on-line site, where participants can offer feedback. Their guidelines for the responses are to consider: Which ideas seem compelling and why; which ideas made them uncomfortable and why; what questions arose as a result of the reading? This practice of writing and response seems to foster the growth of their critical thinking skills; deepens their knowledge of issues; and supports the philosophy that their classmates' responses to their ideas are as significant as the professor's. They are also asked to recommend articles that they feel are pertinent for us to read concerning the issues being studied.

Music

From teaching in high school, at Morehouse College, and studying the Southern Freedom Movement, I learned that music is an integral part of the African culture (Wynne 2002). A number of studies also indicate that the use of music effectively facilitates the discussion of difficult concepts and skills (Moffett, 1991; Gardner, 2008). To create a welcoming space for all cultures as well as to use effective tools to study abstractions, I share music, whose themes I believe relate to concepts we are exploring. Later, students bring their music to explain concepts being investigated. Students repeatedly insist that music helped them better explore and remember theories like "Critical Race Theory" or "Culturally Responsive Pedagogy."

Videos

To keep ideas current, and because we live in a digital age, I include videos that are relevant to many issues being studied, from educational sites, Youtube. org, and TED.com. Videos like Howard Zinn's, *the People Speak* (Zinn, 2010) have become a staple in my curriculum. Within such videos, students can learn the variety of freedom struggles in this country and can begin forming their own sense of social agency. The videos are always followed by open-ended questions that students consider with their small groups. They continuously evaluate the videos, suggesting the "good, bad, and ugly" of each.

What Worked? What Did Not Work?

The last five minutes of each session is devoted to the students anonymously writing what activities or discussions worked for them; and what did not work. This evaluation helps us understand that teaching/learning is a continuous cycle of success and failure. And that my growth as a professional is tied to their honest reflection on how the class either facilitated or hindered their learning. This mechanism, I believe, reminds me and my students to see ourselves more clearly as peers in the struggle for truth.

Mantra at the End

From studying African-centered curriculum and practices, I became a believer in the power of affirmations. Because that and studying the Southern Freedom Movement convinced me of the value of community building in educational spaces, I end all sessions, with us standing in a circle, repeating the mantra, "None of us is as strong as all of us." On the first day, I explain the history of choosing to end my classes with the mantra; what standing in solidarity might mean for us as educators and for dismantling hegemony. Thereafter, I invite students to volunteer to lead the mantra at the end of sessions. I've also experimented by asking students to create mantras. One student's creation that I particularly liked was "None of us is free until all of us are free." But students, most often, later choose to end the class with the same mantra we used on the first day. Many students have reported that they later have used this mantra in their K-12 classrooms.

In Conclusion

This may be the last time a spiritual sung during the Southern Freedom Movement (1961; Freedom Song), still compels me to understand the sacred nature of each moment of instruction. The power of that song and that moment in time it was sung in the building of this nation remind me of how fragile the experience of building community is. It reminds me that each semester probably is the last time that my students and I are together, exploring the depth of oppression and the breadth of possibilities for transformation. So each classroom moment must be grounded in the integrity of discovery, a willingness to explore the unknown. Philosopher Martha Nussbaum indicates that this kind of exploration "says something very important about the human condition of the ethical life: that it is based on a trust in the uncertain and on a willingness to be exposed; it's based on being more like a plant than like a jewel, something rather fragile, but whose very particular beauty is inseparable from its fragility (Nussbaum, 1989, p. 448). Because of this ethical conundrum of beauty and fragility, maybe no classroom moment should be corrupted by the tyranny of grades, of sorting students, of rigid adherence to syllabi or bell curves or boring lectures. And possibly, the space and time for story, for expressing feelings of isolation and cultural separation, time for tales of victimization and liberation, along with candid confessions of denial, ultimately, can help us effectively juggle the ominous and the optimistic.

Who knows—if we have the courage to face our collective stories, they, like the wild geese in Mary Oliver's poem, may lead us toward "our place in the family of things" (Oliver, 1996).

References

Baldwin, J. (1995). *Sonny's Blues*. New York: Penguin Books Ltd. p. 87.

Becvar, R. and Canfield, B. (1997). *Group Work: Cybernetics, Constructivist, & Social Constructionist Perspectives*. New York: Lov Publishing Co.

Civil Rights Data Collection. (2014). "Data Snapshot: School Discipline." *U.S. Department of Education Office for Civil Rights*. March. Accessed June 16, 2014 from http://www2.ed.gov/about/offices/list/ocr/docs/crdc-discipline-snapshot.pdf

Delpit, L. (1995). *Other people's children: Cultural conflict in the classroom*. New York: The New Press.

Delpit, L. (2012). *Multiplication is for White People: Raising Expectations for Other People's Children*. New York: The New Press.

Delpit, L. & Joanne Dowdy (Eds.). (2002). *The skin that we speak: Thoughts on language and culture in the classroom*. Delpit. New York: The New Press.

Freedom Song. (2000). AlphaVille with Carrie Productions, Danny Glover. TNT. DVD.

Freire, P. and Macedo. D. (2001). *Literacy: Reading the Word and the World*. London: Routledge.

Focus Group Transcripts. (2014). Student e-mails, 2014; Student on-line responses to readings, 2013–14.

Gardner, H. (2008). *Multiple Intelligences: New Horizons in Theory and Practice*. Boston: Basic Books.

Harding, V. (1990). *Hope and History: Why We Must Share the History of the Movement*. Maryknoll, New York: Orbis Books.

Harding, V. (1997). *We Changed the World: African Americans 1945–1970*. USA: Oxford University Press.

Hilliard, A. G. III. (1995). *The Maroon within Us: Selected Essays on African American Community Socialization*. Baltimore, MD: Black Classic Press.

Hilliard, A. G. III. (1998). *SBA: The Reawakening of the African Mind*. Gainesville, FL: Makare Publishing Co.

Hilliard, A. G. III. (2014). What Do We Need to Know Now? In Au, W. (Ed.). *Rethinking Multicultural Education: Teaching for Racial and Cultural Justice*. Milwaukee: Rethinking Schools. pp. 25–38.

hooks, bell. 2003. *Teaching Community: A Pedagogy of hope*. New York: Routledge. p. 33.

hooks, bell. 2003. p. 197.

hooks, bell. 2003. p. 197.

Hsieh, S. (2014). Jury Fails to Reach Verdict on Murder Charge in Michael Dunn Trial. *The Nation* February 15 (Accessed June 16, 2014).

Moffett, J. (1988). *Coming on Center: Evolution of English Education*. New York: Boyton/Cook.

Moffett, J. and Wagner, B. (1991). *Student Centered Language Arts K-12*. New York: Heinemann Publishing Co.

Moses, R. E. (2014). Unpublished Keynote Address. Educational Testing Service Institute for Student Achievement. June 30.

Moses, R. & Charlie Cobb. (2001). *Radical Equations: Civil Rights from Mississippi to the Algebra Project*. Boston: Beacon Press.

Nussbaum, M. (1989). Interview. Bill Moyers: A World of Ideas. In Flowers, B. S. (Ed.) New York: Doubleday Dell Publishing. p. 448.

Oliver, M. (1986). Wild Geese. *Dream Work*. New York, NY: The Atlantic Monthly Press.

Palmer, P. (2007). The Courage to teach: Exploring the inner landscape of a teacher's life. San Francisco: Jossey Bass.

Perry, T., Steele, C., and Hilliard, A. G. III. (2004). Young Gifted and Black: Promoting high achievement among African American students. Boston: Beacon Press.

Poreles, J. (2014). "Pete Seeger, Champion of Folk Music and Social Change Dies at 94." *The New York Times* January 29: A20.

Ransby, B. (2003). *Ella Baker & the Black Freedom Movement: A radical democratic vision*. Chapel Hill: The University of North Carolina Press. p. 335.

Rivera, C. (2013). Black college students face persistent gaps. *LA Times* December 05. Accessed June 16, 2014 from http://articles.latimes.com/2013/dec/05/local/la-me-ln-college-blacks-20131205

Robles, F. (2012). A shooting in the neighborhood, *The Miami Herald* (Broward & Keys edition) March 16: A2.

Smith, M. D. (2014). White people have to give up racism. *The Nation* February 14: 1.

Student e-mails. (2014). Student on-line responses to readings, 2013–14.

Tatum, B. (1997). *"Why Are All the Black Kids Sitting Together in the Cafeteria" and Other Conversations about Race.* New York: Basic Books.

This may be the last time, Old Negro Spiritual sung in African American churches but originally recorded by the Staple Singers in 1961, and often sung later by the Student Non-Violent Coordinating Committee youth when leaving meetings during the years of the Southern Freedom Movement. Sung recently at Freedom Summer 50th Anniversary Congress, June 29, 2014.

Weimer, M. (2002). *Learner-centered teaching: Five key changes to practice.* San Francisco: Jossey Bass.

Wynne, J. T. (2005). Education, Liberation, and Transformation: Teaching African American Students within a context of culture. In Gallien, L. and Peterson, M. S. (Eds.). *Instructing and Mentoring the African American College Student: Strategies for Success in Higher Education.* Boston, MA: Pearson Education, Inc.

Wynne, J. T. (2002). We don't talk right. You ask him. In: Delpit, L. and Dowdy, J. K. (Eds.). *The Skin that We Speak: Thoughts on Language and Culture in the Classroom.* New York: The New Press. pp. 215–216.

Wynne, J. T. (2012). Grassroots leadership: leading by not leading. In: Wynne, J. T., Delpit, L., and Miles, R. E. (Eds.). *Confessions of a White Educator: Stories in Search of Justice and Diversity.* Dubuque, IA: Kendall Hunt Publishing Co.

Zinn, H. (2010). *The People Speak* DVD. A&E Home Video.

The dark & the dazzling: Children leading us back from the edge[1]

by Joan T. Wynne

One of my favorite activists, Bryan Stevenson, Director of Equal Justice Initiative, in a TED talk, said to an audience interested in innovation, that "It's the mind-heart connection that compels us to not just be attentive to all the bright and dazzling things but also to the dark and difficult things" (2012).

For educators, part of the "dark and difficult" is the huge growth of the school to prison pipeline and its impact on our black, brown and poor children—and on our society's dream of becoming a real democracy. Another difficult part is exploring strategies and taking action that will change public policies which continuously create the inferior schools where these children are forced to attend. Schools where guards stand at the doors and roam the halls; where bathrooms hold no toilet paper; where rain water leaks down stairwells; where exhausted teachers have lost faith in our children's hunger to learn. As teachers we must collectively grapple with the reality that we live in a racist country, where too many of us reap benefits from our unearned power and privilege that negatively impact children of color. Because approximately 76 percent of public school teachers are white and mostly female (Characteristics 2013), our responsibility is to use that power and privilege to confront and eliminate injustices and inequities in schools.

Writing to teachers years ago, my late friend and mentor, Asa G. Hilliard, III, educator, psychologist, and historian, insisted that: *"Revolution, not reform, is required to release the power of teaching. . . . Virtually, all teachers possess tremendous*

---

[1] Keynote Address, The 14th Annual South Florida Education Research Conference, June 6, 2015. A version of this speech was earlier published as Wynne, J. (2014). Foreword. In *Transforming the School to Prison Pipeline: Lessons from the classroom.* Debra Payne & Tonette Rocco. Rotterdam, The Netherlands: Sense Publishers.

power which can be released, given the proper exposure. We can't get to that point by tinkering with a broken system. We must change our intellectual structures, definitions and assumptions; then we can release teacher power" (Hilliard 1997).

Hilliard's clarion call seems vital if we ever hope to create schools worthy of our children and our teachers. As did Hilliard, we must question current belief systems that:

- establish racism in schools;
- deliver authoritarian pedagogy;
- foster an obsession with student behavior in lieu of the pursuit of academic excellence; and
- institutionalize the blaming of students and parents for the consequences of demoralizing instruction.

We must openly challenge the arcane and dangerous "structures and assumptions" that prevail in schools, pushing our Black and Brown children into the sinister, corporate "school to prison pipe-line" and, by doing so, bankrupt our nation of the benefit of these young, untapped brilliant minds.

This is a huge issue in Florida, since its school to prison pipeline as of 2013 was the largest in the nation (Hing 2013). Another disturbing reality in the state is that Black students are just 21 percent of Florida youth, but make up 46 percent of all school related referrals to law enforcement (Hing). So, addressing racism is crucial to any legitimate study of the pipeline or the demand for quality education for every mother's child.

Many of the urban schools, where I observe and where my graduate students teach, carry the same stench of offensive and obsolete curriculum and pedagogy. Too many of these schools, in fact, operate like prisons, where students of color—especially those forced to live in poverty by an economic system that demands there be "losers"—are daily maligned and rigidly controlled as though they already wore orange jumpsuits. Because of this badgering of certain youth, I often think that the school to prison pipeline is in reality a prison to prison pipeline.

Affirming my experiences in public schools, Henry Giroux in his latest book, *Youth in Revolt,* asserts that we are criminalizing the behavior of young people in schools" (Giroux 2013, p. 10). Giroux declares that "young children are being arrested and subjected to court appearances for behaviors that can only be called trivial" (p. 10). In Florida, even a 5 year old child was handcuffed and arrested for a temper tantrum (CBS 2009). Given the state's racist history and policies (King 2012), no surprise that this 5 year old was black.

But we should explore as well another facet of this assault on children in schools. The privatized prison system is one of the fastest growing industries in the nation (Rappleye 2012). The industry needs a continuous flow of prisoners into these jails to capture the public dollars; thus, here, enters the demand for criminalizing youth for the least infraction while also increasing the detention of the immigrant poor in these prisons. The GEO Group and the Corrections Corporation of America (CCA) are the two largest privatized prison companies, with profits per year of 3 billion dollars (Rappleye 2012). Not only do these companies demean society by receiving such abundant profits for incarcerating people, they also drive local and national policy about immigration and criminal justice. Riding the waves of this corporate tsunami catching our poor children in its undertow are banks like Wells Fargo who hold significant equity shares in CCA (Rappleye 2012). These shares further the national economic interest in pushing students out of school and into prison. It's another case of "follow the money" and you find out who is driving the policy.

Consciously or not, the structure and practice of "inner-city" schools aids the corporations in dictating these policies. In these schools situated deep in the belly of most cities, obedience, not academic excellence, is the prime attribute desired for their students at the bottom. Obedience prepares them not just for prisons, but also for the military and for low paying jobs. In the schools where most poor children attend, scripted curricula and stupidly designed testing, all delivering multi-billion dollar profits to corporations, stifle the creative curiosity of our young children kicked to the curb by a society who doesn't believe in them, nor care about them.

Hundreds of years ago, Great Britain created a colonial educational system to sustain its empire. And it worked extremely well to keep everyone in the proper place in a well-structured, hegemonic hierarchy. Teachers at the front doling out information, students sitting in rows powerless and obedient, sucking up filtered information that the elite chose for them. That system is still alive and well in many countries across the globe. And, yes, the U.S.A. continues to use it. Yet it most often colonizes only black, brown, and poor white students. And what better colony than a school-to-prison pipeline. All of these "dark and difficult things" that Bryan Stevenson challenges us to examine, I hope we can explore during this conference.

But as promised, I will also talk today about the things that dazzle: like student-centered, creative, non-punitive teaching. I want to talk about models of education that are right now in schools interrupting the cycle of tyranny, mediocrity, and warehousing of young, imaginative students who daily suffer the slings and arrows of society's outrageous failure to provide quality education for all of its children. I have been lucky to experience first-hand two of those models. Since 1997, I have visited and/or worked with the children that Bob Moses leads. I have met with them in Mississippi, in Boston, in New York City, in Los Angeles and in Miami. Many are the students whom this nation has ignored or punished.

Yet Moses' youngsters personify hope for education. They are part of the Algebra Project (AP), a program dreamed up, founded, and delivered by Moses (Civil Rights icon and MacArthur Genius Fellow) and his regional teams. His project takes the alienated and underperforming kids—and serves up accelerated learning in mathematics, not remedial pabulum. Its primary interest is in the students' intellect, not their "good behavior." Contrary to traditional math content, AP's curriculum changes as the need of the students change. AP teachers must learn how to quickly modify their plans for teaching tomorrow according to what was learned today. This kind of creative curriculum flies in the face of test-driven, standardized, static, regurgitated models in use most often today in failing schools. Yet because of AP's demand for creativity, not only students, but also their teachers begin to think more critically and imaginatively about their work.

For thirty years, in the Algebra Project classrooms, the progeny of slaves and sharecroppers, children of new immigrants, and youth from Appalachia enjoy the instruction typically reserved for what society deems "the gifted." Steeped in an experiential, student centered pedagogy, AP listens deeply to the voices of the youngsters they educate. And it raises those voices into the public sphere. In cities and towns around the country AP students talk about mathematics at national and state conferences, local school boards, college classrooms, and community events.

Explaining the need for AP's work, Moses insists that "The absence of math literacy in urban and rural communities is as urgent an issue today as the lack of registered voters was 40 years ago . . . solving the problem requires the same kind of community organizing that changed the South then. For, if we can succeed in bringing all children to a level of math literacy so they can participate in today's economy, that would be a revolution (Cass 2002)." AP isn't waiting for a "superman" or for society to clean up its act; rather, AP continually finds what Moses calls the "crawl space" within and outside schools to reach the students that society has chosen to leave behind or send to jail. AP is grounded in a history of grass roots organizing that understands clearly that those at the bottom must demand the education they deserve. Consequently, AP develops students as a cohort, fostering a community with their teachers and their parents.

Another beacon for hope is AP's offspring, the Young People's Project (YPP), designed, run by and for young people. Directed by Maisha Moses, it develops students into math literacy workers who go into their communities during after-school hours to teach younger children that math is interesting, fun, and doable. YPP uses the youth culture, its rhythms and rhymes, drums, hip-hop, videography, youth participatory action research, math games, all as vehicles to teach—and to extricate youngsters from the colonial vise that holds them tightly to the bad education that gets them ready for prison.

In its sixteen year journey, YPP continually evolves as its prestige and local power grows. Because of its openness to the organic nature of change—and as a result of grants awarded by the National Science Foundation, it has begun to develop young leaders to challenge and influence public policy. These youth are engaging our alienated students.

YPP's capacity for authentic encounters that can shift quickly into the urgency of any current event is illustrated best with their "Finding our Folks" campaign. Within weeks after the debacle of Katrina, these disenfranchised youth began organizing students and young adults from across the south to "Find our Folks." Along with the New Orleans Hot 8 Brass Band, YPP went to Atlanta, Baton Rouge, Jackson, Mobile, New Orleans, and Houston to find the hurricane's dispossessed. They networked with community agencies, churches, schools, colleges, friends in each city who might support the tour and its work with dispersed populations (Wynne 2012). Their vision for this tour spoke to our demands for educational transformation. They said:

We seek to raise the voices of Katrina's survivors and connect them with the voices of America's survivors, the brothers and sisters in all corners of the country who remain on the margins of citizenship. We seek to use the tools of education, documentation, healing, and organizing to explore and discuss the conditions that led to the devastating impact of Katrina; to join the voices of resistance, the veterans of past and continuing movements, with the voices of Hip-Hop, Blues and Jazz; to celebrate African and indigenous cultures as they have been expressed in New Orleans and throughout the world; to find our folk, to reconnect the individuals, families and communities that are scattered across the country, living in exile. In finding our folk, we hope to find ourselves (YPP 2007).

What better antidote to oppressive models of education might we find than the YPP's visionary alternative to the school to prison pipeline—young people leading youth, using their imagination and skills, their art and music, inviting the wisdom of their elders, reaching back to all of the nation's cultural roots, in order to lead America into a more just, equitable, and creative twenty-first century education. This is a paradigm shift that I could easily wrap my brain around.

Might this shift also be needed to shake the foundations of Colleges of Education (COE)? Shouldn't every Teacher Ed program in Florida, indeed, in the nation deliberately and emphatically address these difficult issues of hegemony within their courses? I implore all COE's to investigate AP's and YPP's work; to invite the young into their "classroom management" courses to teach teachers how to liberate students from the archaic systems that enslave both teachers and children. And isn't the very notion of "management" an antiquated concept? Dan Pink insists it is, when talking to business owners who desire innovation. Drawing upon his behavioral science research on what motivates people to think new, Pink suggests that "management" is a tool for compliance and, thus, is contrary to autonomous, creative thinking and innovation (Pink 2009). If Pink is correct and if we want to engage youngsters in critical thinking, shouldn't we stop managing them and start delivering instruction that inspires them to create the new; that engages their intellects; that amplifies their voices?

Or better still, maybe we simply get out of their way and allow them to learn how to act like citizens of a democracy, willing to grapple with the hard questions as well as attend to "all of the bright and dazzling things." In such a scenario, might teachers, then, become inspirational guides, "living the question," not giving the answers—and certainly not relegated as police, meting out punishment in dreary urban "inner-city" schools?

But if we are honest, maybe the real questions we must ask ourselves are:

- Do we really want to *inspire* the progeny of slaves and sharecroppers, the children of recent Black and Brown immigrants, the children in Appalachia?
- Or is our real desire to keep them in a system that will guarantee someone else will pick up our garbage, flip our burgers, dig in the bowels of our mines, pluck the feathers off our chickens, pick our tomatoes sprayed with poisons, and otherwise work for slave wages? Is that the hidden agenda of what we require for "other people's" children?
- Or might we just get out of the way so that our children can lead us back from the edge of the dark?

References

Cass, J. (2002) The Moses factor. *Mother Jones*, May/June 2002 issue 3. http://motherjones.com/politics/2002/05/moses-factor

Characteristics of Public and Private Elementary and Secondary School Teachers in the United States. (2013). Institute of Education Sciences: National Center for Education Statistics. US Department of Education. https://nces.ed.gov/pubs2013/2013314.pdf

Giroux, Henry, Introduction to *Youth in Revolt* on Truthdig.com, Feb 2, 2013 p. 10. http://www.truthdig.com/arts_culture/item/youth_in_revolt_20130202/

Handcuffed 5-Year-Old Sparks Suit CBS/AP/February 11, 2009, 7:27 PM. http://www.cbsnews.com/2100-500202_162-690601.html

Hilliard, III, Asa G (1997), "The Structure of valid staff development." *Journal of staff development.* Spring, Vol.18, No.2.

Hing, Julianne, Florida's school to prison pipeline is largest in the nation, *Color Lines News for Action*, Feb. 12, 2013. http://colorlines.com/archives/2013/02/in_2012_florida_arrested_12000_students_in_school—and_that_was_an_improvement.html

King, G. (2012). Devil in the grove: Thurgood Marshall, the Groveland boys, and the dawn of a new America. New York, NY: HarperCollins Publishers.

Pink, Dan, The Puzzle of Motivation, TED.com, August, 2009. http://www.ted.com/talks/dan_pink_on_motivation.html

Rappleye, Hannah, The end of the for-profit prison era?, Salon, Feb. 20, 2012. http://www.salon.com/2012/02/20/the_end_of_the_for_profit_prison_era/

Stevenson, Bryan , We need to talk about an injustice, TED.com, March, 2012. http://www.ted.com/talks/bryan_stevenson_we_need_to_talk_about_an_injustice.html

The Young People's Project (YPP) (2007) Finding our folk. DVD. Chicago, Ill: YPP youth.

Wynne, J. (2012). We who love freedom cannot rest: Young people transforming their worlds, *Confessions of a white educator: Stories in search of justice and diversity*, Wynne, J., Delpit, L., Miles, R. (eds), Dubuque, IA: Kendall Hunt Publishing Co. 2012.

Voices of those we cage —and a different kind of witness

by Chaundra L. Whitehead

If there is anywhere in the world where there is a predominance of not only control and subjugation, but also the caging of humans, it exists in prisons in the United States of America. It might shock some of our citizens of the USA that our "leader of the free world" is also the leader of incarceration. The United States has the highest incarceration rate in the world (Tsai & Scommegna, 2012). At the end of 2011, there were about 7 million offenders under the supervision of the adult correctional systems in the United States. This equates to about one in every 34 adult residents in the U.S. being under some form of correctional supervision, which includes incarceration, probation, and parole (Glaze & Parks, 2012). Many of the imprisoned have very little hope to be seen or heard from again, with about 50,000 serving life sentences without the possibility of parole. About 3,000 people are sentenced to death. Given the rates of mass incarceration in the United States, the voices of many, who have suffered unjustly in a court system that is stacked against them (Alexander, 2010; Stevenson, 2012), are missing each day from our workplaces, schools, and communities. These voices are to be found behind bars, unseen and unheard by society because of either frivolous or minor infractions against the laws of a legal system that far more often prosecutes the poor than it does the rich for the same or worse crimes. Too few can or do speak for the imprisoned poor.

For almost 10 years, I have been telling the stories of imprisoned people, as just that, people who are confined to prisons, not inmates, degenerates or criminals, but people. I tell their stories with a distinct inability to do it justice. Witnessing is an act of caring for your fellow human being. Being a true witness requires courage in the face of those who wish to continue to silence the stories of caged individuals.

My first teaching position at a correctional facility arose from a series of fortunate occurrences. I was in a telephone customer service position I greatly disliked, when we were informed that we were going to be laid off in a couple months. I was excited and saw this as my chance to look for full-time work in adult education. I had been a volunteer tutor at the public library and worked part time at an adult reading center, but now I wanted to find a full-time job that could use the same skills. I saw an advertisement in the local newspaper for an Adult Basic Education Instructor at a nearby prison in the next county. I applied and was offered the position soon after.

I was a novice teacher to say the least. I had only taught in one-on-one settings, now I was going to be responsible for reading, math, and language arts for two classes a day, each three hours long with about 25 incarcerated women on a 4th- to 6th-grade performance level. This was my Adult Basic Education II (ABE II) class. Now what was I going to do with them? No one really told me what to do. There was a two-week training on correctional facility policies and procedures, such as safety, suicide prevention, and key control. That is the typical employee-training program at most correctional facilities. Then I was given a week to do lesson plans and prepare my classroom. Luckily another teacher was hired for ABE II at the same time, so we had each other to bounce ideas around and come up with a plan. We also had to share materials. There was only one class set of most of the books that we both needed, so we coordinated a schedule for the dictionaries and other important books. No matter how much planning a new teacher does, however, we are hardly ever ready. Being ready for my incarcerated students seemed like a different type of ready. Was I truly ready to be a nonjudgmental promoter of learning?

For the first few months I was overwhelmed with lesson plans, grading, attendance form submissions, classes interrupted or cancelled by institutional incidents, standardized test scores, and the general management of 25 personalities at once. Eventually I found my way, and I relied heavily on hands-on-activities with limited supplies, watching videos and having discussions or worksheets to accompany them, division of the class into small groups for activities, plays, and reading aloud. Essentially I tried to do everything, but lecture. If I did need to do whole group direct instruction, it was limited to 20 minutes. With such diverse learning needs and levels in one class, lecture was not the most productive means of instruction. If lecture was the least effective, quiet independent work was a close second. This was the method of choice for many other teachers at the institution, but with low literacy levels, short attention spans, and adult women who may take various medications that cause drowsiness, quiet-time work was limited. But I did find that classical or new age music could lessen the pain of "quiet-time" work.

In my class, there were also lessons on topics that were not in the books on the shelf such as a lesson on propaganda during election time. When each holiday came around, we learned its history and meaning. I offered information that

I believed might broaden their understanding of what was happening in the world around them. I also served as the Literacy Coordinator, providing trainings for those incarcerated women who wanted to become tutors. I created and managed the Lunchtime Tutoring program, which was successful and well received. My position as an ABEII instructor was instrumental in developing my understanding of correctional facilities, criminal justice, and crime.

I enjoyed my work so much that I had the crazy notion of becoming a director or principal of a school in a prison. I was told by my supervising principal, who was retiring, though, that I would need a master's degree to take on the position. Off I went to get a master's degree. Then all of this "prison stuff" I did, took off. For the past five years, I have been a volunteer with Alternatives to Violence Project (AVP), a conflict resolution training program offered to incarcerated people. Whether conduction research or being a volunteer, AVP is an organization for which I would choose to work precisely because whatever the role, the AVP program promotes dialogue, empathy, and community building. They engage the prisoner as a fellow human being.

Many people do not feel comfortable working in or visiting prison facilities. Some AVP volunteers have come once and not returned. When teaching at a prison full time, I remember the high teacher turnover rate. I always felt that some of these people who chose not to return, did so not out of fear, but because they recognized the hypocrisy and inequality which existed inside the prisons. Nothing like the society script they had been told about prison turned out to be true. The prison was simply not the humane rehabilitation facility they had expected.

Why do we believe that we should be fearful in a correctional setting? Because that is the script that has been told to us. Certainly, timidity is not a useful quality for working in a correctional setting, but when has timidity been useful anywhere? People respond to bold authenticity. Some qualities that are valued in correctional facilities, much like anywhere else in society, seemed most often to be honesty, sincerity, and humor. As an educator moving and working in that space, I became aware of the contradictions and flaws ever present. Yet I began to understand that I was accountable to the people who live in those cells, to tell their stories as a counter narrative to the dominant script. I have visited several prisons in different parts of the country, and they can be quiet or loud. In either scenario, though, no one's real voice is heard.

Way too often I see the phrase "Lock them up and throw away the key," in news story comments online. I wonder if the people who use this phrase have ever really stopped to think of the implications of removing someone from society for life, especially for nonviolent offenses or even worse, conspiracy charges, which often equates to no real charge, just a suspicion of involvement in something the power structure finds offensive.

How has America become number one in harsh, often inhumane, punitive treatment of fellow human beings, without the public registering outrage or demonstrating shame by this statistical abomination? Of course, after the pictures of our nation's torture of international prisoners suspected as terrorists, why would I ask that question?

Nevertheless, as a nation we seem to choose to believe the scripts we have been told over the years about crime. We choose to believe that we are safer locking everybody up; that crime is out of control; that harsher punishments are needed. And, of course, the best story ever told is that we needed a war on drugs. But the media seems to be rampant with deception, misinformation, covering up of injustices, pandering to privilege and oppression.

Experience in a correctional facility and dialogue with an incarcerated person or someone returning home after incarceration often reveals the truth that many of them are not much different from us. The dominant language we are accustomed to hearing and speaking has been used to diminish the stories of incarcerated people and reframe them as less than human, revolting, unintelligent. For, often we hear the adage that if the imprisoned were intelligent, they would get away with "it" as many other Americans do each day—like the gang on Wall Street. I would argue that the defining factor is not intelligence but power and money. As Bryan Stevenson, lawyer, Founder and Executive Director of the Equal Justice Initiative, said in a Ted Talk (2012), "We have a system of justice in [the US] that treats you much better if you're rich and guilty than if you're poor and innocent. Wealth, not culpability, shapes outcomes."

Those outcomes limit the ability of millions of people to think and create. In our nation's prisons, individual needs, thoughts, and ideas are not valued, encouraged, or rewarded. How is this rehabilitation? When thinking skills are continually reduced, how is an incarcerated person to develop the skills they need to have a successful return to society? Contrary to society's distortions about the humanity of people it chooses to cage like animals in a zoo, worth and value are actually abundant in the prisons where I've worked. Surprisingly, in the most oppressive and repressive human conditions, creativity still manages to flourish. I hear the voices of incarcerated people who find a way to write and speak from behind the walls. I see them read and reflect. I witness acts of kindness between them.

Squandering talent through the use of serving long sentences seems unproductive and a waste of human potential. I experienced this waste once when I was assigned a teacher's aide, Heather, who was a professional woman, excellent with accounting and convicted of some fraudulent activities which gained her a 10-year sentence. At the end of the 10 years, she was expected to find a job, hope her skill set was still relevant, and earn enough money to pay restitution. She was an excellent teacher's aide, managed my gradebook, helped students one-on-one, and kept the class tidy. Yet I always thought it was such a waste of talent that she was there grading the student papers instead of contributing to the larger society outside the prison walls. I was thankful, though, that she was able to maintain some of her professional skills. At the time, I truly felt that she could teach the class, so why was she incarcerated for 10 years, rather than a shorter sentence, and more community-based restorative justice strategies?

I learned that she was there because the more money a person steals, the longer they are expected to be banished from society. Fortunately she did her time and was released. Soon after release, she contacted me to tell me she was on this side of freedom, and within two weeks, she had a job and purchased a car. As we chatted online, I was so excited to read that she had been given an opportunity. Heather was motivated and she had a great support system. She also provided a glimmer of hope for the work I do by stating "You had an impact on me at the very beginning. I always told my family how much I enjoyed working for you because it felt like a normal working relationship. I enjoyed our lunchtime discussions. Having just come to prison is was nice to be able to have intelligent conversations." Incidents like this continually persuade me that most people want to be acknowledged and heard, regardless of their circumstances. Why should a criminal conviction render a person unworthy of the most basic conversational exchange?

When I left working at the prison, I tried to make a quiet exit. I told my class one day before I planned to leave that I did not want them to plot a surprise party, or have time to get too sad. But that plan failed. On my last day, at the end of class, I had one student who stood there looking at me, crying and asking why I had to go. Who, she asked, was she going to talk to? And who would fill the void. As she stood there, with the heavy weight of sadness, I violated my employee protocols and gave her a hug.

The AVP program had the opportunity to hold a full day workshop inside the prison, where dozens of outside AVP people came to have training and dialogue with the inside people. I overheard one person questioning "Are they always this happy?" Soon she got up the nerve to comment to one of the inside facilitators about how happy everyone seemed and the response was "Just because this is prison doesn't mean we go around sad every day." Society would have us believe the people who have made mistakes do not deserve happiness, joy, accomplishment, or any of the other positive emotions representing the human condition. Some people do have hard days, great sadness, remorse, and regret, but we will never know the dimensions of their humanness unless incarcerated people are allowed to have a voice. Stevenson insists that he believes that a murderer is not just a murderer; a thief is not just a thief. Most humans, he suggests, are multifaceted, complex beings. Certainly those were the ambiguous dimensions that I observed in the prisons. Granted there are recalcitrant, who probably might cause us to challenge this belief, but those were not the people with whom I came in contact.

Redefining the narrative of voices from prison requires redefining the script of fairness and integrity in our criminal justice system, which continues to crumble before the eyes of Americans and the world. While the evidence exists that justice for some happens, many in our country still hold on to the notion that there is a fair and equitable punitive system for all. If only those who still believe in the fairness of the criminal justice system had a chance to hear the voices I hear regularly, they might reconsider the script that has duped them into distortions of prison realities, of erroneous notions of fairness and legal equity. To really understand the horrors that our democracy has created inside its jails and prisons, everyone should read, *The New Jim Crow* by Michelle Alexander (2010).

In the Marvin Gaye tune "Can I get a Witness," he inquires "Is it right to be treated so bad, When you've given everything you had?" Returning citizens can echo this same refrain post release as they are continuously subjected to exclusion from voting, housing, employment, and opportunities (2010). How long must punishment continue after punishment has been completed? Once again, there is a script expressing that those who have been convicted of committing a crime are not worthy of reintegration, that their penitence must last their natural life. Sharing the stories of those who are denied voice, silenced, unheard has been a validating experience for both me and my imprisoned students. The sharing has allowed the silenced to know, "I am listening, I hear you" and it lets the silencers understand that, "I know you are trying to silence them, but their stories will be told."

References

Alexander, M. (2010). *The New Jim Crow: Mass incarceration in the age of colorblindness.* New York, NY: The New Press.

Glaze, L.E. and Parks, E. (2012). Correctional populations in the United States, 2011. (NCJ 239972). Washington, DC: U.S. Department of Justice/Bureau of Justice Statistics, 2012 November.

Stevenson, B. (2012). We need to talk about an injustice. *Ted Talks.* Ted.com. Retrieved from: http://www.ted.com/talks/bryan_stevenson_we_need_to_talk_about_an_injustice?language=en

Tsai, T. & Scommegna, P. (2012, August). U.S. Has World's Highest Incarceration Rate.

Population Reference Bureau. (2012). Retrieved from http://www.prb.org/Publications/Articles/2012/us-incarceration.aspx

Let the human spirit in the room[1]

by Joan T. Wynne

"**A**n important component of African indigenous pedagogy is the vision of the teacher as a selfless healer intent on inspiring, transforming, and propelling students to a higher spiritual level." When I first read this passage by Asa G. Hilliard, III (*SBA*, 1997, pp. 69–70), I felt as I did when the Berlin Wall fell or when Nelson Mandela walked out prison doors. I never thought either would happen in my lifetime. Neither did I think that anyone with a respectable reputation, indeed, a renowned scholar like Hilliard, in a white university would ever have the courage to publicly frame education within a context of spiritual transformation. Seeing that in print, I felt as though somewhere in my psyche, walls had fallen down and a liberator had been set free.

My years in white universities as a student and as a professor had indicated to me that matters of the intellect and matters of the spirit are as separate as church and state. That the purpose of my education might become the "transformation toward a new spiritual level" was certainly never remotely discussed or assumed. Typically, scholars who entertain such ideas are relegated to fringe groups in their disciplines. Because of the distortions of fundamentalists and most religions on such issues, many of us academics may feel justifiably uncomfortable. Nevertheless, for fear of being thought anti-intellectual, or worse, unworthy of academia, I kept the idea of a connection between spirituality and intellectual pursuits suppressed in my conversations with other mainstream professors. My experience in colleges and universities

---

[1] A version of this essay was first published as Wynne, J. (2005) Education, Liberation, and Transformation: Teaching African American Students within a context of culture. In *Instructing and mentoring the African American college student: Strategies for Success in higher education*. Louis B. Gallien, Jr. & Marshalita Sims Peterson (Eds). Boston: Pearson Education, Inc. (pp. 101–121).

around this issue taught me that Paulo Freire (1987) was probably right when he suggested that "The intellectual activity of those without power is always characterized as non-intellectual" (p. 122). I found that scholars who openly spoke of the spiritual within a context of intellectual discourse typically were outside the academic circles of power. I remember back in the 1980s attending a conference in Denver, Colorado, called Exploring the Spiritual in the Teaching of English. It highlighted the work of Language Arts scholar and researcher, James Moffitt, who was a giant in the Language Arts field at the time and an active member of National Council of Teachers of English (NCTE). Only 80 teachers and professors showed up from the association that, in that era, boasted 10–15,000 active members or 43,934 paying members (Hogan, NCTE). So, many noted scholars are often ignored if they speak of the spirit!

Yet, as I thought about the writing of this chapter, I kept coming back to Hilliard's wisdom as one of the distinguishing characteristics of effective pedagogy with African-American students. I learned it when teaching African-American students at an inner-city high school. I learned it when teaching at a premier, all male, historically black college (HBCU); and I learned it again when working with African-American teachers in an urban teacher leadership master's degree program. In all three experiences, there seemed to be an innate sense of the "spiritual" aspirations of an entire people being integral to educational journeys. Jacob Carruthers (1999), a professor of Inner City Studies, concurs in *Intellectual Warfare*, saying that the "Restoration of African civilization is not possible without a return to African spirituality" (p. xv).

As a white woman, I feel presumptuous writing about effective pedagogy for African-American students. So, I can only offer my story from the perspective of one who first learned about "good teaching" from African-American teachers and scholars. Master teachers like Mattie Williams, Dorothy McGirt, Baby Ruth Brantley and Oliver McClendon took me under their wings my first year out of college, teaching at an African-American high school. They taught me how to expect and demand the best academic performance from all students, especially those living in poverty. Later on, scholars, teachers, and leaders like Lisa Delpit and Asa Hilliard, III taught me the theory that explained the practice that had been modeled at Howard High School. Alonzo Crim, Robert Dixon, and Bob Moses taught me how to hone my practice when teaching disenfranchised students. Thus, any wisdom I share came from those educators and those places where, no matter the physical structure, the educational process became a "sacred space" (Hilliard SBA, 1997).

The research literature and my experiences in the classroom indicate that there are specific strategies that create optimum learning conditions for African-American students. Yet, some of those studies and experiences have also persuaded me that regardless of the strategies, something far more profound than methodology connects students of African descent with the pursuit of academic excellence. For, along the way as I worked with African-American students, I did observe, and probably engaged in as well, some "bad" instruction that seemed antithetical to what is considered pedagogically sound. Nevertheless, many African American students survived such instruction.

It is only recently, however, that I've begun to understand the reasons that students of African descent can endure ineffective teaching strategies in HBCU's when they often cannot in mainstream colleges. That is not to say that there are not thousands of African-American students who, nonetheless, achieve in mainstream colleges without these conditions being present. Rather, they excel in spite of those colleges, not because of them.

Some of the conditions, beyond pedagogy, yet, bound within the culture, that I believe facilitate academic success for African-American students are:

- the assumption of the spiritual connection to educational pursuits;
- the infusion of music into the educational experience;
- the explicit discussions of challenging an oppressive society;
- the expectation and demand for excellence in the midst of a nurturing environment;
- the developing of personal relationships with faculty;
- the belief in the collaborative nature of the educational journey.

All of these were integral parts of the total Morehouse College experience, an HBCU where I taught for 10 years. Much of what I now consider a quality educational experience for any student, but especially for African-American students, was crystallized for me at that college.

Spiritual Connection to Educational Pursuits

When explaining the ancient, education traditions of Africa, Hilliard (SBA, 1997), who often spoke at the college, said, "Our educational and socialization process was always situated in a sacred space. This space served to clarify purpose and emphasize the divine nature of the process." At Morehouse, part of that "educational and socialization process" was obligatory attendance at chapel twice a week. In that space, students heard renowned persons of African descent—ministers, scholars, politicians, or heads of state—speak of the ancestral spirits who gave their all so that these young men could be at that college. At the end of such meetings at chapel, students resoundingly sang together the "Alma Mater." When the song's reference to the "Holy Spirit" emerged, all reverently lowered their voices and bowed their heads as they whispered the two words. I had never before experienced, first, a student body who all knew and sang their "Alma Mater," nor, secondly, a secular college that made reference to the "Holy Spirit." This attention to the divine, outside a specific religious context or denomination, poured out beyond the chapel walls. The legacies of spiritualists/educators like Howard Thurman, Martin Luther King, Jr., Benjamin E. Mays reverberated not only in the chapel but also in the halls of the academy. The memorializing of those legacies is a ritual considered part of the "Mystique" of the college.

Many of my students, whether they were in the writing, literature, speech, or education seminars, unabashedly found appropriate ways to connect their personal spiritual experiences to their writing, their speeches, or classroom discussions, no matter the assigned topic. I learned early in my career at Morehouse that "touching the spirit" was a collective assumption throughout the campus. No hesitation there to connect the intellectual with the spiritual. Caruthers insists that, "The road to African liberation begins at the door of that 'Good Old African Spirit'" (p. xv). And if education is not "liberating," then it becomes, more often than not, propaganda for maintaining the societal status quo.

For mainstream professors in colleges or universities where the spiritual is ignored or shunned, creating opportunities for students to connect their spiritual heritage to discussions of content in a specific discipline is a culturally responsive strategy that can be quite effective in fostering stronger engagement of African-American students in college classrooms. In such discussions, the professor is not obligated to validate or dismiss any particular belief system—only to establish a safe space for the students to bring those spiritual analogies into classroom conversations. I once observed a mainstream professor, who was a professed atheist, sit respectfully quiet as student after student began to connect her spiritual beliefs to the topic at hand. The energy in the room, due to his acquiescence to their desires to connect their own spiritual stories to the abstraction being grappled with, grew into a vigorous, synchronized exploration of the self and the discipline.

Infusion of Music

Part of the spiritual experience at Morehouse was music. The college's award-winning Glee Club, usually opened and closed every chapel session. Their sometimes thundering renditions of old spirituals often left me so charged that I, too, felt the call of their ancestors to produce the best teaching performance possible for those who had inherited these heroes' struggle. Moreover, I became convinced, after a number of years attending chapel, that the messages and music, the total education experienced within that "sacred space," seemed to increase student determination to "hang in" with those difficult courses or the ones that might bore them into distraction. And, because of those chapel experiences, some students, who might have just barely slipped through the admissions door, seemed to get the extra boost they needed to study more diligently. It's what Delpit (1997) seems to intimate when she suggests that African-American students learn best when they "connect to something greater than themselves."

Using music as ritual and as a collective everyday experience is deeply rooted in the African cultural experience. I was reminded of that when working in Alexandria, South Africa one summer. I listened often as black South African workers, building homes in a Habitat for Humanities project, spontaneously burst into song when passing bricks to one another or when carrying food from one home to another; at the beginning and end of informal social gatherings; or in the middle of any mundane task such as washing dishes together. In that same tradition, during the Southern Freedom Movement, freedom fighters burst into song together in buses, churches, marches, and jails whenever fear became intense, struggle became burdensome, or short-term victory was won (King, 1986; Reagon, 1998). Regardless of the song, it seemed to invite the "spirit" into the human space. Music in the collective seems an integral part of African lives and struggle. How sterile our white institutions of learning must seem to such a musically sophisticated people.

Using Music in the Classroom

Though I have no training or talent in music, because of the powerful use of it in the King chapel and my success in using music in high school classrooms, I began to play taped musical selections in my college literature and composition classes when students were writing. For many, their writing became more fluent while the music was playing. In literature classes, I brought songs whose lyrics and/or rhythms related to themes, metaphors, or forms being studied in specific genres. I often asked students to bring to class their choices of music to relate to what we were studying. On tests, I found that the students could demonstrate more effectively their conceptual understanding of those lessons that had been connected to their music. Many educational researchers have documented the use of music as a means of teaching a diverse range of skills from mathematics to poetry (Moffett & Wagner, 1983). The Algebra Project, initiated by Robert Moses, a mathematics educator and prominent Civil Rights Activist, sometimes uses African drumming to teach algebraic concepts. Howard Gardner's research (Gardner, 2000) defines music as one of the distinct Multiple Human Intelligences. To leave it outside the classroom door once students complete the third or fourth grade seems negligent on our part.

Nature Vs. Nurture

Hilliard (1999) has argued that in America, there is a continuing "nature vs. nurture" educational debate about African-American learners. Many Eurocentric scholars, represented by the likes of Murray and Hernstein (1994) of the infamous *Bell Curve*, purport that the nature of the student defines his potential to learn and achieve. Because of these and similar educational theorists, the nature or capacity of African-American learners to academically excel is more often than not questioned throughout our society, not just in our schools. Using his own educational experiences and research as well as the work of Shinichi Suzuki, "a teacher of world-class musicians who asserted that talent was not inborn but must be trained," Hilliard (1988) affirms that the nature of every human is to learn and that all students optimally learn when they are nurtured. It's rather, Hilliard explains, the "nature of the nurture" that promotes academic achievement, not the nature of the student. Delpit (1997), too, suggests that when teachers create "a sense of family and caring," students of color are more apt to excel.

That kind of nurturing exists at many of the HBCU's where I have taught or visited. The support system for excellence and the belief in the students' capacity to excel is so strong throughout these colleges that most of their students can survive "bad" instructional practices found within a few classrooms. Traditionally, the nurturing of African-American students, especially in the segregated "colored" schools in the south, began with academic excellence as not just an expectation, but a demand by their teachers (Siddle-Walker, 1996). Without that expectation and without taking the responsibility to insure that students learn, questions of pedagogy seem irrelevant. For, we all know the research that suggests we get what we expect, regardless of the methodology (Clark 1989; Good 1981 & 1982; Rosenthal & Jacobson, 1968; Venter, 2000). Delpit (1997), who received the MacArthur genius award, admonished every teacher of African-American students, including elementary teachers, that "Whatever methodology or instructional program is used, demand critical thinking." That demand, for African-American educators, grows naturally from a place of nurture. In too many mainstream college classrooms and in some HBCU classrooms, a nurturing spirit is sorely missing. Hilliard (2000) insists education in the United States is characterized by its "pathological preoccupation with capacity."

Best Practices

Nevertheless, if we are white professors teaching African-Americans in a mainstream college where students' lives on the campus, outside the classroom walls, do not have this kind of nurture or support, then, I believe, we must diligently engage in "best practices" in our classrooms. Along with the indigenous African vision of a teacher, the framework for a discussion of best practices might include a definition found in Vincent Harding's (1999), *Hope and History*. In that text, Ronald Massanari says, "Being a teacher refers less to one who gives answers and expects conformity . . . and more to one who is capable of providing contexts and stimuli so each learner can discover for him or herself. Such teachers are skillful intermediaries and guides in the search for meaning and self-understanding" (p. 1) That kind of skillful teaching within a cultural "context" is, in my experience, the basis for the academic success of many African-American students in any classroom. And, probably, it is, as Massanari suggests, the basis for teaching students of any ethnicity. Many African-American students, as mentioned earlier, can achieve academic excellence in spite of the absence of such a framework for teaching, even in majority white universities. However, those who fail to achieve at that level probably fail because of the other kind of teaching that caters to "giving information, answers, and demanding conformity," within a Euro-American cultural context—a practice that Dr. Alonzo Crim (1999), the first African-American superintendent of the Atlanta Public School System, called, the "Sage on Stage" model. To increase the rate of success for all African-Americans in colleges, I believe, requires a shift away from that model. It requires an inter-active, participant-centered approach to instruction.

Education for Liberation

Within that shift from conformity into a "search for meaning and self-understanding," I believe, is the demand for a pedagogy and a curriculum that is grounded in a philosophy of education for liberation. The Morehouse campus abounds in those conversations—in history classes, in African studies, in African-American literature classes, in meetings in chapels, in campus-wide colloquium, etc. When taught outside a liberation context, knowledge learned in schools can become not only meaningless to African-Americans and other students of color, but worse, a means to maintain an oppressive society. Culturally responsive pedagogy "prepares students to effect change in society, not merely fit into it" (Ladson-Billings, 1992, p. 382).

In the Americas in the 20th century, great teachers like Ella Baker, Septima Clark, Paulo Friere, Fannie Lou Hamer, Vincent Harding, Myles Horton, Benjamin E. Mays, and others led the way in teaching how to educate to liberate. Indebted to their courage and intellectual integrity, many educators have learned how, as Hilliard (Tapping the Genius, 1997; Structure, 1997) suggests, to invite students, faculties, and communities to engage in conversations that question mainstream society's epistemologies as well as its assumptions about education, power, and social justice. Without those questions in mind, the disciplines of physics, literature, science, history, mathematics, etc. often become intellectual scaffolds to sustain hegemony. For African-Americans, living within a society that has for 400 years distorted past and present stories of history, economics, civilizations, and superiority, such a dialogue is imperative, if these students are to assert themselves in an accurate historical context (Loewen, 1996). Moreover, if our society is to progress beyond materialism, militarism, domination, and greed, all students, regardless of ethnicity, need to explore knowledge in the context of liberation. So as a classroom strategy, what does that look like?

First, in any college classroom whether teaching business or humanities, a professor might begin each new semester with an exploration of the many facets of Education for Liberation. This can cause lively discussions of discovery of self and of the depth and breadth of human knowledge, as professors and students try to examine just what liberation means? Who are we liberating? From what? And for what? What does liberation look like? Feel like? What does it have to do with studying physics, chemistry, mathematics, engineering, literature, history, art, etc? Freire (1970) insists that there is "no such thing as a neutral educational process." It either sustains the status quo of the presently known, he suggests, or it uses what it knows to transform the world. If we choose transformation, then we must do as Hilliard (Structure, 1997) suggests, "change our intellectual structures, definitions and assumptions" that presume and foster white privilege and superiority. This means that in every discipline these conversations must be part of the strategy we use to engage our students in investigating the individual epistemologies of our particular content area. Can the laws of physics be seen only through a Eurocentric cultural lens; or is it possible that other cultures and other ancient traditions can offer new perspectives on those laws? In-service teachers (Perry, 2001) at Wheelock College in Boston have discovered methods of scientific inquiry different from the traditional Western model as they have immersed themselves in the Haitian culture.

The Common Good and Liberation:

Many African-American scholars argue that rooted deep in the culture of people of African descent is a curriculum, pedagogy, and practice that insist on the necessity to learn for the greater good of the community (Delpit 1997; Hilliard, SBA, 1997; Ladson-Billings 1994; Siddle-Walker 1996; Wilson 1998). When the purpose for learning any discipline is explicitly stated within a context larger than self-aggrandizement, these scholars indicate, the achievement level of African-American students is favorably impacted. Benjamin E. Mays (1983), the President of Morehouse College for 27 years, who saw his life's purpose as being "born to rebel," proclaimed that the purpose of education was not only "to train the mind to think" but also "the heart to feel . . . the injustices of mankind; and to strengthen the will to act in the interest of the common good" (p. 5). We know from such scholars' work that African-American students take their studies more seriously when they assume that the purpose of exploring a discipline is to make a more just and equitable reality for the "whole" (Harding 1999; Hilliard SBA 1997; Moses & Cobb 2001; Siddle-Walker 1996), James Banks (1997) insists "When the school fails to recognize, validate, and testify to the racism, poverty, and inequality that students experience in their daily lives, they are likely to view the school and the curriculum as contrived and sugar-coated constructs that are out of touch with the real world and the struggles of their daily lives" (p. 16). The work of Herb Kohl (1994) indicates that when our curriculum and our pedagogy omit these realities, many students of color choose to resist learning anything from us. At Morehouse, many students come from economically privileged backgrounds, yet there was a concerted effort at the college to remind those students that their economic status demanded that they use their intellectual talents to battle against the poverty of their people. They were encouraged to understand what former SNCC member, Charles Cobb, once said of the students in Mississippi Freedom Schools, "What they must see is the link between a rotting shack and a rotting America" (Payne 1997, p. 5).

Strategies for Liberation Education

Learning disciplinary content and exploring liberation are not mutually exclusive, as some professors might assume. Steeped in a tradition that honors a "pedagogy of the oppressed" (Freire 1998/1970), a science professor might, for example, encourage students to examine scientific content, laws, theories, etc. in a context of thwarting the use of science as a weapon against oppressed peoples. She might ask her students to ponder the probabilities that if they learned science well enough they might, indeed, together with their newly formed scientific community, be the instruments in discovering the end to world hunger, cancer, pollution, high infant mortality rates, etc. Or the physics students might together discuss how to use the principles of physics, like those used to split the atom, to support life instead of death and destruction. For a people whose guiding principle of educational traditions for over 5,000 years is spiritual transformation and liberation, studying to get a job or to make excessive amounts of money pales in the light of these grander purposes. For oppressed people, Ella Baker insisted that radical education "means facing a system that does not lend itself to your needs and devising means by which you change that system" (Grant 1998). A first step in changing that system in education for African-American students, could mean facilitating open dialogue in the classroom investigating the assumptions of oppression embedded in every discipline studied. For many of us as professors, such discussions might unfold unconscious biases as well as wisdom.

In the humanities, raising questions of liberation is often more common than in the sciences. An English professor might ask students to connect the purposes of effective writing with countering the misconceptions in printed media about the disenfranchised. After ample student driven discussion of larger contexts for learning to write than passing tests or better ways of competing in the job market, a professor might offer students opportunities to hone their skills by writing letters to editors, members of Congress, mayors, etc., about issues of social concern in their immediate college or home communities. They might also suggest ways to develop web sites or chat rooms for students to discuss issues of social justice. In addition, that same professor when teaching literature might ask students to look at the literary canon not only for its aesthetic qualities, but also in the light of the unexamined racist, sexist, and other hegemonic notions that pervade Western literature as well as to question the choice of works admitted into that canon. In small groups, students might then debate the issues, thereby, strengthening their oratorical and dialogic skills, and, then, use what they are learning to educate students in K-12 institutions. In their exploration of racism and oppression, they might read to youngsters in surrounding schools of the story of an unschooled sharecropper named Fannie Lou Hamer (Harding 1999; Moses 2001) who turned a national Democratic convention upside down by demanding to be seated. Some English professors, a history professor, and a few sociology and psychology professors at Morehouse used service-learning techniques like these to enhance their college students' acquisition of and honing of skills in the individual content area.

Empowering students to use their skills as they learn them in a productive way to better their communities is a liberatory act. The "Service-learning" literature prolifically chronicles the successes of such instruction in student acquisition of new skills as well as its positive impact on the communities these students serve. One of the characters in Barry Lopez's (1990) fables says that, "Sometimes people need a story more than food to stay alive" (p. 60) I believe that the stories of people of color, their histories, their cultural legacies have been ignored or mutilated so often in the United States that their children need and deserve accurate cultural narratives told in schools and universities to "stay intellectually alive."

Through the Algebra project, Bob Moses and his colleagues have taught complicated conceptual material to unschooled adults, the children of those adults, and their teachers in poor, rural, and inner city communities. Along with their new mathematical expertise and higher order thinking skills, these parents and students have become politically active in challenging the inadequacies of their schools, their teachers, and the systems that told them they couldn't learn algebra "because they are dysfunctional."

The work of Moses, Delpit, Freire, Hilliard, etc. implies that rigorous intellectual growth is a possibility for every college student regardless of his or her SAT scores, prior knowledge of content, or skill base—if the belief system is there at the college that we leave no student behind. Braced by that belief and willing to discover and employ new methods of instruction, every professor can teach any student. If we read Moses' successes with students, whom the larger society assumed could not and would not learn complicated abstract thinking, those of us who teach African-American students in colleges, regardless of our ethnicity, should feel a new sense of hope for facilitating success for students who don't now excel in our discipline. It doesn't matter if their reading, writing, and mathematical skills are inadequate when they come to us. Informed by Moses and others' work, we can assume that anyone can be brought from behind, perceiving a sense of purpose larger than self, given the right instruction, and encouraged to persist at the "hard work" of mastering a subject. As Hilliard says, it is the quality of the instruction, not the quality of the student that creates academic excellence.

Building a Community of Learners

To be able to explore the questions of justice and equity within a classroom, and for students to feel safe enough to risk exposing what they don't know in a specific discipline, a teacher must first build a Community of learners. Most indigenous cultures are rooted in a strong sense of communal values. With the primary focus on individual rights in our U.S. culture, our sense of community is too often neglected. In many college classrooms, competition is the guiding principle, a principle that is outside the African worldview (Diop 1989), a view described by Chibueze Udeani (1989) as "the consciousness of a lively unity with community . . . where cooperation, collective responsibility, and interdependence are the key values" (p. 1). In contrast to that, the predominant Euro-centric worldview is one that relies on competition, independence, separateness, and individual rights (Carruthers 1999). Stark differences exist between the two within the context of seeking knowledge. As educators, how do we create a sense of balance among both, where the individual and the community are equally valued? How do we dance with the creative tensions of the dualities? Can we, as educators in college classrooms, continue to separate our work from the community's work? These questions might make worthy discussion with our students within classrooms as community is sought.

Especially, for African-American students, taking the time to build a community within the classroom makes the most sense. Furthermore, if we have the integrity to honor the ancient traditions of the culture of the students we are teaching, then we must pay attention to the social nature of the African educational experience. Often on the Morehouse campus, I saw the reflection of Hilliard's research (SBA 1997) which found that "Education, to our [African] ancestors was regarded as a social, rather than an individual process. Serious efforts were taken to establish the social bonds necessary to create a cohort of learners who not only were students, but who would be lifelong brothers and sisters in the most profound sense of those words" (p. 9). Instinctively, Morehouse capitulated to that ancestral wisdom and those ancient practices. Though deliberate attempts to establish social bonds might not be practiced in every classroom, the emphasis of brotherhood outside the classroom walls sustained campus life and academic achievement.

Moreover, numbers of scholars suggest that there is scientific data from ancient Egypt to modern physics, which indicates the interdependence of all humanity, all species, and all components of the universe from the subatomic level to the formation of the galaxies (Berry 1990; Eisler 1987; Thomas 1974; Swimme 1992). Given those assumptions, why would we model in our classrooms a format of isolated thought and competition, a format incongruent with what we accept as true in cosmic terms? Building a community of students in the classroom seems, then, not just educationally sound, but also well-grounded in ancient and modern scientific theories.

For those of us who teach where the campus life does not offer that sense of community for African-American students, or for those of us, who have consistent problems with student failure, I suggest we, especially, give classroom time to build a community of learners. My students during course evaluations have repeatedly asserted that their being part of such an experience assisted their performance in the classroom. Because I am convinced of the efficacy of this bonding, I use at least 30 minutes of the first class period of all my courses to begin establishing those bonds. Thereafter, I establish small collaborative groups who will become peer editing teams, literature discussion circles, speech critique groups, or textual analysis response groups in any discipline. Important to the construction of these groups is at least one session dedicated to the simulation of just what makes good teams. Because the mainstream culture of the United States primarily promotes competition, too few of us come to college with an adequate background in just what it means to be an effective team player and little experience in group roles that lead to individual and group success. Nevertheless, we can find guides to facilitate such a process. Research literature and popular bookstores are replete with examples describing specific activities that create social bonding, team process, and group success (Campbell & Smith 1997; Felder & Brent 1994; Felder & Brent 2001; Haller et al 2000; Johnson & Johnson 1989 & 1995; Maton & Hrabowski 1999; Starfield & Bleloch et al. 1994). Such success with group process in college classrooms was recently validated by a group of African-American graduate students. These teachers comprised three different, graduating cohorts of an urban teacher leadership master's degree program. As a deliberately formed cohort, these students attended together every course in their five-semester program. When asked during exit interviews to evaluate the program, all graduates remarked that the bonding of the cohort influenced their success more than any other component in the program. This type of peer support system is enormously important if we want to foster the intellectual growth of African-American students in a mainstream college.

With the pressure on professors to cover material, to raise standards, to produce adequately prepared graduates ready either for a competitive market or for graduate school, many believe that bonding is a "nice idea," but too much fluff and too little substance. However, after many trials and errors of others and mine, I have come to agree with Parker Palmer (1993), who says that, "In the absence of the communal virtues, intellectual rigor too easily turns into intellectual rigor mortis" (p. xvii).

The Developing of Personal Relationships with Faculty

Professors at Morehouse spent many hours developing mentor relationships with their students. Professors felt an obligation to know their students beyond the classroom. Many a professor met students during late evenings to tutor or counsel them. One of the professors there, a departmental chairperson, not only used his night hours to tutor college students, but also tutored high school students who showed promise in science, but did not have adequate instruction in the high school. He performed these uncompensated tasks in the midst of writing texts, grants, research, and teaching a full load. I used to tease him that he "needed to get a life." His practices, however, reminded me of the African vision of the teacher as "selfless." In the indigenous African context of education, serious learning happens when teachers have established a personal bond with their students. In the Swahili tradition, this relationship of passing on knowledge through direct contact with people who are skilled craftsmen and instructors is referred to as fundi (Moses & Cobb 2001; Grant 1998). Unlike many white universities whose major focus is chasing research dollars, at Morehouse teaching is considered a serious and meaningful responsibility, the act of a fundi.

At the college, it was not an uncommon practice for professors to invite their students in small groups to their homes. Long before the administration officially initiated advisory groups for all freshmen, many professors chose to occasionally meet students at their homes. In my classroom, at the end of each semester, nearly 100% of the students, on evaluation cards I issued, commented on the benefit for them of the meetings at my home in creating a harmony for struggling with difficult questions and concepts. In my experience with African-American students in high school, college, and graduate school, this practice seemed to cement relationships that made room for a "mutual criticism of thought" (Palmer, p. 74). Many African-American scholars insist that relationship building is a key value in the African culture, and, thus, African-American students perform best for those teachers, whatever their ethnicity, who have authentically bonded with their students.

Other Issues of Culture

Intertwined within discussions of relationship building and other elements of African-American culture lay questions about culture in general. How do we respect each other's cultures; learn from all the variations; recognize the "hidden dimensions of unconscious culture" (Hall 1989); and move as Edward T. Hall suggests "Beyond Culture"? How do we grapple with the thoughts, feelings, communications and behaviors that are molded by our separate cultures? How do we reckon with the good and bad in every culture? And, perhaps, most importantly, through the investigation of culture, can we begin to break the chains of a hegemonic society where all citizens are held captive, not only the disenfranchised?

For most professors in the U. S., issues of culture are deeply embedded in how we teach. Because most of us were schooled in a Euro-centric (or a British) model of education, including those who have come to the university from previously colonized countries (Carruthers & Harris 1997), we seem obliged to consider the limits of teaching within that one cultural frame. Connecting our classroom instruction to the culture of our students to help unfold their brilliance has been validated by a host of educational researchers (Delpit 1995, 1997; Hilliard SBA 1997; Irvine 2000; Ladson-Billings 1993; Wilson 1999). Yet, in my numerous years of sitting in meetings with white university professors, I have been perplexed by our attempts to look outside the context of the African-American culture, in fact, to look among ourselves, for answers to pedagogical problems in teaching students from another's culture—a practice that seems not only arrogant, but also stupid. We seem to assume that our wisdom, emanating from our one cultural perspective, is somehow universal—that our truths are not grounded in our particular cultural belief system, rather somehow gleaned from a cosmic logic. Delpit's research (1995) indicates that many mainstream teachers' confusion of culturally relevant instruction is common no matter where we teach—in African-American communities, in indigenous communities in Alaska, Papua New Guinea, in elementary through college classrooms. Along with

Delpit's, my experience, too, suggests that many of us in mainstream contexts seem confused as well about the significance of culture in the personal and the political lives of all people.

Because of institutional and societal failures to recognize diverse cultural realities and wisdom, can we who teach African-American students in college assume that our content knowledge is enough to optimally support the intellectual growth of our students? Though expertise in a discipline is crucial, a culturally responsive context for teaching that discipline seems equally significant to the academic achievement of African-American students, as it is for all students. Too few students achieve at their highest potential when the instructional climate is alien to their cultural experience. White students are always taught in the United States within their cultural context. But, for African-American students, and most students of color, whose culture and history have been denied or distorted in our schools, teaching within a cultural context becomes a mandate of intellectual integrity.

Sometimes when confronting the racist epistemology that dictates policies and practices of most of our institutions, especially education, I sink into disillusionment and hopelessness. In those moments I remind myself, however, that part of my hopelessness is driven by my own racism. Being white and a product of mainstream schooling, I have unconsciously absorbed many notions of supremacy. One of those is the assumption that if white people don't find a solution to the problems we have created in schools that supposedly serve African-American youth, then those youth are all doomed. I now understand more clearly, however, that what we really need to do is get out of the way of those African-American teachers, scholars, and researchers who already know the "way out of no way" (Young 1994). For, the reality is that, with or without us—their teachers, as Richard Wright (1941) proclaimed in *12 Million Black Voices*, "Hundreds of thousands [of African-Americans] are moving into the sphere of conscious history" (p. 147) a history that includes Hilliard's assumption of intellectual and spiritual transformation.

Summary

Two of the philosophical and instructional constructs for the classroom, discussed in this chapter are not only valuable but also imperative for delivering consistently positive academic results and for grounding all of our classroom work in intellectual integrity.

The first is discussed in the chapter under the category of *Nature Vs. Nurture*. The nature of the learner, in colleges and universities, is too often questioned. Without a record of past high performance or high test scores accompanying admittance, a student's ability to withstand the rigor of the college classroom is strongly doubted. What this chapter suggests is that, as instructors, when we do not believe in the capacity of all students to achieve at high levels, regardless of SAT scores, previous skill-based competence in a discipline, or ethnic or socio-economic history, we stunt the intellectual growth of those who are in our classroom, and we weaken the nation's capacity to profit from its human intellectual capital. Too much research and too many life stories emphatically demonstrate that those who work hard to pursue excellence, regardless of previous manifestations of talent, can and do achieve at high levels when they know that their teachers expect from them and demand excellence. Within such a climate of respect and nurture, the students perform well, regardless of the methodology that those professors use (Hilliard, Delpit, Steele). Septima Clark and others in the Southern Freedom Movement proved this over and over again, while teaching illiterate adults in the rural south. Bob Moses continues that tradition in the Algebra Project. Asa G. Hilliard, III creates that for graduate students. As professors, we need to school ourselves in those lessons.

The second imperative is discussed under the category *Education for Liberation.* Denying our students the opportunity to examine the faulty notions of a history and epistemology rooted in oppression, which taints all of our individual disciplines, is a negligence that hinders honest intellectual discourse. Within a discourse of liberation, African-Americans like Vincent Harding seem to be asking educators the right questions. Harding (1999) wrote that, "Langston Hughes, our poet/teacher, said, 'We, the people, must redeem our land . . . And make America again.' What does it mean to redeem a land, to remake a nation? Who are 'the people' who must do it? And who are the teachers, and what is the curriculum that will prepare us for such a task?" Theresa Perry, Charles Payne (Perry et al. 2003; Payne 1995, 1997) and hundreds of other African American scholars suggest that a curriculum grounded in the old African-American traditions of liberatory education is a first step in transforming our students, our schools and colleges, ourselves, and our nation.

Therefore, if we really want to call forth in the classroom the intellectual dimension of African-American students, we need to honor their histories which demonstrate that struggles for liberation have been an on-going movement in America since the days of slavery, that their ancestors for centuries have been pushing America to reach its dream. These stories are powerfully instructive. They privilege a narrative that counters society's diminishment of their cultural vigor and intellectual traditions (Perry et al. 2003). When students investigate science, mathematics, philosophy, and the humanities within a context that acknowledges the ancient Black civilizations that existed while Europe was still in the dark ages, possibilities emerge for new ways of thinking about each discipline, about knowledge, and about the making of knowledge. If we ignore the significance of examining cultural truths, then no matter how creative or "cutting edge" our strategies are, they become meaningless and lead nowhere except to further buoy a spiritually and intellectually corrupt "military industrial complex." If students are reading and writing historical and cultural distortions, and ignoring the impact of those distortions on sustaining a hegemonic worldview, who cares what strategy we're using, or how well the students read and write. In such classrooms, I think about the words of Maori writer, Patricia Grace who said that, "Books are Dangerous" because most books lie about indigenous people's values, actions, customs, culture, identity, and, ultimately, their existence (Smith, 1999, p. 35). When we do not confront the erroneous constructions of knowledge embedded in all of our disciplines, are not our classrooms dangerous as well?

Martin Luther King, Jr. said that, "The American Negro may be the vanguard of a prolonged struggle that may change the shape of the world, as billions of deprived shake and transform the earth in the quest for life, freedom and justice" (Harding, 1998, p. 108) From reading the stories of the long history of African people's resistance to oppression, I believe that the "American Negro" has been in the vanguard for over 400 years, struggling, changing, challenging the society to transform itself, and if we as teachers cannot usher those ancestors' children to the top of their game, then we need to step aside and allow those who do know how to do it.

References

Banks, J. (1997). *Educating citizens in a multicultural society*. New York: Teachers College Press. p. 16.

Berry, T. (1990). *The dream of the earth*. University of California Press.

Campbell, W. & Smith, K. (1997). *New Paradigms for College Teaching*. Minneapolis: Burgess Publishing Co.

Carruthers, J. H. (1999). *Intellectual warfare*. Chicago: Third World Press. p. xv.

Carruthers, J. H. & Harris L. C. (Eds). (1997). *African world history project: The preliminary challenge*. Los Angeles, CA: Association for the Study of Classical African Civilizations.

Clark, D. (1989). High expectations. *Effective schools: Critical issues in the education of black children*. Detroit: National Alliance of black School Educators. p. 33.

Crim, A. A. (1999). Psychological aspects of leadership. A course taught at Georgia State University, Atlanta, GA.

Delpit, L. (1995). *Other people's children*. New York: The New Press.

Delpit, L. (1997, September). Ten factors for teaching excellence in urban schools. Speech at Urban Atlanta Coalition Compact Town Meeting, Atlanta, GA.

Diop, C. A. (1989) *The cultural unity of Black Africa: The domains of matriarchy & patriarchy in classical antiquity.* London: Karnak House.

Eisler, R. (1987). *The chalice & the blade: Our history, our future.* New York: Harper & Row.

Felder R. M. & Brent, R. (1994). Cooperative learning in technical courses: Procedures, pitfalls, and payoffs. *ERIC* Document Reproduction Service, ED 377038.

Felder, R. M. & Brent, R. (2001). Effective strategies for cooperative learning. *Journal of Cooperation & Collaboration in College Teaching* 10 (2), 69–75.

Freire, P. (1998/1970). *Pedagogy of the oppressed,* translated by Myra Bergman Ramos. New York: Continuum.

Freire, P. & Macedo, D. (1987). *Literacy.* New York: Bergin & Garvey. p. 122.

Gardner, H. (2000). Intelligence reframed: Multiple intelligences for the 21st century. New York: Basic Books, Inc.

Good, T. L. (1981, February). Teacher expectations and student perceptions: A decade of research. *Educational Leadership* 38, 415–422.

Good, T. L. (1982, December). How teachers' expectations affect results. *American Education* 18, 25–32.

Grant, J. (1998). *Ella Baker: Freedom bound.* New York: John Wiley & Sons.

Hall, E. (1989). *Beyond culture.* New York: Anchor Books Edition/Double Day Dell Publishing Co.

Haller, C. R., Gallagher, V. J., Weldon, T. L., & Felder, R. M. (2000). Dynamics of peer education in cooperative learning workgroups. *Journal of Engineering Education* 89 (3), 285–293.

Harding, V. (1999). *Hope and history: Why we must share the story of the movement.* New York: Orbis Books. p. 1.

Harding, V. (1998). *Martin Luther King: The Inconvenient Hero.* New York: Orbis Books. p. 108.

Hilliard, III, A. G. (1988). Testing and misunderstanding intelligence. Paper presented at Puget Sound Educational Consortium, Seattle, WA.

Hilliard, III, A. G. (1997). *SBA: The reawakening of the African mind.* Gainesville, FL: Makare Publishing Co. pp. 69–70.

Hilliard, III, A. G. (1997, October). Tapping the genius and touching the spirit: A human approach to the rescue of our children. The Ninth Annual Benjamin E. Atlanta, GA: Mays Lecture.

Hilliard, III, A. G. (1997). The structure of valid staff development. *Journal of Staff Development* 18 (2), Spring.

Hilliard, III, A. G. (1999, February). The spirit of the African child. Unpublished speech at the Urban Atlanta Coalition Compact Town Meeting, Atlanta, GA.

Hilliard, III, A. G. (2000). Awaken the geniuses of children: The nurture of nature. Unpublished speech for Skylight 6th International Teaching for Intelligence Conference (Cassette produced by: Chesapeake Audio/Video Communications, Inc. 6330 Howard Lane, Elkridge, MD, 21075 (00227-1160).

Hogan, R. (1974). On Playing Chess and on Counting NCTE Members. NCTE For the members. Urbana, IL: NCTE publications. Retrieved from/ library/NCTEFiles/Resources/Journals/EJ/1974/0638-nov1974/ EJ0638Members.pdf

Johnson, D. & Johnson, R. (1989). *Cooperation and competition: Theory and research.* Minneapolis: Burgess Publishing Co.

Johnson, D. & Johnson, R. (1995). *Creative controversy: Intellectual challenge in the classroom,* 3rd ed. Minneapolis: Burgess Publishing Co.

King, M. (1986). *Freedom Song: A personal story of the 1960's Civil Rights Movement.* New York: Morrow, Inc.

Kohl, H. (1994). *'I Won't Learn From You': And other thoughts on creative maladjustment.* New York: The New Press.

Ladson-Billings, G. (1992). Liberatory consequences of literacy: A case of culturally relevant instruction for African American students. *Journal of Negro Education* 61 (3): 378–391.

Ladson-Billings, G. (1994). *The dreamkeepers.* San Francisco: Jossey-Bass.

Loewen, J. W. (1996). *Lies my teacher told me: Everything your American history textbook got wrong.* New York: Simon & Schuster.

Lopez, B. (1990). *Crow and weasel.* San Francisco: North Point Press.

Maton, K. I. & Hrabowski, III, F. A. (1999). Enhancing the success of African American students in the sciences: Freshman year outcomes. Baltimore County: University of Maryland.

Mays, B. E. (1983). *Quotable quotes of Benjamin E. Mays.* New York: Vantage Press.

Moffett, J. & Wagner, B. (1983). *Student centered language arts and reading, k-13: A handbook for teachers.* New York: Houghton Mifflin Co.

Moses, R. & Cobb, Jr., C. (2001). *Radical equations: Math literacy and Civil Rights.* Boston: Beacon Press.

Murray, C. & Hernstein, R. (1994). *The bell curve.* New York, NY: The Free Press.

Palmer, P. (1993). *To know as we are known: Education as a spiritual journey.* San Francisco: Harper.

Payne, C. (1997, March). Education for activism: Mississippi freedom schools in the 1960s. Paper presented at AERA conference, Chicago. p. 5.

Payne, C. (1995). *I've got the light of freedom: The organizing tradition and the Mississippi freedom struggle.* Berkeley: University of California Press.

Perry, T. (2001, April). Task Force on Black Education Report. Panel for AERA conference, Seattle, WA.

Perry, T., Steele, C., Hilliard, A. G. (2003). *Young gifted and black: Promoting high achievement among African-American students.* Boston: Beacon Press.

Reagon, B. J. (1998). 'Oh freedom': Music of the movement. In Greenberg, G. (Ed.). *A circle of trust: Remembering SNCC.* New Brunswick: Rutgers University Press.

Rosenthal, R & Jacobson, L. (1968). *Pygmalion in the Classroom: Teacher Expectation and Pupils' Intellectual Development.* New York: Holt.

Siddle-Walker, V. (1996). *Their highest potential: An African American school community in the* segregated south. Chapel Hill, N.C.: The University of North Carolina Press.

Smith. L. T. (1999). *Decolonizing methodologies: Research and indigenous peoples.* London: Zed Books Ltd.

Starfield, T., Smith, K., & Bleloch, A. (1994). *How to model it: Problem solving for the computer age.* Edina, MN.: Interaction Book Co.

Swimme, B. (1992). *The universe story: From the primordial flaring forth to the ecozoic era—A celebration of the unfolding of the cosmos.* San Francisco: Harper.

Thomas, L. (1974). *The lives of a cell—Notes of a biology watcher.* London: Bantam Books Edition.

Udeani, C. C. (1989). The search for meaning in the traditional African worldview. Upper Austria/Caritas Integration project. Kepler University Linz, Austria. Retrieved October 5, 2001 from http://www.stfx.ca/people/wsweet/abstract-Udeani.html

Venter, E. (2000). Expectation of students versus expectation of lecturers of philosophy in a postgraduate course. Philosophy of education in the new millennium: Conference proceedings—International Network of Philosophers of Education, Vol. 3. Sydney, Australia: University of Sydney.

Wilson, A. (1998). *Blueprint for Black power: A moral, political and economic imperative for the twenty-first century.* New York: Afrikan World InfoSystems.

Young, A. (1994). *A way out of no way: The spiritual memoirs of Andrew Young.* Nashville: Thomas Nelson Publishing.

Wright, R. (1941). *12 Million Black voices.* New York: Thunder's Mouth Press. p. 147.

PART 6

To love. To be loved . . .
Never get used to the disparity

To love. To be loved . . . To never get used to the unspeakable
violence and the vulgar disparity of life around you.
To see joy in the saddest places. To pursue beauty to
its lair. To never simplify what is complicated or
complicate what is simple. To respect strength,
never power. Above all, to watch.
To try and understand.

—*Arundhati Roy*

What will become of your life?

by Isabel Souza-Rodriguez

I always hated concrete. Sure, I have benefitted from and appreciated the many structures in my life that utilized concrete to offer me support, an even path, or even shelter. Mostly, I grew up hating the way that concrete made my surroundings hard, impenetrable, and unresponsive. I can't run my fingers through concrete. I can't put my ear against it and hear beautiful messages of a live world. The most it ever did was to echo the beatings of my own heart. I still remember what it felt like having my ear against the concrete wall of my parent's bedroom, those nights that my sisters ran and crawled into my bed. I remember hearing the deepness of my father's voice through that wall—how it made the wall shake, especially with the sudden thud of my mother's body slamming against it. I remember not being able, against my better wishes, to will that wall into softening before her impact. There is a crisp finality in impacting concrete. A deep silence always follows for a few moments as the compounds consume every last thread of the momentum that just came upon it. Surviving it always creates the void of that unavoidable question, "What will become of your life . . . now?"

I heard this question again in December of 2011. I had been drinking excessively, and the series of events that followed led to my confrontation with this question as I felt the weight of two bodies pressing down against my back. A broad hand cupped my skull and pressed my face down against the pavement. I realized, beyond the sound of this question, that my hands were pinned tightly against my back. Two officers were restraining me, protecting me . . . from myself. Not 60 seconds earlier I had struck, with the full force of my body, the love of my life. I didn't even see him until his body was already ahead of my fist, flying backward with all of my energy, and slamming into the side of a moving SUV that was passing right behind him on the street in that instant. As the concrete printed itself onto my cheek, I could hear the officers screaming to me, "We're taking you to jail" and my love screaming somewhere behind them, "Please don't take him! Please don't take him! Please!!!"

I didn't deserve being released by the officers in that moment. I had lost control. In an instant, I now understand, a trigger from my childhood made me react violently and defensively against my father who wasn't even there that day. It wasn't my father that had reached for my shoulder. It was my fiancé. So it was clear to me, then, as we traveled in silence back to our home, crying and barely able to understand what had just happened, that I knew I could no longer continue to avoid seeing a therapist.

As a Latino man, I know the stigma in my culture against seeking mental health support. I was raised to believe that "mental health" was a figment of people's imagination, and that all therapists were nothing more than professional con artists. I internalized that for so many years that I wasn't paying attention to the severity of my own problem. I needed to find help . . . for my mind. No diet could ever cure the narrative of my own thoughts. No physical practice could ever build up my internal strength to defeat trauma. I understood this finally after my explosion on December 11th. Immediately afterward, I looked into providers and scheduled my first appointment.

The day before my therapist appointment, I met for breakfast with one of my best friends from middle school—one of the hardest periods of my life. I asked her candidly, "How is it possible that we survived?" Neither one of us had an answer.

In my first session, I shared with my therapist my recollections of the **bodies** that made up my years in middle school; flashbacks of my peers who were always more dead than alive, stuffed to capacity with medications that were supposed to have made them "feel better" or "hold themselves together." Remembering how those bodies constantly fell apart, became pale, fragile, tore at the extremities, ached, and fell to the ground suddenly, repeatedly, needing to be carried to "administration" where parents would come to carry them farther away to institutions where their entire world would become boxes of concrete. I recanted to my shrink how I grappled through those years, barely making it, desperately hoping not to become another needless casualty.

"I'm not sure how we survived it," I said.
"We did . . ." my friend replied, "and I think that's why we're such good friends."

I began to see quite clearly in my therapy sessions that the therapist had no particular healing affinity, nor magical powers. She didn't generally say very clever things nor were her responses much more interesting than any other conversation I ever held with a friend in childhood. I appreciated though, being able to find a complete stranger who could tell me, "I'm SO glad you made it today" knowing that she meant it, and especially that she could understand how "today"makes it such a special victory. I did learn through her, though, that Yes, I managed to survive middle school, but I need to remember and to appreciate that I survived today too. The lesson will remain that perhaps if I survived today, I might be able to tap into that same strength tomorrow.

I resent any parent that still makes their kids feel stupid for wondering if their minds and hearts also need medical care, just like our bodies. That's like denying a kid eye and dental exams for years, simply from superstition. I feel that I could have just as easily gone blind. I could have completely lost sight of my very self.

My therapist one day explained, "I'm surprised at the level of conversation I've been able to have with you. People who have lived your experiences generally become so far removed from reality that it's hard to achieve any coherent dialogue with them beyond a few disjointed sentences." I laugh at how incredibly un-reassuring it is to think that somehow I adapted some unnatural ability to survive trauma. That doesn't give me any comfort. It really just makes me feel somewhat undeservingly lucky. I remember reading a Margaret Atwood novel once about a woman who felt like the word, "shatter." I spent over a year reflecting on that book and how closely I connected to that character. I've been on the verge of shattering for the 14 years I've known I've needed therapy.

Therapy is just a step. A single liberated stride on an uncharted path of self-healing. It isn't that life "gets better" all of a sudden. But without that therapy experience, I wouldn't have the words to describe to you how incredibly wonderful it feels right now to know that "I gave myself a chance" and trusted my instinct well enough to have taken that first step, in whatever direction that may take me. How often do we ever "give ourselves a chance?"

It seems much easier for me to believe in others than to believe in myself. I used to go to any lengths not to do it—not to "fail"—as if personal care were a definitive form of failure. I seemed to want to sacrifice 14 years of my life to self-doubt, when my very bones seemed to yearn for self-love, or acknowledgement, or gratitude. I often see a mind . . . a heart . . . a spirit somewhere inside me, running like a 5 year old to each dark corner of me, whispering, "I am here."

I regret that we still live in a world where mental health is far beyond accessible to everyone who deserves it. Still, I believe it can be possible for all of us, if we as a community could dare to believe that mental health is as important in our lives as our physical health: our exercise, our eye exams, our immunizations, our hygiene, our diet. It is possible to care for our whole selves! I'm learning that it is possible to show love and compassion for the entirety of who I am, and not just my physical parts.

I tell my therapist about my life of activism, and she replies, "I was an activist like you when I was young. My body shifted and my capacities became different, so now I bring my activism to this room, where every day I fight very hard for good people to have faith in themselves, and for misunderstood people to see the fullness of their astounding beauty."

I remember again, my friend telling me: "We're friends because we are survivors." I grieve the fact that not all of us who had every right to be here with us today made it—and that the best of us might be needing constantly to brace for the impending impacts and lashes of each new day of resilience. For, I, too, am unsure if I will find my way back in that void of the questions hidden within concrete.

So if you've ever wanted to reach out to someone anonymously to ask for proper individualized attention to everything beyond your physical self: DO. If you've been postponing it for years because of something someone you loved said to you: SCREW THEIR IGNORANCE, AND TAKE CARE OF YOURSELF. You are way too precious to be set aside as a secondary priority. Sometimes we must be our #1 priority. Our lives and others may depend on that basic respect.

Knowing that I might be close to taking my own life, my therapist, during my initial session, recommended scheduling another appointment for a date four days away. Ironically, she accidentally wrote the appointment on the wrong page of her calendar, so her office was locked the day that I came back to see her.

I had a moment of panic for a split second as I stared at my hand grasping the knob of her locked office door. Yet it was that moment that I realized the true function of the sessions of therapy. I didn't really need to talk to her about anything specific, or brilliant, or insightful. I just needed to come back. I needed to be able to reassure myself that I cared about my mind enough to be willing to offer it continued, undivided medical attention. I realized this, released the doorknob, and felt peace. I haven't missed a single one of my appointments since.

What is going on?

by Alexa Ovalles

"Mom, what is going on? What are these people doing here?"

Those are the words I remember asking her at 10:00 p.m. when my dad's family were outside our bakery on June 12th, 2003. It was dark, 60 degrees, and the only lights shining were from the lamp posts and the cars. By the time we arrived home, seated in a corner of the bed, Mom said: "We can't find your dad."

A seven-year-old girl might not understand the severity of the situation, but when I heard that rough voice coming from the phone saying "We have him," it was clear that this was more than just a disappearance. The people behind the voice wanted money. The amount was ridiculously high, and a miracle would be needed to sell the farm, the bakery, and get him back. We were just recovering from a two-year separation of the family when my dad's kidnapping happened. Weeks later, from our balcony, I saw my mom with my little Barbie suitcase. Her words were "Bye" but her face spoke a different story. Where was she going? I did not know, yet it seemed just like a normal day.

That night was my cousin's birthday. We were in front of the cake when my aunt suddenly led my sister and me to the car, then drove us to my grandma's house. Lights, noises, reporters, and at the end of the hallway, there was a dirty long bearded man. It was my father. He did not look like what I remembered him. He had been kidnapped for two months—which had seemed like years.

In those woods, in the jungle, these Colombian abductors hold their victims neither with chains nor ropes, but with the fear of a soldier's armament. They are an organization where phones do not exist and the messages are sent by gunshots to the air. Thank God, my father was secure now. Unfortunately, his liberty came with a price. Higher than any currency exchange, a life. The exact same day he returned, the same day my mom disappeared. That last day I saw her from the balcony, she was set to have a face-to-face interview with the kid-nappers to give some money she had gathered for my dad's rescue.

It was already August, very late at night, wearing a brown wig, she drove a rented car. Maybe it was his heartbreaking voice on the tape saying that he loved us and how he hoped we could be together that moved my mom to go after him. She expected to see him, but . . .

"Mrs. this is not enough. We'll release your husband, but you must come with us," said the guerrillero when she gave him a hollow tire filled with cash. It was either the trade or my dad's death. Right after she accepted the terms, they released him and kept her.

On the other side of the border from my mom, there was my dad wobbling, finding an exit from the jungle. He ran into the mud and started rolling downhill, where he ended near a principal road that connects to our home-town. I still wonder how he didn't die while falling from that mountain. Just as he got on his feet, a taxi passed by and gave him the ride to my grandma's house. He was physically free, but still shackled to their extortion. He knew that the battle was not finished yet.

Back in the jungle, the first week of her kidnapping, my mom was losing her mind. Being a woman surrounded by seven men is not a good picture. The days were long and the nights were more so. The only light she saw was from the sun or the moon. She was trapped and had nowhere to go. "One night, while I was sleeping in a hammock hung between two trees, something fell from the top and rubbed me closely. It was a snake," she said. Another day, they were walking and she saw a big scratch in a trunk. Clearly some big ani-mal had left its mark.

There was no escape from her captors. If she tried, she would end up caught and killed by her abductors or by a dangerous animal. Her prison was a place where there was neither bathroom nor kitchen, just trees, ground, rain, bugs, and fear. She feared dying or worse, being raped by each of the seven.

Often people in danger's way have suggested that when death is close, scenes from one's life flash before them. During those times, people of faith suggest that their God is always close, closer than one's fear. There was only one thing my mom's abductors allowed her to keep along with the men's clothing she had brought to my father—a Bible. Being raised a Christian, she spent her days reading and her nights praying. She told us later that she discovered how her reality was in that book. The scriptures became alive for her. While captive, something moved where she put her hand in a tree. It was a chame-leon. She read this chameleon as no other than God's message of love for her. She thought she heard God whisper to her: "Just as he hides from his enemies, so I hide you from yours."

Sometime after the initial shock of her captivity wore off, my mom started meditating and praying Psalms 23. "Even though I walk through the darkest valley, I will fear no evil for you are with me; your rod and your staff, they comfort me." Miraculously, she started to become more patient, more peaceful, believing that God's will would be done. The hope of returning home, she said, began to grow.

Weeks passed by and few notices came from the status of the mission, as they used to call it. My dad tried to sell some properties, but he couldn't raise enough of the ransom demand, and ended up mortgaging every property he had. Once he gathered the money and gave it to them, she was guided outside the woods.

My mom explained, "We walked for hours until we made it to a small village. There, one of my captors told me: 'Don't say a word to anybody. If they ask something, you are my wife, and we're just waiting for the bus that will take us to the nearest place.'"

After they arrived in the closest city to the border between Colombia and Venezuela, her captor said: "I am sorry, Ms, but this is the job I chose." With those words, he went his way. My mom was free.

It took her almost a day to get to Rubio, my mom's hometown. I can't forget her words about the return: "When I was in a corner of the street, at about 500 feet away from home, I stopped walking and broke down crying. I hadn't cried until I finally realized it was over."

Neither my little sister nor I knew about her kidnapping during that month and a half. I was told she was in a spiritual retreat. She was, indeed. I might say, one that changed our entire lives forever. Nowadays, I thank God for bringing back my family, for giving me the understanding that life might last years or can easily be gone in a second. Money, properties, material things don't matter when you're losing your loved ones. Then you get to admit that love, honor, and gratitude cannot be taken for granted.

There are a lot of stories that root who I am today, but my parent's bravery and sign of true love is, perhaps, a special seed inside of my heart. Their story has strengthened me and filled me with courage to never give up on anything, even when it's hard to see the light, to look first at the need of others before being selfish and egocentric; to care about what I have and not complain about what I do not have; to honor and appreciate my family and surroundings; to respect others; to give without expecting anything in return—"What you sow, you shall reap."

I would love to say that everything was perfect after we were all reunited as a family, but though one chapter may end in joy, another kind may quickly begin. The first month after our ordeal, my dad didn't want to go out of our apartment. He struggled to overcome the fear of being abducted again. His and my mom's fears dominated how they raised us thereafter. Their fears and insecurity became ours. I struggled to liberate myself from fear.

With time, our lives improved, but our hearts needed healing. Two years later, because of a new threat, my family had to flee to Miami, a city where many seem to be pursuing a second chance; where many seem to be running away from a conflict, trying to save their lives. As I write these words, I know that my family's journey is not finished. We are slowly remaking our lives, embracing change, and rooting ourselves once again in another place and time.

My great grandmother's battle

by Monica Penichet

Pulling up to my great grandmothers house I was a little scared and nervous. It was the first time I had gone to see her and the same day she had chemotherapy. I didn't know what to expect. Was she going to look different? Was she going to act different?

As soon as my great grandfather opened the door to their house I automatically smelled the familiar aroma of Cuban spices and the greasy smell of plantains. I walked into her kitchen and there she was stirring a pig pot of Arroz con pollo. "Abuela what are you doing?" I asked her.

"I'm cooking your favorite meal, why do you ask?" she said.
"You should be resting not cooking; you just got home from four hours of chemotherapy."

To all of us standing around her, she said "I'm not dying, so stop treating me like a baby, I am going to continue to live my life the same way I always did. So, Monica and Jonathan, go set the table."

At the dinner table, no one really wanted to speak about the whole cancer thing but I did. I was 11 years old at the time and I was curious. I waited until the whole table got quiet, stuffing their faces with food.

I started off with a compliment "Abuela this Arroz con pollo is amazing!" With a typical sarcastic remark, She replied: "What do you think, just because I have breast cancer, it will be bad?" My brother laughed at that, then, my mom hit him upside the head; and I laughed at that.

Her remark gave me the perfect opportunity to ask about the chemotherapy. "It was actually really uncomfortable and tiring, for four hours you are hooked up to machines and an IV stuck in your skin." Because of my horrible Spanish skills, my mom translated most of my questions.

"Are there any side effects after the chemotherapy?"

"I will eventually lose my hair, I will throw up occasionally; there will be days I won't want to get up from the bed. But through all the side effects, I will continue my daily routine because if I give up I am not teaching you and your brother the right lesson."

After eating and washing dishes, we were sitting in the living room. As always I was right next to her. Everyone was talking amongst themselves, and I turned to her, "Abuela, why are you being so strong?" and for a second she didn't say anything just looked at me; the whole room got quiet in seconds. My great grandmother grabbed my hand and said "I am strong for you and for the rest of this family; I will not let a little disease ruin me and each and every one of you. When something terrible in your life occurs you can't let it affect the way you live and that is why I will continue to invite the whole family for pool parties, and I will continue to cook everyone's favorite meal."

Finding out she had breast cancer was not easy for me. I was probably the one who took it the hardest. I broke down crying right on her lap because I automatically thought I was going to lose her. People told me to be strong and to have faith, but at 11 years old I didn't know how to be strong for something like cancer.

That day that she cooked us all my favorite meal "Arroz con Pollo" I understood what people meant to be strong. I started researching everything that had to do with Breast Cancer to get a better understanding of what she was going through. I found out she had to remove her breast; and I was so shocked that I asked her "Abuela can you live without a breast?"

"Yes, of course, but I don't think your great grandfather will be too happy about it being removed." She continued to make jokes in the midst of the ensuing disease.

She continued to live her life as though she had never been diagnosed with breast cancer; but when she started to lose her hair and went bald, her suffering became even more real to me. For the longest time after her hair fell out, she didn't want to leave her house; but if she had no other choice, she would wear a scarf wrapped around her head and forge on.

My great grandmother is what some call a high-maintenance old woman. She weekly went to the salon to do her hair and nails. She also loved to be the center of attention; if you didn't call her even one day out of the seven days in the week, you would end up on her "bad" list. It was understandable, though, because she did so much for me and my family that the least we can do is call her every day.

While growing up, from my great grandmother, I learned not only life lessons, but how to cook, how to speak Spanish, and how to treat guests when they visit. She never really said "Hey, Monica, let's go teach you some things." Rather, being at her house every other day, I just watched her and listened to her and observed the way she carried herself.

I am always amazed by her strength through her fight with breast cancer. Seeing her go through it for so many years, I believe, helped me develop strength. People every day are struggling with new problems, illnesses, financial situations, work, school, family problems, and social injustices. Fortunately, for me, my great grandmother demonstrates how to remain strong in the midst of pain, disappointment, and suffering. Her "toughness" reminds me that when fighting for justice, I must stay true to who I am, keep maintaining my daily routine and responsibilities, while trying to help others "fight the good fight."

Recently I lost my grandmother, daughter of my great grandmother, and I stayed strong.

History lessons learned and paid forward

by Ruba Monem

Teaching history is important, and, sometimes, reminders of its importance are found in the least expected places. Many years ago, I attended a Native American festival. Before going, I anticipated it becoming a valuable cultural experience, yet I underestimated the impact it would have on my role as a history teacher. The festival itself was quite an education. I remember being captivated by the artifacts and visual depictions of Native American culture and spirituality. I moved from exhibit to exhibit and tried to take in the flood of information. I listened to folktales and watched mesmerizing dances performed by Native men and women dressed in full regalia. After one of the performances, I made my way to one of the female Native performers to let her know how much I enjoyed the production. Both polite and gracious, she started to make small talk with me. Being the history enthusiast that I am, I proceeded to ask her several questions about her tribal ancestry and customs. She did not seem to mind answering my many questions. In fact, she told me that she enjoyed my genuine interest in her culture. At that point, I told her I was a history teacher. I remember that she smiled and told me that teaching was a special gift.

We spent about 45 minutes discussing various aspects of the festival and Native Peoples' contributions to the Americas. During the conversation, she asked me questions about Native American history. As a history teacher, I was a little embarrassed that I could not answer some of her questions. This eye-opening encounter with my ignorance forced me to examine my dearth of knowledge about a crucial national narrative. I admitted to her that I needed to brush up on the history of North American indigenous communities. She encouraged me to look for sources of factual information developed by various tribes of the Americas, and not to rely solely on mass market American history textbooks. She believed that most history books failed to provide an accurate portrayal of Native American historical record nor adequately described the injustices and cruelty inflicted upon Natives by a hegemonic, Eurocentric society. My new friend gave me the names of a few authors and asked me to promise her that I would learn more about the saga of Native peoples in this country and pass that along to my students.

Later, I asked her what the most important message was that I should take back to my students. She answered me with two words, "The truth." Of course, I knew enough to know that I did not know "the truth" of the Cherokee, the Iroquois, the Lakhota, the Navajo, the Miccosukee, the Seminole, and hundreds of other First Nations communities. But, she told me that her concerns revolved around the lack of awareness about the brutal treatment of Native tribes as well as their fallacious depiction in popular media. She believed it was important to dispel Native American stereotypes and gross distortions of facts. She wanted me to separate the fact from the fiction. I promised her I would do my best to honor her wishes. We continued to discuss the particulars of her tribe and my new friend left me with the question, "If the children are not taught, how will they know?"

After the festival, I spent countless hours researching Native American history. I knew that I had a responsibility to share a part of our country's history that is largely ignored or totally bypassed in many American history classrooms. All too often, the presence of Native Americans in texts is relegated to being the backdrop to the events experienced by White Americans. Based on the limited pages in textbooks and the limited class time devoted to First Nation's history in K-12 social studies pacing guides, the public falsely assumes that the history of Europeans in the Americas is far more important than that of the 12,000 year old Native American civilization. I soon learned exactly what my new friend meant when she referred to Native Americans as the "invisible voice."

The relationship between Whites, Native Americans, and other minorities is complex, and that complexity must be discussed and acknowledged. I knew I would be doing a great disservice to my new friend, my profession, and my students if I failed to address this issue. I knew it would not be easy. Injustice? Rape? Murder? Racism? Social dominance? These issues are all sensitive subjects to broach with adolescents; therefore, I carefully considered how I would go about presenting the information. I knew that if I engaged my students in an honest unraveling of these concepts, my students were capable of analyzing the information and making the necessary connections. I asked my students, in collaborative groups, to investigate the definitions and examples of the concepts of injustice, rape, murder, and racism. Due to their living in a large urban city, these ideas were familiar to my students. But, introducing the concept of social dominance was a bit more challenging. I had to provide them with several examples in order for them to recognize social dominance and be able to provide me with examples of their own. Once they under-stand the concept, however, they started to piece together the social, eco-nomic, and political consequences of dominance on society. This type of gradual release required encouragement and patience on my part as a teacher and our joint willingness to learn on the part of my students. Once this exchange took place, my students were ready to process the information on their own and draw parallels between the past and the present.

Adolescents are amazing individuals and their willingness to learn about the past is boundless. Their passion for justice is even more admirable. Far too often, teachers underestimate their students' ability and desire to learn. Once this desire to learn is unleashed, there is no containing it. I set out to promote a dialogue about Native Americans that extended beyond folktales, spirit guides, and rituals. Based on responses, I have received from my students, I believe that I have started to achieve this goal. For example, during one class-room discussion, a student pointed out that Native Americans living on res-ervations is a form of segregation. While discussing the issue with his peers in class, he concluded that this was unfair and illegal, and that it was not a deci-sion made by Natives. Rather, he insisted, it was a decision forced on the Natives by a more dominant group in society. My students recognized that a race-based hierarchy was established hundreds of years ago and continues to be maintained generation after generation. These adolescents began to understand that skin color continues to be used as a means by which hege-mony (dominance) is forced on American institutional systems. And they now insisted that, yes, American cultural hegemony manifests itself in the form of segregation of Native Americans from Non-Native Americans; Whites from non-Whites; etc. Further, when we discussed the murder of mil-lions of Native Americans beginning with the arrival of the Europeans, my students drew comparisons between the genocide of the Natives and the genocide of other ethnic groups in history—indeed, powerful connections made by adolescents.

Because of my serendipitous conversation years ago with the Native Ameri-can woman at the festival, which led me to further research, I somehow influ-enced my students as well as myself to think about history on a deeper level and to respect all of the inhabitants of the earth, past, present, and future, regardless of skin color or ethnicity. Certainly, I learned from my adolescents that they are capable of drawing parallels between hegemony and racism. Adolescents are capable of questioning why some groups are singled out while others are forgotten. And adolescents care more about social issues than we may think.

Perhaps, if we open up a dialogue with our students about social dominance, they will lead the way in advocating for positive changes that benefit all groups. Adolescents are smarter than most adults give them credit. They critically seek truth and possess the voices and passion to become change agents. Lighting the spark that motivates them to seek and share the truth about marginalized populations and the reasons for their marginalization seems a privilege for me.

I have spent countless hours teaching American history to nearly a thousand students. I have often asked myself if I'm honoring the promise I made to the Native American friend I made many years ago. I do not need to look further than my students, though, to assume that I am.

One of my favorite student-posed questions continues to be, "Why don't people know about this?" I tell them some people know about it and choose not to share the information. But now that they themselves know the information, they are responsible for sharing it with others. After all, if the story is not shared, then the story ceases to exist. I know my students are sharing these stories because I often teach history to their younger siblings or family members who recount these stories to me. The adolescents that I am grateful to teach understand that the group with the loudest voices is the group who probably will be remembered. I believe these adolescents can break the sound barrier.

Books that are a must read for teachers:

Campbell, J. H. (1998). *Bloodlines: Odyssey of a Native daughter.* Tucson, AZ: University of Arizona Press.

Deloria, J. V. (1988). *Custer died for your sins: An Indian manifesto.* Norman, OK: University of Oklahoma Press.

Dunbar-Ortiz, R. (2014). *An indigenous peoples' history of the United States.* Boston: Beacon Press.

Eagle, A. F. (2010). *Pipestone: My life in an Indian boarding school.* Norman, OK: University of Oklahoma Press.

Eastman, C. A. (2003). *The soul of the Indian.* Mineola, NY: Dover Publications.

LaDuke, W. (1999). *All our relations: Native struggles for land and life.* Cambridge, MA: South End Press.

Thinking outside the binary box: Queer(ing) research and practice

by Danny Glassman

Biology is destiny, or at least that is what our society would want us to believe. From the moment we are born, we are inducted into a gender system of identity that labels us either male or female. Being labeled male or female comes with a long list of expected behaviors, traits, and aptitudes that we must adhere to in order to be accepted in society. If we do not meet up to the high standards our society places on our gender identity, then we fear being and are often labeled an outsider. Few of us, if any, actually meet the super macho or super femme gender types, however. From the colors of the clothes that society tells us we are "supposed" to wear to the expected sexual partners we are "meant" to have—we are the result of society's lens of what "should" be our gender and sexual identities.

Early in life, I learned what price I had to pay for both my sex and gender. I was in the sixth grade. I had learned plenty about my sex and gender by this point, but this was the first time I began to understand how both constructs drew boundaries around me, even if I was not fully aware of what those boundaries were at the time. I had always been the type of child who tumbled around on the floor and did cartwheels around my family. Sensing I might have a little too much energy for my own good, when I was younger my mother took me to the doctor to see if maybe I was hyperactive. As it turned out, the doctor told my mother I was actually not hyperactive, but what he called overactive instead. I simply did not have an outlet to make good use of all my energy. He recommended to her that she get me involved in something to take out my energy. This began my parent's search to find something for me to do—baseball, basketball, Boys Scouts, you name it. My parents pretty much gave me the opportunity to see what might be the right outlet for all my energy. Obviously, these were all activities that would be typical and acceptable for my gender as a boy. Unfortunately, however, all those activities I was either not interested in or simply not good at. I had a different idea in mind. I wanted to learn more gymnastics, since by this time, I had already mastered a back handspring with no formal training. However, the only other people I knew who took gymnastics in my school were cheerleaders. The only next logical step, then, was for me to become a cheerleader!

Certainly, I was capable of becoming a cheerleader, but there was one thing I was not: female! It was unheard of in the small, rural town in Arkansas I grew up in for a guy to be a cheerleader, not to mention the stereotypes that went along with being that. I did not want to be called a sissy or even worse names for being in a "girls" activity. If I tried out, I would basically be breaking a rigid social norm and risked being socially ostracized. Somehow, maybe against my mother's and my better judgment, I mustered the courage and went ahead and tried out despite the consequences. After tryouts, when the list was announced for my school's seventh-grade cheerleading squad, I made school history by being the first male ever to not only try out, but to make the cheerleading team! Since it was such big news in my little town, I was even interviewed for our local newspaper and an article was published entitled, "Busy Seventh Grader Tumbles over Gender Barriers." Barriers? I just wanted to tumble and, at the time, I did not realize there was something I needed to tumble over! It was a bittersweet victory, for sure. As I basked in the glory of finally finding a place where I could hone my gymnastics abilities, my triumph was darkened by ridicule and taunting from other students for challenging established gender expectations and roles.

At such a young age, I learned a vital lesson that our current gender system taught me through my place in cheerleading: some activities are for males and others are for females. According to our cultural norms, you do not mix the two. I would later learn that we should not mix a lot of different aspects of our lives either: from marrying outside of our race to having sexual relations with our own sex. "We have become," as queer theorist Michael Foucault writes, "a society of normalization" (1985, p. 8). What Foucault was referring to is our sex and gender system, which advocates that in order to be "normal" one must be either male or female, which means accepting the many social norms of what being either means. If someone stands outside of either box, they are seen as the "Other" and, usually, either changed to become "normal" or oppressed for remaining different. This experience of gender, as well as many others throughout my life, has opened my mind and heart to seeing gender, sexuality, and other social constructs of identity through less binary, strict, and rigid thinking. It was not until later in life that I would discover a theory that helped further my own understanding of sex and gender and help me put words to what I had seen throughout my life. It was when I discovered queer theory that I was truly freed to see outside of binaries of sex and gender to something more fluid, open, and real.

I am unsure of how I even missed being "touched" by queer theory before I was a doctoral student, but it was not until then that queer theory found me. I am surprised because my personal and professional background should have led me to queer theory sooner than it did. As a White, gay-identified man who grew up lower middle-class in rural Arkansas, I might have learned about queer theory in my own lived experience, whether in conversations or research about gay identity when I was coming out as a teenager or later as an under-graduate studying gender and sexuality, but somehow I never did. As an edu-cational administrator who took graduate courses in psychosocial and identity development, I might have heard the concept referenced in course discussions or content, but somehow it never came up. It was not until I was taking a doc-toral-level qualitative research methods course that queer theory finally reached me. In that class, we were required to consider each of our epistemo-logical and theoretical frameworks that guided our research and practice.

If it took me as long as it did to be exposed to queer theory, I suspect it might take even longer for other educators to learn about and, more importantly, to use queer theory. A paradox in education settings, specifically postsecondary, is: "Although colleges and universities are the source of much queer theory, they have remained substantially untouched by the queer agenda" (Renn, 2010, p. 132). In hopes of welcoming more educators to the use of queer theory that my own life has shown validity for, this piece serves as an intro-duction to the historical development, key tenets, and uses of queer theory in educational research and practice for the purposes of creating more inclusive educational settings, where students in K-16 can find a place to "belong" in schools as I so longed for when I was growing up.

Historical development of queer theory

Queer theory is based upon the work of poststructural theorists Foucault (1976/1978), Derrida (1967/1978), and Lyotard (1984) and more recently, Butler (1990) and Sedgwick (1990). These queer theorists deconstructed and challenged the validity of heteronormative discourses and practices of gender and sexuality that promote heterosexuality as the normal and preferred sexual orientation. In the 1990s, when gay and lesbian studies proliferated at many universities, the phrase *queer theory* emerged as a result of dissatisfaction with the slow response given to the AIDS epidemic by state agencies and politicians (Morris, 2000). The purpose of queer theory was as "a reaction and resistance to this cold eye of do-nothing, see-nothing, hear-nothing" public policies and philosophy (Morris, 2000, p. 16). Queer theory was the response to society's lack of acknowledgment and acceptance of gender and sexual identities that did not fit nicely into the boxes of male, female, or heterosexual. Queer theory criticizes and critiques mainstream ideas of what gender and sex are and pushes for a broader perspective of gender and sexual identities.

The term *queer theory* was first invoked by Teresa de Lauretis (1991) in the introduction of an issue of the journal *differences*, entitled "Queer Theory: Lesbian and Gay Sexualities," as a means of asking the questions that might strip the myths away from the mainstream concepts of sexual and gender identities as binary, fixed, and static. At its core, queer theory resists and challenges mainstream and dominant discourses of sexual and gender identities and normative practices that marginalize, oppress, and silence the queer community (Plummer, 2005). It suggests that biology and humans are not encased in only two forms of male and female; rather nature and evolution have created more freedom in expression of the form a human takes, and not just humans, but many other species. Furthermore, "queer research invites discourse that challenges heteronormativity as well as binaries related to gender, sexual orientation, [and] religion . . . ." (Levy & Johnson, 2011, p. 6). As I reflect on my own experience growing up gay in the South, had I known about queer theory then, it may have offered me the opportunity to see past the rigid expectations of masculinity and sexuality placed on me at that time. My decision to join my school's cheerleading team, and later the marching band's color guard, might have been much easier and safer had tenants of queer theory been known to my family, my school administrators, my teachers, and me.

Key tenants of queer theory

Three concepts of queer theory are important to consider in relation to educational research and practice with lesbian, gay, bisexual, transgender, and queer (LGBTQ) students, which are heteronormativity, performativity, and liminality. Taken together, these three tenets of queer theory provide a useful framework for educators' understanding of behavior, performance, and resistance of heteronormativity. First, *heteronormativity* challenges the use of heterosexuality as the norm to understand gender and sexuality (Warner, 1991) and calls for greater emphasis on gender and sexual fluidity. For example, heteronormativity categorizes sexuality and gender into two distinct groups, heterosexual/homosexual and male/female, and positions these two sexualities and genders as opposite and different from one another. Queer theory argues against demanding that sexuality or gender must be two distinct and fixed categories. The theory counters the argument that all humans must either exist as men or women with no latitude for multiple variations. Foucault challenges conventional assumption theories because he insists that identities consist of multiple components that are in constant flux (1991).

Second, queer theory contends that sexual and gender identities are socially constructed and that the expression or performance of identity is unstable and ever changing (Butler, 1990). Queer theory focuses more on incongruence, than congruence, between sex, gender, and desire (Jagose, 1996) and works to "disrupt discourses that enclose selves, pin down desires" (Morris, 2000, p. 23). According to Foucault (1976/1978), normative discourses of identities are used to maintain heteronormativity through regulatory spaces in which identities are formed, reinforced, and reproduced. Butler (1990) contends that individuals construct their sexual and gender identities through everyday behaviors or performatives (Butler, 1990) that are dependent upon "the time and place in which they exist and the individuals who enact them" (Abes & Kasch, 2007, p. 621). Morris (2000) explained, "Ultimately, queer identities are performances . . . and these performances are radically unstable since the queer self is not bound by any particular label or desire" (p. 21). There is a distinction between performance and performativity: performance presupposes a preexisting subject, whereas performativity contests the very notion of the subject (Osborne & Segal, 1994). Gender and sexual expression are changed both at the individual and societal level, and a person's gender and sexuality are influenced both within and outside of oneself. Therefore, sexual and gender identities are always being created and changed through individual actions, rather than actions representing an already determined or static identity (Butler, 1990). Since actions are never repeated in exactly the same fashion, individual identity is always shifting because of how identity is uniquely expressed. Built upon the identity formation theories of Foucault and Butler, queer theory counters the normative discourse of fixed, stable identities and articulates a view that identity based on categorizes is meaningless since identities are fluid and always in flux. If this idea of queer theory had been embraced in my childhood, I would have been freer to express and enjoy all of my interests and identities.

Lastly, the concept of liminality is useful in understanding binaries between sexuality, gender, and space and forms of resistance. Liminality was first discussed by Arnold van Gennep (1909/1960) and later further explored by Victor Turner (1967) in characterizing rites of passage in various cultures. Liminality comes from the Latin word *limen*, meaning "threshold," which implies a transitional state or space between two distinct and stable states or spaces (Abes & Kasch, 2007). In terms of heteronormativity, "liminality is a resistance strategy in which elements of heterosexuality and nonheterosexuality are incorporated into one identity that rejects normalized definitions of either heterosexuality or nonheterosexuality" (Abes & Kasch, 2007, p. 621). Therefore, within an individual state or space, persons can perform their sexuality or gender in combination or in contradictory ways to heteronormativity. These strategies of resistance are related to the opposition of power structures (Foucault, 1976/1978; Torres et al., 2009) that work to maintain heteronormativity. Taking me as an example, my expression of my interest in gymnastics and cheerleading were in defiance of traditional and heteronormative expressions of male identity in sport that is often maintained through power structures, such as male dominance and patriarchy.

Queer theory in educational settings

My own personal journey and professional experience as a higher education administrator validates my belief that the use of queer theory in educational research and practice as a critical theoretical lens helps challenge the complexities and fluidity of how gender and sexual identity are expressed by LGBTQ students. According to Ruffolo (2006), "the use of queer theory as a critical research lens" can help us as teachers and students resist society's demand that we all conform to someone else's view of what is normal. He indicates that understanding queer theory might help us reject all efforts to make us feel forced to assimilate into the power structure's boxes of culture, class, race, behavior, belief systems, etc. This rejection, Ruffolo believes can "bring about an equitable and democratic society where binary discourses are reworked" (p. 4).

Tenets of queer theory, specifically heteronormativity, performativity, and liminality, provide a framework for educators to understand and deconstruct conventional notions and discussions, ones distorted by the power structure, about male/female being the only "normal" categorizing of humans around sexual and gender identities. The concept of heteronormativity is useful in acknowledging the fluidity and multiplicity of LGBTQ students' identities and normative discourses that resist or reinforce dominant forms of sexual and gender identities within educational contexts. Performativity is also helpful in understanding how sexual and gender identities are uniquely expressed through actions within educational settings. Lastly, liminality provides a critical means of recognizing how these notions about what is normal are both maintained and resisted through power structures (Foucault, 1976/1978), sometimes at the same time, in educational research and practice.

Recommendations for queer(ing) educational research and practice

Using queer theory in educational research and practice is useful for researchers and practitioners in a number of ways. First, queer theory can be a useful tool to help educators understand students (Abes & Kasch, 2007), as well as teach their students about the complexities of identities (Morris, 2000). Using queer theory assists educators to "move outside of linear models to consider the influence that students are having on their environment to reshape their contexts" (Abes & Kasch, 2007, p. 633). For me, this creates a lens to see and recognize students outside of their sex, gender, or other social identities as more whole and ever changing people with multiple and sometimes conflicting identities. Queer theory's emphasis on identity fluidity and complexity is helpful in considering against linear models of sexual identity development (Cass, 1979, 1996; McCarn & Fassinger, 1996). Although it might be easier to think of students' personal development as a straight line, queer theory helps us see that identity development is never straight or linear, but rather multifaceted and, sometimes, like the universe, seemingly messy in how it develops.

The emphasis of queer theory on identity performance and movement can be beneficial for educators who fight against the labeling of students' identity. Often, labeling of identity has been done in damaging ways and "queer theory teaches that naming kills" (Morris, 2000, p. 27). Instead of labeling particular identities or gendering certain activities, educators can use queer theory to give voice in research and practice to the multiplicity of evolving and shifting identities and expressions. Unlike many stage and lifespan student development theories (Cass, 1979; D'Augelli, 1994; McCarn & Fassinger, 1996; Rhoads, 1997; Stevens, 2004), queer theory articulates a very different view of development as always evolving and never "arriving" at a stage of development (Abes & Kasch, 2007). From a queer theory perspective, students are not in a linear trajectory of developing, they are always in a state of constantly becoming (Turner, 1967). The focus of queer theory on performativity (Butler, 1990) and movement (Morris, 2000) can also be helpful in educational research and practice to resist labeling static identity, rather than celebrating fluid subjectivities. Whether in research or practice, classifying students into identity categories risks silencing their multiple and shifting subjectivities.

Conclusion

In order to solve the paradox of educational settings being sources of just queer theory, but not being queered themselves, not being liberated as institutions from neatly categorizing our students as an either/or, educational research and practice must increase the use of queer theory to further scholarship and policies that challenge rather than maintain dominant discourses and labels of sexual and gender identities and, indeed, all identities. Teachers and schools are challenged to think critically about how research and practice are inclusive of all our students, including those who identify as LGBTQ, and should work toward rather than against social justice. It is hoped that this chapter has served as your introduction to queer theory and that moving forward, you will queer educational research and practice in your schools and communities so that what is normal becomes more like a rainbow of acceptance where not only gender bias, but classism, racism, sexism, ableism, and all the other "isms" can be eradicated as we move toward making democratic schools more of a reality than a myth. If what is "queer" is looked at through a multifaceted lens, maybe then, our institutions will become safer and more inclusive of everyone's evolving identities, where being different might be the norm.

References

Abes, E. S. & Kasch, D. (2007). Using queer theory to explore lesbian college students' multiple dimensions of identity. *Journal of College Student Development* 48, 619–636.

Butler, J. (1990). *Gender trouble.* London: Routledge.

Cass, V. C. (1979). Homosexual identity formation: A theoretical model. Journal of Homosexuality 4 (3), 219–235.

Cass, V. C. (1996). Sexual orientation identity formation: A western phenomenon. In: R. P. Cabaj & T. S. Stein (Eds.). *Textbook of homosexuality and mental health.* Washington, DC: American Psychiatric Press. pp. 227–251.

D'Augelli, A. R. (1994). Lesbian and gay male development: Steps toward an analysis of lesbians' and gay men's lives. In B. Greene and G. Herek (Eds.). *Contemporary perspectives in gay and lesbian psychology* (Vol. 1, pp. 118-132). Newbury Park, CA: Sage.

de Lauretis, T. (1991). Queer theory: Lesbian and gay sexualities: An introduction. *Differences: A Journal of Feminist Cultural Studies* 3 (2), iii–xviii.

Derrida, J. (1978). *Writing and difference.* (A. Bass, Trans.). Chicago: The University of Chicago Press (Original work published in 1967).

Foucault, M. (1978). *The history of sexuality: Volume 1, An introduction.* (R. Hurley, Trans.). New York: Vantage Books. (Original work published 1976).

Foucault, M. (1985). *The use of pleasure: The history of sexuality* Vol. 2. New York: Random House.

Foucault, M. (1991). *Discipline and punish: The birth of a prison.* London, Penguin.

Jagose, A. (1996). *Queer theory: An introduction.* New York: New York University Press.

Levy, D. & Johnson, C. W. (2011). What does the Q mean? Including queer voices in qualitative research. *Qualitative Social Work* 10 (2).

Lyotard, J. F. (1984). *The postmodern condition: A report on knowledge (Theory and history of literature* Vol. 10. Manchester, United Kingdom: Manchester University Press.

McCarn, S. R. & Fassinger, R. E. (1996). Revisioning sexual minority identity formation: A new model of lesbian identity and its implications for counseling and research. *The Counseling Psychologist, 24*, 508–534.

Morris, M. (2000). Dante's left foot kicks queer theory into gear. In S. Talburt & S. R. Steinberg (Eds.). *Thinking queer: Sexuality, culture and education* (pp. 15-32). New York: Peter Lang.

Osborne, P. & Segal, L. (1994). Gender as performance: An interview with Judith Butler. *Radical Philosophy* 67, 32–39.

Plummer, K. (2005). Critical humanism and queer theory. In N. K. Denzin & Y. S. Lincoln (Eds.). *Handbook of Qualitative Research* 3rd ed. Thousand Oaks, CA: Sage. pp. 357–373.

Renn, K. (2010). LGBT and queer research in higher education: The state and status of the field. *Educational Researcher* 39 (2), 132–141.

Rhoads, R. A. (1997). A subcultural study of gay and bisexual college males. *Journal of Higher Education* 68, 460–482.

Ruffolo, D. V. (2006). Queer(ing) scholarly research: Decentering fixed subjects for implicated subjectivities. *Higher Education Perspectives* 2 (2), 1–22.

Sedgwick, E. K. (1990). *Epistemology of the closet*. Berkeley: University of California Press.

Stevens, Jr., R. A. (2004). Understanding gay identity development within the college environment. *Journal of College Student Development* 45 (2), 185–206.

Talburt, S. & Steinberg, S. R. (2000). *Thinking queer: Sexuality, culture, and education*. New York: Peter Lang.

Torres, V., Jones, S. R., & Renn, K. A. (2009). Identity development theories in student affairs: Origins, current status, and new approaches. *Journal of College Student Development 50* (6), 577–596.

Turner, V. (1967). *The forest of symbols: Aspects of Ndembu ritual*. Ithaca, NY: Cornell University Press.

Van Gennep, A. V. (1960). *The rites of passage*. London: Routledge & Kegan Paul (Original work published 1909).

Warner, M. (1991). *Fear of a queer planet: Queer politics and social theory*. Minneapolis: University of Minnesota.

APPENDIX: VIDEOS RELATED TO THE THEMES IN EACH SECTION

Striving for Social Justice is the most valuable thing to do in life. ~ *Albert Einstein*

So I marvel, rejoice, and give thanks, looking forward to the continuing movement of creation, believing that the best is yet to come for us all. ~*Vincent Harding*

Do not think that love, in order to be genuine, has to be extraordinary, what we need is to love without getting tired. ~*Mother Teresa*

Part 1: A human being is part of the whole

- Louie Schwartzberg: Nature, Beauty, Gratitude. *TED.com* http://www.ted.com/talks/louie_schwartzberg_nature_beauty_gratitude
- Ernesto Sirolli: Shut up and listen. *TED.com* http://www.ted.com/talks/ernesto_sirolli_want_to_help_someone_shut_up_and_listen
- Jane Goodall: What separates us from chimpanzees? *TED.com* (roots and shoots)
- Ron Finley: A guerilla gardener in South Central LA. *TED.com* http://www.ted.com/talks/ron_finley_a_guerilla_gardener_in_south_central_la
- Powers of Ten. *Youtube.com*: https://www.youtube.com/watch?v=0fKBhvDjuy0
- John Legend & Common. *Glory.YouTube.com* https://www.youtube.com/watch?v=HUZOKvYcx_o
- *American Experience: Freedom Riders.* (2011). DVD.PBS documentary.Laurens Grant. Boston: WGBH.
- Howard Zinn. (2009). *The People Speak.* DVD documentary. Produced by Matt Damon, et al.

Part 2: Develop the genius within the young

- AlgebraProject/YPPMiami:http://www.youtube.com/watch?v=boeT69PrMRY
- Ken Robinson: Shifting the paradigm in schools: http://bit.ly/o3Epsg
- TED.com/Ken Robinson: "How schools kill creativity"

- No More: The children in Birmingham. *YouTube.com*:https://www.youtube.com/watch?v=hCxE6i_SzoQ
- Sugata Mitra. Hole in the Wall. *TED.com* http://www.ted.com/talks/sugata_mitra_build_a_school_in_the_cloud.html

Part 3: The spirit of agency

- Kevin Breel: Confessions of a depressed comic. *TED*.com https://www.ted.com/talks/kevin_breel_confessions_of_a_depressed_comic
- Rita Pierson: Every kid needs a champion. *TED.com* http://www.ted.com/talks/rita_pierson_every_kid_needs_a_champion
- Jackson Katz: Violence against women; it's a men's issue. *TED.com* http://www.ted.com/talks/jackson_katz_violence_against_women_it_s_a_men_s_issue
- Bob Moses on Freedom Summer. Legendary civil rights activist and educator Bob Moses joins Rev. Sharpton to discuss his role in the summer of 1964*MSNBC.com* http://www.msnbc.com/politicsnation/watch/bob-moses-on-the-freedom-summer-290118211650
- Sebastiao Salgado: The silent drama of photography http://www.ted.com/talks/sebastiao_salgado_the_silent_drama_of_photography
- Maysoon Zayid: I got 99 problems . . . palsy is just one http://www.ted.com/talks/maysoon_zayid_i_got_99_problems_palsy_is_just_one
- Ron Finley: Gardening in L.A. *TED*.com http://www.ted.com/talks/ron_finley_a_guerilla_gardener_in_south_central_la

Part 4: The world in language

- Tim Wise talks about the "n" word. *YouTube.com*: https://www.youtube.com/watch?v=2MnmmDiQSdA
- Malcolm London. High School Training Ground. *TED.com* http://www.ted.com/talks/malcolm_london_high_school_training_ground
- Ernestine Johnson: Spoken word answer to 'talking white.' *YouTube.com* https://www.youtube.com/watch?v=ShrWgdHEwHs
- One Minute Insight: Why Bilingual Brains Rock! https://www.youtube.com/watch?v=rhpVd30AJaY
- John McWhorter: Txting is killing language. *TED.com* https://www.ted.com/playlists/117/words_words_words
- Krista Tippet: The Alchemy of Pilgrimage. http://www.onbeing.org/program/paulo-coelho-the-alchemy-of-pilgrimage/6639
- Parker J. Palmer: What is a Divided Life? https://www.youtube.com/watch?t=18&v=gCvIZpMo8aY

Part 5: The problem is cultural

- A trip to the grocery store -White privilege https://www.youtube.com/watch?v=GTvU7uUgjUI
- BBC Scientific Racism: The Eugenics of Social Darwinism. *YouTube.com* https://www.youtube.com/watch?v=3FmEjDaWqA4
- Bree Newsome & the Confederate Flag http://www.democracynow.org/2015/7/6/bree_newsome_as_sc_lawmakers_debate
- Bryan Stevenson: We need to talk about an injustice. *TED.com* http://www.ted.com/talks/bryan_stevenson_we_need_to_talk_about_an_injustice
- Diversitytrainingfilms.com Presents: The Color of Fear-The 'Red Ground' Scene. *YouTube.com* https://www.youtube.com/watch?v=-vAbpJW_xEc
- John Legend's acceptance speech for Oscar. http://time.com/3717055/oscars-2015-best-original-song-john-legend-common-selma/
- Vincent Harding: Civility, History, and Hope. Krista Tippet audio. http://www.onbeing.org/program/civility-history-and-hope/79
- Tim Wise: White Privilege. *YouTube.com* https://www.youtube.com/watch?v=J3Xe1kX7Wsc
- You throw like a girl. http://omeleto.com/200170/
- Derrick Jensen on Civilization. *YouTube.com* https://www.youtube.com/watch?v=QLiDcLua58I
- *Freedom Song.* (2000). DVD. TNT. Danny Glover, producer. Warnervideo.com
- *American Experience: Freedom Summer* (2014). DVD. PBS documentary. Produced by CyndeeReaddean. Boston: WGBH.

Part 6: To love and be loved

- Vincent Harding: Are you ready to heal George Zimmerman? *YouTube.com* https://www.youtube.com/watch?v=twD7XDOOIyU
- Native Americans resistance to name of Red Skins. https://www.youtube.com/watch?v=mR-tbOxlhvE
- The US Border Patrol: "Honor First"? Or taking justice into their own hands? *YouTube.com*https://www.youtube.com/watch?v=oByurQPpMxc&list=PLUhG_g8CbAJ7vP-2wtVv_F2tL9OKY-U70&index=3
- Crossing the line at the border "Need to Know." http://www.pbs.org/wnet/need-to-know/security/video-first-look-crossing-the-line/13597/
- Kids react to gay marriage. *YouTube.com* https://www.youtube.com/watch?v=8TJxnYgP6D8
- Educating kids about gender norms. *YouTube.com* https://www.youtube.com/watch?v=MHN1gqrXMUM

CONTRIBUTORS

Martha Barantovich is an Instructor in the department of Leadership and Professional Studies in the College of Education at Florida International University. Her area of focus is on social, cultural, and historical foundations and mindfulness practices. Her number one rule for her students is that they learn to ask deep questions regarding any issue they are addressing. She was a high school teacher for nine years before she obtained her doctoral degree in Curriculum and Instruction: Instructional leadership, from Florida International University in 2006. She is an advisory board member with E-SToPP, Eradicating the School to Prison Pipeline, and works with young students in Liberty City, teaching them yoga and mindfulness. Her work also takes her into urban high schools as a mentor to teachers who are working with students taking college level courses.

Mary-Alison Burger is a current candidate for a Master's of Science in Urban Education at Florida International University. She completed her undergraduate education, Summa Cum Laude, from the University of Florida with disciplinary foci in Cultural/Medical Anthropology & African Diaspora studies. Her research interests were East African culture, language, and history, African-American history, race, class, and gender studies, and global health disparities. At University of Florida, she was awarded a William J Fulbright Group Project's Abroad Scholarship to study KiSwahili in Arusha Tanzania. While there she reflected on her own historical identity in the United States, and shifted her research inquiry to structural violence, white privilege, institutionalized racism, and damaging systemic power paradigms. Upon completion of her Master's, she anticipates teaching highschool students and to eventually pursue her Ph.D. In summer of 2015, she will work alongside Civil Rights icon and President of the Algebra Project, Bob Moses, to continue her research and to learn how to advocate for justice and socialchange.

Eric J. Cooper earned two masters and a doctorate at Columbia University. Eric is the President of the National Urban Alliance for Effective Education (NUA). He served in a similar position as Executive Director for the NUA at Columbia University's Teachers College and as Adjunct Associate Professor for seven years. Prior to this position, he was the Vice President for In-service Training & Telecommunications for the Simon & Schuster Education Group. He has worked in the capacities of Associate Director of Program & Research Development for the College Board, Administrative Assistant in the Office of Curriculum for the Boston Public Schools, and Director of a treatment center for emotionally disturbed students, in addition to working as a teacher, researcher, counselor, and Washington Fellow. He is a Huffington Post opinion writer, and the host of NCEBC Talk Radio. He was honored in 2005/2006 to speak at the prestigious Aspen Institute's Ideas Festival.

Mario Eraso holds a Ph. D. from Florida International University (FIU) in curriculum and instruction, with emphasis on science, technology, engineering, and mathematics (STEM). After working for six years as a structural engineer designing precast, steel, and concrete buildings, he went back to school to do his doctoral work in how students learn geometry when integrating technology in the classroom and being immersed in constructivist learning environments. He has taught all grades in middle and high school, as well as undergraduate and graduate courses for three years at Texas A&M University-Commerce. He currently works at the School of Computing and Information Sciences at FIU, as STEM coordinator. Prior to his position at FIU, he taught mathematics and robotics at a private middle school in south Florida. Mario develops his own teaching material because he believes every lesson and assessment needs to be customized to current students' needs.

Danny Glassmann is the Associate Dean of Students at University of Tennessee. He served as Assistant Dean of Students at Oglethorpe University in Atlanta, Georgia. He received his Ph.D. in Counseling and Student Personnel Services from The University of Georgia. His research interests include college student and identity development, social justice, multicultural populations and competencies, safe spaces, and technology. Glassmann worked in the Office of Staff Development and Student Conduct at UGA and served as the Assistant Director of Residence Life and Multicultural Center at Elon University. His professional background includes experience with residence life, student conduct, multicultural affairs, and lesbian, gay, bisexual, and transgender (LGBT) life. He has served in leadership roles on local, state, and national professional organizations and currently serves on the Directorate Board of the ACPA Commission for Assessment and Evaluation, Executive Board of the Consortium of Higher Education LGBT Resource Professionals, and the Atlanta Pride Committee.

Alyssa Nicole Hernandez was born in 1996, but has the soul of a teen who grew up in the 1980s. Jamming to Cyndi Lauper and wishing she were a Goonie, she is most certainly an old soul. Born and raised in Miami, she is the eldest of three sisters and not to mention quite the momma's girl (and proud!!). She treasures her family and is grateful for her authentic friends. Intimidated by what the future may hold, she still strives towards becoming a great nurse practitioner someday. She likes to live with the optimistic mentality of: "No Bad Days".

Pamela Hernandez obtained her B.A. from Florida State University in Communications and English. Currently, in the Urban Education Master's Degree program at Florida International University, she has served over 1,700 hours in an underserved community as an academic interventionist in an under-resourced school. As a result of her service, she received the Eli Segal Education Award. Passionate about working with students in urban communities, she is eager to work for educational equality. She plans to continue teaching students about social justice issues and raising the voices of disenfranchised students, so that they may demand their right to quality education.

Debby W. Kelly is a native of Atlanta, Georgia and started her community service as a young girl beside her mother and father. She has been recognized for her leadership in the Harvard Business School Partners (President); Cathedral of Christ the King Church and School, Atlanta (President PTA); St. Michael Church and School, Houston (President PTA); Epilepsy Foundation, Houston and Atlanta (board officer); Young Audiences, Atlanta (board member); Georgia Shakespeare, Atlanta (Board President); Women's Leadership Group of Boys and Girls Clubs, Washington, DC (steering committee); Food and Friends, Washington, DC (volunteer) and International Neighbors Clubs, Washington, DC (President). Debby's proudest achievement has been rearing three sons: Jason, Wynne, and Sam. She resides in Washington, DC with her husband, Dennis, and their dog, Mugsy.

Maria K. Lovett is a Clinical Assistant Professor in the College of Education at Florida International University and Director of the Education Effect, a university community school partnership. With an extensive background in documentary production, teaching youth media, and social foundations of education Maria uses media as a tool to fight for social justice both in the classroom and the community. As an educator and researcher in the field, Maria has taught youth media production and participatory action research projects in cities across the United States. In Miami, she also works with students from the Algebra Project and the Young People's Project to advance multiple literacy skills and promote community action.

Ruba Monem has been a middle school social studies teacher in South Florida for nearly a decade. She completed her doctoral degree from Florida International University where she serves as an adjunct instructor in the Department of Teaching and Learning. Whether teaching middle school students or preservice teachers, she believes that educators are responsible for facilitating a dialogue about social justice and nurturing the next generation of leaders. Her research interests include social studies instructional strategies in urban settings, technology integration, and special education.

Carlos Gonzalez Morales lives and works in South Florida. His primary work over the past two decades has been to invite soul spaces within the unlikely environment of institutional education. His work is ephemeral and intentionally marginal. He is currently focused on exploring loss and (re)creation, while working with students in a small fragment of a pine rockland and a center for adults with intellectual disabilities. He teaches English along with monkey-wrenching skills at Miami Dade College. He was an endowed chair at MDC for seven years and also taught at FIU in the English Department as well as in the College of Education/Algebra Project Summer Institutes for high school youth.

Omo Moses was born in Tanzania, East Africa, in 1972. He is a founding member of the Young People's Project (YPP), a non-profit organization that seeks to "organize young people to radically change their education and the way they relate to it." Formerly, the YPP Executive Director, he worked with high school and college students and community members to develop local and national governance structures; secured funding for local and national initiatives; developed relationships with educators, community members, and mathematicians across the country to build local capacity and to position YPP to have a national impact. One of four siblings, growing up in Cambridge, MA, he led his high school basketball team to a state championship in 1990.He attended Pittsburgh and George Washington Universities on full athletic scholarships. At George Washington, majoring in mathematics and minoring in Creative Writing, he received the Black Issues in Higher education Sports-Scholar Award and Creative Writing award. He is now completing a book to be published in 2016.

Robert P. Moses is one of the leading civil rights icons from the 1960s. He was the former field secretary for the Student Nonviolent Coordinating Committee (SNCC) and the main organizer of the Freedom Summer project, which was intended to end racial disenfranchisement. In 1982, he received a MacArthur "Genius" Fellowship and used the money to create the Algebra Project, which serves ten thousand students in twenty-eight cities nationwide and follows the philosophy of grassroots community organizing to promote math literacy. In 2001, with Charles Cobb, Moses published

Radical equations: Civil Rights from Mississippi to the Algebra Project. In 2010, along with Theresa Perry, Joan Wynne, Lisa Delpit, and Ernie Cortez, he published *Quality Education as a constitutional right: Creating a grassroots movement to transform public schools.*

Alexa Ovalles is 19 years old and was born in San Cristobal, Venezuela where she studied Medicine and plans to continue that study eventually in Miami. She has practiced dance since she was six years old and piano is her favorite instrument. She discontinued her music classes when attending Medical School. She puts 100% of her energy into her academic pursuits. Her life revolves around college, church, and work.

Monica Penichet is 19 years old and is majoring in Forensic Science at Miami Dade College. She was born and raised in Miami, Florida. Her ancestors are from Cuba. She spends most of her free time with my family and friends soaking up the sun at the beach or pool. Her goal in life is to live, laugh, and love always.

Matthew Rubenstein was born in Miami, Florida in 1984. He spent his adolescent years exploring the everglades and the wild areas that surround Miami. Shortly after graduating from high school, he enlisted in the United States Army and was assigned to the 173rd Airborne. After fulfilling his four year obligation in the Army, he came home to manage a local zoo. He has spent countless hours in the Everglades exploring and photographing the life in the swamps and surrounding ecosystems. He is currently working on a degree in criminal justice and hopes to work for the Fish and Game service as a Conservation Officer.

Alex Salinas is a Senior Associate Professor of Communications at the Inter-American Campus of Miami Dade College, where he has taught composition, literature and creative writing courses since 2003. Raised in Miami, he grew up aware of the invisible walls of fear that separate communities based on ethnicity and class. He has developed a communications pedagogy rooted in civic engagement, while coordinating countless partnerships with non-profits and student organizations. He currently serves as a Council Member at the Earth Ethics Institute, which promotes sustainability in curriculum and institutional practices. In 2009, he helped found a 17-year project to support the education of 30 children in Nicaragua called TengoUnSueño that has become a pivotal part of his life's work. Alex hopes that part of the text for every class lies in the space between joy for the beauty of the world and activism in the face of its injustices.

Sarah Schultz is originally from Pembroke Pines, Florida. She graduated with a bachelor's degree in Elementary Education from Florida Gulf Coast University in 2011 and has been teaching third grade since then. Sarah is currently pursuing a Master's degree in Urban Education at Florida International University and is passionate about social justice issues. Sarah believes that every classroom should have a rich, multicultural curriculum and create a welcoming classroom environment that allows students to freely express themselves.

Isabel Sousa-Rodriguez is a Doctoral candidate in the Department of Sociology at the Graduate Center of the City University of New York. Isabel conducts qualitative and ethnographic research on the identity struggles of undocumented youth in their transition to adulthood and of the impacts of legal status on mothering strategies. Isabel's research is rooted in their own experience as a formerly undocumented immigrant that fled Colombia seeking, and being denied, political asylum in the United States. They are gender non-conforming, national recipient of the Freedom from Fear Award and currently serves on the national selection committee for the DREAM.US Undocumented Youth Scholarship Fund.

Gerson Sanchez was born to Nicaraguan immigrant parents in Arlington, Virginia. His family moved around often, until they finally settled down in Greensboro, North Carolina. He remained in North Carolina throughout his high school and undergraduate career. He now resides in Miami, Florida and is currently attending Florida International University pursuing a Master of Science in Higher Education Administration in conjunction with a certificate in African and African Diaspora Studies. The harsh realities of hegemony and bigotry that he endured in North Carolina have led him to write *The Lost Voice of a Spic*. This is but a small epigraph that provides insight into the young mind of a first generation Latino, growing up in North Carolina.

Chaundra L. Whitehead is a doctoral candidate in Adult Education and Human Resource Development at Florida International University, has over 10 years teaching experience in literacy, vocational, and correctional education. Her research interests are conflict resolution, correctional education, urban studies, and adult basic education. She is a Research Assistant with a university-community partnership in Miami at a historical urban high school. She enjoys facilitating many different types of adult training workshops and programs. She actively volunteers as a facilitator with Alternatives to Violence Project in South Florida prisons. She has an M.S. from FIU and a B.A. from Florida A&M University.

Joan Wynne's multitude of students, from Howard High School, Morehouse College, Georgia State University, and Florida International University, as well as educators like Lisa Delpit, Asa G. Hilliard III, Robert P. Moses, have influenced her research about transformational leadership, un-learning racism, and building partnerships among youth, parents, schools, and communities. Her last 10 years have been dedicated to researching the work of the Algebra Project and the Young People's Project. Her passion for being in and learning from the communities where her students live started at Howard High School and has continued throughout her career. She strongly believes in the scholar as activist; that the academy is informed and enriched when its professors are involved in and learning from the cities, towns, and neighborhoods that house their universities. Her newest edited book, *Confessions of a white educator: Stories in search of justice and diversity*, explores what works and doesn't work in public education.

CPSIA information can be obtained
at www.ICGtesting.com
Printed in the USA
LVHW020532010519
616186LV00004B/5